Staging Frontiers

Diálogos Series

Kris Lane, Series Editor

Understanding Latin America demands dialogue, deep exploration, and frank discussion of key topics. Founded by Lyman L. Johnson in 1992 and edited since 2013 by Kris Lane, the Diálogos Series focuses on innovative scholarship in Latin American history and related fields. The series, the most successful of its type, includes specialist works accessible to a wide readership and a variety of thematic titles, all ideally suited for classroom adoption by university and college teachers.

Also available in the Diálogos Series:

For additional titles in the Diálogos Series, please visit unmpress.com.

William Garrett Acree Jr.

Staging Frontiers

The Making of Modern Popular
Culture in Argentina and Uruguay

University of New Mexico Press • Albuquerque

© 2019 by the University of New Mexico Press
All rights reserved. Published 2019
Printed in the United States of America

ISBN 978-0-8263-6104-2 (cloth)
ISBN 978-0-8263-6105-9 (paper)
ISBN 978-0-8263-6106-6 (electronic)

Library of Congress Control Number: 2019948070

Cover illustration: cover of *Caras y Caretas*, September 9, 1905
Designed by Felicia Cedillos
Composed in Minion Pro 10.25/13.5

For

Sophia Acree

Mi sol, mi luna, fuente de alegría, mi alma, mi hija—
te amo hasta el infinito

Cecilia Hanan Reyes

Exemplar of resilience and courage, whose smile and laughter can change
the world; master teacher; and my dearest friend

Rebecca Lynn Chiz Acree

Pillar of strength; remarkable storyteller; endless source of creative energy;
giver of boundless love; and my mother

Contents

~ℓ

Illustrations

Map

Figures

Acknowledgments

Writing a book about popular culture in Latin America prior to the twentieth century can be daunting. Part of the challenge stems from the availability of sources that allow us to peer into that world over time and get a sense of the meanings people got out of or attributed to the experiences they had. Another aspect of the challenge relates to learning about the ways and frequency with which people interacted with activities or objects that made up the popular culture landscape, and with each other precisely because of this landscape. A final element of this challenge revolves around the fleeting character of so many sources for accessing those activities and objects. This is especially apparent with the forms of entertainment that were central to the development of modern popular culture in Argentina and Uruguay—equestrian shows, acrobatic feats at circuses, extravagant showmen and women, and the gaucho drama hits that moved from circus pit to theater stage to silver screen.

The daily experiences of those shows were supposed to be ephemeral, though we know the impacts of attending such performances often endured, and in surprising ways. There are records of ticket sales, photographic collections of performers and performances, advertisements detailing the day's entertainment fare, and correspondence among actors, authors, and impresarios. Likewise, there are accounts of motifs, songs, and characters that saw their debut in circus dramas and then went on to galvanize members of country-themed social clubs and crowds at carnival. Yet to appreciate the enduring power of those ephemeral experiences and the transformative influence of popular culture more broadly, we must pair records of the sort mentioned with news of and reaction to shows in decades of newspapers from small towns to big cities. We have to visit these social clubs, listen to scratchy recordings from rural musicians who made it big thanks to the circus or theater, and talk with aficionados of theater history or private collectors of all things gaucho.

Developing an understanding of the lasting impact of the ephemeral comes from a months-long discussion of Argentine and Uruguayan circus families with a history buff around his 2 × 3 foot kitchen table, set in the 6 × 8 foot living room of a studio apartment, as the television blasts out the afternoon's latest *chisme.* Or from pouring over a trove of theater and circus documents passed on from one collector to another, glimpsing rich details in between the movements of a cat that crawls back and forth from your shoulders to the table where everything is sprawled out. I could go on. But simply put, developing this understanding means having lots of ephemeral experiences that also leave their lasting impressions.

So, searching for the sources behind modern popular culture in Argentina and Uruguay was daunting. At the same time, it provided eye-opening opportunities for discovery and for making connections with sources and people. It was a process that was exhilarating, remarkably formative, and, best of all, incredibly fun. And I had a lot of help along the way.

Many years have passed since I first started thinking about the themes, people, places, and historical phenomena featured in this book. Over that time I have benefited enormously from conversations with family, friends, colleagues, librarians, archivists, collectors, students, and strangers. All of these exchanges have enriched my understanding of popular culture in general as well as my specific interests. Similarly, many individuals, organizations, and institutions have supported my research and the necessary time to piece together the story of *Staging Frontiers.* I want to recognize them here.

To begin, my family have given me not only unyielding encouragement but also the gift of time. Cecilia Hanan Reyes has been one of my greatest teachers over the past fifteen years. I'm indebted to her for her patience, her insistence on appreciating how the greatest happiness can spring from the smallest of things, the shortest of moments. Sophia Acree was born right after I completed chapter 3, which means that the second half of the book, like my life, is so much richer. No doubt because of all the playtime we enjoyed together.

I have long admired the University of New Mexico Press's Diálogos series, and I am deeply honored to be a contributing author now. Clark Whitehorn and Kris Lane are an amazing team. From the very first conversation I had with Clark about this project he has been deeply engaged in its development and has been supportive every step of the way. In every sense, Clark is a model editor and I am so thankful to have had the chance to work with him. Likewise, it has been a true privilege to work with series editor Kris Lane who, like Clark, has been closely connected to the book from its beginning. I have benefited from his expert editorial eye as well as his keen sense of narrative arc and argumentative structure. And I'm immensely grateful for the time and energy Clark, Kris, and the rest of the UNM Press team, including reviewers and the Editorial Board, have devoted to my book in all stages of the process.

I am also grateful for incredible research support I have received for this project. In 2010 and 2011, I had the good fortune to be a Fulbright Scholar in Uruguay. Special thanks to Patricia Vargas of the Fulbright Commission in Uruguay for helping with all aspects of my work while there, for facilitating connections with other Fulbrighters, and for continuing to promote educational exchange. Thanks as well to Ana Frega in the Department of History at the Facultad de Humanidades for her support of the project, and her suggestions for sources to consult during my fellowship. In summer 2012 a Faculty Research Grant from the Graduate School at Washington University in St. Louis, Missouri, funded critical research in Buenos Aires. During the 2013–2014 academic year I was honored to receive a National Endowment for the Humanities Fellowship that allowed me to dedicate all of my time to writing. And during fall semester 2016 I was lucky enough to be a Faculty Fellow at the Center for the Humanities at Washington University in St. Louis, where I wrote two chapters and thrived off of the intellectual exchanges with colleagues and Center staff. Research support of the kind I have enjoyed is imperative for humanities scholars and made *Staging Frontiers* possible, period.

So many friends and colleagues have, in a variety of ways, been instrumental in bringing this project to completion. Over countless meals Paul Ramírez shared feedback on grant proposals, the initial outline of the book, and on several chapters. His comments were always spot on. I'm thankful for his help in making a better book, but mostly for the conversations and friendship we have shared over the years. Christopher Conway read just about as many drafts of chapters as I have. I am grateful for his insights and perspectives, for the steadfast encouragement, and for being a wonderful friend. I'm also thankful for the invitation to present to Conway's colleagues and students at the University of Texas at Arlington. I was lucky to count on Yuko Miki, too, who offered her guidance with early framing of the argument and shared rigorous yet constructive criticism of proposal drafts. I have spoken with Alex Borucki about Creole dramas and Rioplatense cultural history more times than either of us can recall, in places stretching from Montevideo to Chapel Hill, North Carolina, to St. Louis. Always looking forward to our next conversation. Last, Stuart Day, Juan Carlos González-Espitia, and John Chasteen—longtime friends, mentors, colleagues—helped with many elements of the project, from thinking about ways to approach the types of performances at the heart of the book to supporting grant proposals to thinking about the transformative value and power of the everyday, mundane experience.

Additionally, at Washington University in St. Louis I am surrounded by outstanding colleagues in Romance Languages and Literatures and beyond. Special thanks go to: Paige McGinley, Julia Walker, Rob Henke, Pannill Camp, and the Department of Performing Arts for their ongoing interest in my work and the chance to present as part of the PAD Colloquium; Jean Allman, Rebecca Wanzo, Kathy Daniel, and Barb Liebmann at the Center for the Humanities for creating an inspiring humanities hub on campus, and for a transformative faculty fellow experience; Bret Gustafson, Kurt Beals, Stephanie Kirk, Tim Moore, Elzbieta Sklodowska, Harriet Stone, Peter Kastor, Diana Montaño, Christina Ramos, Ignacio Infante, Samuel Shearer, Mabel Moraña, Ignacio Sánchez Prado, Andrew Brown, Tabea Linhard, Javier García Liendo, Liz Childs, Lynne Tatlock, Joe Loewenstein, Rita Kuehler, Barbara Schaal, Adrienne Davis, and Holden Thorp. I have learned a great deal, too, about popular culture and cultural marketplaces in conversations with undergraduate and graduate students over the past decade. Speaking of students, Becca Fogel and Soledad Mocchi helped gather research material and compile the bibliography, for which I am grateful. My thanks as well to Dexter Zavalza Hough-Snee, Yvonne del Valle, and colleagues from the Department of Spanish and Portuguese at the University of California, Berkeley, for the invitation to share my research there; to Alex Sotelo Eastman, for the invitation to present at Dartmouth and for sustained conversations about shared interests over the years; to Laura Bass and colleagues at Brown University for the invitation to talk about gaucho dramas; to Reid Andrews, Jean-Philippe Barnabé, Paulina Alberto, Matt Karush, Graciela Montaldo, Brian Bockelman, Marcy Schwartz, Mariano Siskind, Alejandra Uslenghi, Ron Briggs, Ariel de la Fuente, Jens Andermann, Jeff Shumway, Mike Huner, Kristen McCleary, Fabricio Prado, Mollie Lewis Nouwen, Jeff Erbig, Mark Sanders, Nicolás Sillitti, and Lina Suk; and to Juan Carlos González-Espitia, Ana Sabau, Daylet Domínguez, Aiala Levy, Lance

Ingwersen, Elizabeth Schwall, and Julia Sarreal for including me on conference panels where I have been able to talk about extravagant circus extraordinaires, playing gaucho, and popular culture on the move.

In Uruguay I am grateful for the research support and assistance I received from staff at the following institutions: the Museo Romántico, Casa Lavalleja, and Casa Giró, all part of the Museo Histórico Nacional, especially Andrés Azpiroz Perera, Ariadna Islas, and Rosa Méndez; the Centro de Investigación, Documentación y Difusión de las Artes Escénicas at the Teatro Solís, in particular Marcelo Sienra; the Archivo Nacional de la Imagen y la Palabra at the SODRE; the Centro de Fotografía de Montevideo, in particular Mauricio Bruno; the Centro Nacional de Documentación Musical Lauro Ayestarán; the Biblioteca Nacional de Uruguay; Eduardo Trujillo and the Sociedad Criolla Elías Regules; and the Archivo General de la Nación. I am also indebted to Nicolás Duffau, Magdalena Broquetas, Juan González Urtiaga, Emilio Irigoyen, and Daniel Vidal for suggestions for sources to explore.

In Argentina my sincere thanks go to Carolina González Velasco, Cristiana Schettini, Julio Schvartzman, Adriana Rodríguez Pérsico, Mercedes García Ferrari, Lila Caimari, Ezequiel Adamovsky, Álvaro Fernández Bravo, and staff at the following institutions: the Archivo General de la Nación; the Biblioteca Nacional, in particular the Hemeroteca; the Instituto Nacional de Estudios de Teatro, especially Susana Arenz, María Rosa Petruccelli, and María Cristina Lastra Belgrano; Juliana María Lozada at the Museo de Arte Popular José Hernández; the Instituto Nacional de Antropología y Pensamiento Latinoamericano; and the Centro de Documentación de Danza, Teatro y Música at the Teatro San Martín.

Map 1.1 Map of the regional performance circuit where hemispheric travelers and Creole drama companies regularly gave shows. Note that the greatest concentration of locations was along the Paraná and Uruguay rivers.

Heterogeneous, Mundane, and Transformative

✦ MONDAY, MARCH 7, 1892: AS TWILIGHT ENVELOPED THE PORT CITY of Buenos Aires, an air of excitement buzzed around the Jardín Florida, one of nearly two dozen entertainment venues dotting the heart of Argentina's capital. Ticket holders made their way inside past curious onlookers, street musicians, and corner food stands, leaving behind one dynamic atmosphere of sights, sounds, and smells for another. That evening at the Jardín Florida was an "outstanding program" put on by the one and only Podestá-Scotti Circus Company, billed as the "Grand Equestrian, Gymnastic, Acrobatic Group, the creators of CREOLE DRAMAS." Variety and authenticity, it seemed, were crucial to the group's claim to fame.

The first part of the show featured all the company stars in miscellaneous acts. Then there was a music competition, consisting of a *payada* (improvisational verse and guitar accompaniment) between *ño Arena* and *ño Isidoro* where "sparks were sure to fly." The Afro-Argentine troubadour Gabino Ezeiza, who was the region's most famous, brought the house down, too. But more than anything else, crowds had come to see the second part of the evening's function: the swashbuckling drama *Juan Moreira*. Based on the story of a real-life outlaw, Moreira was by then Argentina's—and neighboring Uruguay's—most famous gaucho hero, owing primarily to the larger-than-life reputation advanced by the drama, which was the talk of the town. Part of the show included folk dancing, always a crowd pleaser, while another act revolved around an Italian immigrant character known as Cocoliche whose schtick of biting social commentary and outlandishly unsuccessful efforts to blend in with the gauchos (the region's cowboys) guaranteed laughter. On top of all this, the children who traveled with the company also were presented in a handful of scenes from the renowned drama.

That night at the Jardín Florida, then, was no doubt a heterogeneous affair that combined acrobatic stunts with the latest theatrical hits, young actors alongside older ones, musical improvisation with comedy. In effect, there was something for everyone. Far from being atypical, the show that Monday was similar to what one could see every other day of the week that March when the company performed there. The dramatic selection changed from time to time, but spectators attended with a set of assumptions and expectations about their experience. Ads noted that tickets went for "the regular prices," hinting that audiences knew these already, too. So, in addition to being heterogenous, the event was mundane in its familiarity and frequency.[1] Its familiar quality did not keep the show from selling out. Nor did it detract from the value of different social groups mixing and sharing through the evening's performance or prevent attendees from discussing the significant questions raised by what they saw onstage. In fact, the heterogenous and mundane character of what could otherwise be considered a fleeting encounter was also behind the very transformative power such shows had for the world of entertainment as well as for both the production and reception of popular culture. Like the rest of the shows offered by the Podestá-Scotti Company that season (and others), that "outstanding program" on March 7 had an outstanding, outsized impact.

Theater in Argentina and Uruguay, which together comprise the Río de la Plata region of Latin America, has been a predominant form of entertainment since the nineteenth century. Today, theaters abound in Montevideo (Uruguay's capital and most populous city), while its sister city Buenos Aires has its own Broadway on the legendary Corrientes street. In the age of digital culture, the theater remains a social and cultural mainstay of life for Argentines and Uruguayans, from the wealthiest to the economically challenged. In capital cities and small towns alike, hundreds of plays are performed each week, and they are well attended.

Seeing the roots of this theater culture and appreciating its value among citizens require turning away from the formal space of urban theaters (at least initially) to shows presented by traveling Creole Circus troupes in the past, like the famed Podestá-Scotti Company. In the late 1800s these groups "staged frontiers." That is, they effectively put the countryside onstage and represented the transformations the region's export boom and economic modernization were exacting not just on traditional ways of life but also on broader understandings of community. Dramas that spoke to the expansion of the frontier in the region, the accompanying displacement and trials rural inhabitants faced, and the tensions that developed between waves of immigrants and locals in urban and rural contexts, were the heart and soul of the Creole Circus. More generally, these dramatic representations often pitted idealized, heroic frontier figures who were distinctly antimodern against the increasingly powerful and seemingly heartless state. The formula was straightforward and radiated melodrama, which led in turn to staggering commercial success and cultural longevity.

Playing out onstage as well as in daily life was the intersection of state building with powerful strains of nationalism. The meeting of these forces in the many spaces where dramas of antimodern heroes unfolded from the late 1800s through the start of the new century had transformative consequences. Among these were the formation of an enduring theatergoing public and a proliferation of both new places and opportunities for social interaction. Moreover, in addition to providing a captivating experience of rural frontier life onstage for audiences that, for the most part, lived in towns and cities, these events allowed for frontiers of class, nationality, ethnicity, race, gender, and age differences to meet in much more harmonious ways than beyond the confines of the performance venue. The lines separating them were crossed collectively and daily, with far-reaching repercussions.

For a moment then, fleeting as it was, spectators came together in ways previously unimaginable, thanks to popular spectacle. Not that content was unimportant. But audience interaction and participation in such experiences were as meaningful, or more so, than the messages people viewed or heard.[2] The Creole Circus and its dramas, whose characters and themes immediately influenced audience behaviors and jumped from one medium or product to another beyond the tent folds or walls of the show, also led the promotion of iconic frontier and national myths that have permeated Argentine and Uruguayan identity ever since. Most strikingly, the staging of frontiers with their antimodern gaucho heroes constituted the nineteenth-century opening act of modern popular culture in Argentina and Uruguay.

Yet how was all of this possible? How could a bunch of ragtag circus families, many of immigrant descent, and other itinerant performers create what would become one of the most widely attended forms of entertainment for close to two decades, where ranch hands rubbed shoulders with presidents, and whose impacts would long outlive the ephemeral experience of the show? *Staging Frontiers* tells that story.

Beginning in the last third of the 1700s the first formal theaters in Buenos Aires and Montevideo joined with religious festivals to offer new entertainment spaces where crowds gathered and associated in new ways. Patriotic festivities and the uses of spectacle increased during the independence wars, soon to be followed by the arrival of some of the first hemispheric travelers in the 1820s and 1830s. For roughly the next thirty years people across the Río de la Plata went to see acrobats and horse races, along with examples of political theater and an occasional bad opera. Then, in the 1860s, touring equestrian shows from the United States and Europe made their way to the region and dazzled spectators with their stunts. These shows resonated with Argentines and Uruguayans, whom travelers often remarked spent their days on horseback. The decade of 1880, though, marks the point of inflection in this story.

Inspired partly by equestrian and acrobatic spectacles prevalent during the previous two decades, in the mid-1880s short theatrical works were incorporated into circus programs. These plays ushered in what would be an integral component from then on—the *Creole drama*, which was the name-sake and main attraction of the Creole Circus. Creole (*criollo*) was a colonial term denominating Spaniards born in the Americas and their privileged social status. By the second half of the 1800s, however, Creole had come to designate what and who was "authentically" Argentine or Uruguayan and clearly *not* European. Creole dramas told variations of the story of an honest native son, usually a hardworking gaucho, who was persecuted by a corrupt system of justice, sent to fight along the frontier, and who sought revenge for the disruptions modernization wrought.

At face value the story of country life under siege seems simplistic. But this genre of performing the frontier became the backbone of an entire enter-tainment industry, and more, at the turn of the century. Creole dramas facili-tated a more personal theater experience with local content and references that were conspicuously absent from opera or acrobatic performances during previous decades. Audiences thus embraced the dramas, for these repre-sented the same dialogue between tradition and modernity that Argentines, Uruguayans, and hundreds of thousands of European immigrants were experiencing in their everyday lives at the end of the 1800s.

The frontier onstage also spoke to the region's historical character and elements of collective identity. From the late 1700s to the dawn of the twentieth century the Río de la Plata grew from its position as a backwater contraband trading entrepot on the edge of the Spanish empire to become one of Latin America's economic powerhouses and destination for some of the largest numbers of transoceanic migrants in the Western Hemisphere. The "frontier" was very much part of this historical trajectory and narratives of national history in both Argentina and Uruguay. The peripheral frontier position this region occupied in South America was linked to its early bid for independence from Spain in the 1810s. While Argentina achieved nationhood by 1816, Uruguay's independence occurred a decade later, the territory having been the epicenter of conflict among Argentina, the newly formed Brazilian empire, and British commercial interests. In both scenarios, gauchos played critical roles as independence-era soldiers. Their daily life managing livestock involved work that was often violent, dexterity with knives and other tools that were easily transformed into weapons, and expert horsemanship. It was fitting, then, that groups of these men, known as *montoneras*, were recruited to fight and later celebrated in the post-independence years as national heroes, at least for some. Vicente Rossi, for instance, invoked these gaucho soldiers in his survey of the region's theater history: the decade of the 1890s saw "the glorious *montonera* that conquered the future of the Río de la Plata's national theater traditions. The gauchos of parody were victorious just like those of the wars of independence."[3]

Others were more reluctant to praise this local source of pride and turned their attention to European influence, be it in politics, education, philosophy, or science. One source of irritation for this group of Europhiles was the very frontier economy that had been an important source of the region's wealth. Grasslands that stretched south and westward from southern Brazil through Uruguay to Argentina were among the richest grazing areas in the world. Livestock flourished there, so much so that cattle products (beef jerky, hides, fats) dominated the region's economy through the 1850s. Control over this land likewise dominated politics, with conservatives eager to capitalize on the cattle economy, while liberals saw the land, the people who worked it, and the values that were tied to their worldview as obstacles to achieving European-style progress. The frontier had to be tamed. The classic summary of these positions was "civilization versus barbarism," made popular by the Argentine statesman and tireless writer Domingo Sarmiento.

When the balance of power shifted from conservatives to liberals in the second half of the century, the economic focus shifted, too. In Uruguay and later in Argentina, there was a violent military and settlement campaign to push the frontier back and wrest territory from indigenous groups. Sheep herding began taking the place of cattle raising, and then agriculture, especially cereal cultivation, became a primary source of investment, while grains became chief export products. Argentina and Uruguay opened their doors to waves of immigration from the 1870s through 1914. Some proponents of state-sponsored immigration hoped that northern Europeans would make the transatlantic voyage, but to their dismay Italians and Spaniards formed the greatest percentage of immigrants. They came to work the land, to design and build the urban infrastructure of the rapidly expanding port capitals and other cities, to "hacer la América"—that is, to strike it rich and, in the hopes of many, to return home. Most ended up staying, establishing roots and families.

So at the turn of the century, the region was undergoing radical changes on several fronts. There was the economic shift, from livestock to agriculture, where investment in rail lines and shipping were crucial; these lines, in turn, impacted the dynamic of life in the countryside. There was the demographic revolution, spurred by immigration and the flow of rural migrants to urban areas in search of work. And there was the economic and urban growth of the region that resulted in the once-peripheral area enjoying a new reputation in South America as well as globally. These changes brought their share of tensions, too, as we will see. In the face of such transformation, even though Buenos Aires had come to be known as the "Paris of South America" by 1900, and while Montevideo and smaller cities like Salto in Uruguay boasted buildings whose designs came straight from London or Rome, the frontier was not far away, geographically, figuratively, or historically. This fact is one of the reasons Creole dramas resonated so forcefully with audiences.

Another comes from the fact that by the time Creole Circus companies began crisscrossing Argentina and Uruguay in the 1880s stories of good-gauchos-gone bad had been "in the air" for decades thanks to the *gauchesque* literary tradition that deployed rural linguistic modalities and references to folkways in verse, narrative, and periodical publications. Yet it was in the last third of the century that the folksy gaucho toughs crystallized into national heroes. José Hernández's epic poem *The Gaucho Martín Fierro* (1872) was central to this process. But even more influential was the story of Argentina's most famous gaucho outlaw of the time, Juan Moreira, as told by Eduardo Gutiérrez in his "true crime" serial narrative titled simply *Juan Moreira* (1879–1880). *Moreira* became one of the best-selling books in Latin America prior to 1900, and its melodramatic adaptation for the stage sparked the Creole drama movement.

So successful was the dramatic *Moreira* (1886) that authors composed dozens of similar theatrical adaptations of gaucho stories, each drawing crowds day after day. While the print versions of *Fierro* and *Moreira* had been extraordinarily well received, their dramatic adaptations, as well as the explosion of Creole dramas in these years, launched such gaucho protagonists to stratospheric levels of popularity. In the early 1890s the most successful actors of these Creole dramas began to perform them in theaters rather than in tents hoisted above abandoned city blocks or at the entrances to small towns. The audience makeup changed, too, with the urban elite finding reasons to attend these gatherings of the people. From the circus and the theater, the Creole drama craze moved to other media. Cigarette makers marketed Moreira and Fierro brand smokes, while a new surge of gauchesque poetry and prose appeared across both Argentina and Uruguay, with tales of Moreira-like heroes. It was at this time, too, that Creole social clubs, called Creole Societies, formed to celebrate rural traditions. Members "played gaucho"; that is, they dressed in gaucho garb, paraded through town squares and city streets, and held lively dances and, of course, barbecues—a hallmark familiar to every contemporary tourist to the region.

By 1900, however, the Creole drama repertoire had ceased to grow. New entertainment options, which capitalized on the theatergoing public that the Creole drama phenomenon had created, started filling venues. Paramount among these were *zarzuelas* (Spanish light opera) and short, more formal plays called *sainetes* that explored urbanization and the ramifications of massive immigration to the region. The frontier maintained its place onstage, though it and related themes appeared in a much more critical light. Life in tenement housing, conflicts related to workers' unions, and generational differences of opinion also provided story lines for this new entertainment landscape. In the years following the 1910 centennial celebration of independence, a dance that had several debuts in Creole dramas—the tango—attracted devotees, too. Its transatlantic forays in France and the United States launched the dance and its music to new levels of fame in the region in the 1920s, from which point it developed into a Rioplatense icon. Film likewise started competing for audience attention in the early twentieth century. Though one of the region's first silent movies was about Moreira, by the early 1900s Creole dramas stopped appearing in theaters, except for the occasional benefit show for the performers, local politicians, or charity. There was no doubting, however, that the Creole drama phenomenon laid the foundation for the region's ever-expanding theatergoing public and was a catalyst for the Río de la Plata's modern popular culture. The phenomenon's legacy remained ubiquitous throughout the twentieth century, visible in the burgeoning film industry, informing radio theater of the 1930s, 1940s, and 1950s, and returning in a variety of formats in folk festivals across the region.

Creole dramas had catapulted the heroic figure of the gaucho to a new sphere of national visibility that has retained strength ever since. Predictably, vibrations of nationalism ran deep in Creole dramas, and performers as well as playwrights and theater owners were aware of the selling power of staging frontier experiences, especially as these were in full transition. In addition, Creole Circus troupes and entrepreneurs billed performances as family affairs, where there were children actors and sideshows for younger attendees. This blend of the silly and the serious, where mythic gauchos acted alongside whimsical clowns and caricatures of immigrants, where death-defying acrobatics were followed by merry folk-dance scenes, became a centerpiece of life in Buenos Aires, Montevideo, and dozens of smaller towns in rural Uruguay and Argentina.

Staging Frontiers is ultimately about the development of a new entertainment world in this part of Latin America, and its lasting and surprising impact on popular culture. Long before *telenovelas* (television soap operas) or society and entertainment magazines like *Hola* or *Gente* (think *People*), and decades before radio theater or film captivated audiences, Creole dramas and the buzz around them were everywhere. Through the Creole drama phenomenon's rise, its calibration by nationalist sentiments and commercial goals, and its eventual demise at the hands of some of those same forces, there emerged a more resilient theatergoing public, new forms of sociability, and an important strand of modern popular culture in Argentina and Uruguay. The arc of the Creole drama movement was in many senses embedded in the melodramatic representations of the frontier these plays communicated themselves: a surge to prominence (noble gaucho becomes a hero), then, almost as quickly as they rose, Creole dramas come under attack and are replaced by other forms of entertainment (the hero falls prey to the external forces inflicting change on his world). At the same time, the performers, publics, and narratives that together "staged the frontier" were a product of (as well as an expression of resistance to) a pivotal moment in the economic and demographic transformation of the Río de la Plata, resulting in a reconfiguration of social and cultural references. Yet for all of their ramifications and the lasting impressions they left, Creole dramas and their staggering impact have been largely overlooked until now.

Staging Frontiers refines the long-held narrative of *national theater* emerging from the circus, a model historians and literary scholars have elaborated for understanding the roots of the region's theater culture. Aside from the nationalist thrust of this linear model, it is one that centers on the city of Buenos Aires, with little or no attention given to the reception of Creole dramas or to their importance in Montevideo, small towns, and the countryside, where they were every bit as influential. This book also emphasizes the continuous movement that was so central to the appeal of the Creole Circus, manifest in how troupes established and followed a performance circuit stretching across the region, and in constant exchanges between elite and popular cultures through entertainment. In making such aspects central to the story, I aim to offer a more thorough understanding of the impact of Creole dramas and their relationship to the ways in which people interacted in the region, often called sociability. We will see that this relationship was as much (or more) about making money and attracting audiences day after day as it was about specific story lines that could be equated with nation or identity formation. Finally, and where all of these points converge, *Staging Frontiers* argues for a significant shift in our understanding of modern popular culture and the forces underlying its production in the Río de la Plata as developments rooted in the nineteenth century, rather than ones seen through the lens of the twentieth century, which has been the dominant historiographical trend. Of course manifestations of popular culture in Latin America have deep histories stretching back centuries. But when we think of modern popular culture in Argentina and Uruguay, there was a definitive period during which it began to congeal, and that period corresponds to the Creole drama phenomenon.

More broadly, *Staging Frontiers* contributes to the history of popular culture across the Americas. Circus performers from the Río de la Plata were familiar with Buffalo Bill's Wild West Shows, while circus families from the United States, like the Carlo brothers, spent decades working the Argentine and Uruguayan performance circuit. Expanding what we know about the intensity of such cultural flows prior to 1900 can challenge us to see local developments, meanings of frontiers, and nationalist icons in hemispheric or even global perspective.

Our narrative is divided into three parts. The first provides a cultural history of popular entertainment from the 1780s to the 1880s. Chapters focus on the transition from representations of royal power and religiosity to patriotic messaging during and after the wars of independence, and trace the performance circuit that hemispheric travelers created in the region over the nineteenth century. The varying motivations behind "public diversions" during this period as well as modifications to the content of these, and the accompanying shift in audience composition likewise receive much attention in part 1. We then turn to the rise of the Creole drama phenomenon, how it revolutionized the theatergoing experience, and the pervasive impact of the Creole spirit on Rioplatense popular culture. Finally, the story ends with the downfall of Creole dramas. That disappearing act, however, is inseparable from their legacy evident in the consolidation of a theatergoing public, the marketplace of cultural goods that developed over the course of the twentieth century, and the Creole as a lasting source of cultural heritage throughout the region.

This arrangement highlights the frontier of modern popular culture in the Río de la Plata as it came into focus throughout the nineteenth century. Chapters offer a detailed exploration of why it is important to study that frontier in regional perspective, the significance of its existence on the eve of the twentieth century, and the lasting implications of crossing it. At the same time, the book's focus on the making of modern popular culture in the region can advance our understanding of Latin American cultural history more generally. One of the primary ways it achieves this is through sustained attention to repercussions and enduring meanings of what were supposed to be ephemeral events and experiences. Almost by default, records of what went on at the Creole dramas and other forms of popular entertainment are incomplete, as are references to the emotions, sensory stimulation, and daily interpersonal communication that occurred through participation at such gatherings. Threading together existing materials that yield rich insight into these aspects will allow us to re-create portraits of these fleeting moments to see what they offered regularly to inhabitants that was so meaningful, and why.

A second way *Staging Frontiers* seeks to add to a fuller view of Latin American cultural history is with its approach to movement, unforeseen connections, and the power of play to transform public life. Whether we are dealing with cultural brokers who traveled from one town to another or stories and heroes who jumped from print to the stage to the silver screen, blurring the distinctions between high and low culture, movement was a constant force in the making of popular culture. Movement was also tied to unexpected, unplanned connections among people, activities, and cultural goods. Being in the right place at the right time was potentially transformative. Transformative, too, was the power of play to impact public life and feelings of community. That was exactly what was at stake when people went out to see an extravagant display by "Fish Man" (his antics appear in chapter 2), played gaucho at a Creole club, attended gaucho theatrical hits, or joined a Creole carnival *comparsa* to compete with thousands in song, dance, and dress. If we look carefully, before the vestiges and memories vanish, such practices were full of meaning making.

Finally, an outline of several concepts mentioned already and that appear consistently in the book can help readers keep overarching questions in mind. First among these concepts is popular culture. Like Lawrence Levine, I understand popular culture in a straightforward manner: the term refers to goods, objects, and activities that are widely accessible and that are consumed or taken up by significant numbers of people. While there is no set threshold for these numbers given their variation across time, important factors for measuring popularity include availability and accessibility of the cultural expressions or products in question, and the reception of these across social sectors. Popular culture is often public culture and therefore shared.[4] This public and shared character of what we can call popular culture is much more important than any sort of hierarchical appraisal or low/high positioning. It is also central to the understanding of the popular culture industry and marketplace, which comprised the means, methods, and motivations behind the largescale distribution and reception of popular culture.

A second concept is *criollismo*, or what we can loosely understand as the Creole spirit. Criollo was about who and what were local or native—that is, Argentine or Uruguayan; this was the core idea of criollismo. That nativist thrust was manifest in a range of cultural politics and products, Creole dramas being among the most prominent. Ironically, immigrant families and their descendants made up the bulk of Creole Circus performers and played an outsized role in the elaboration of national tropes, which required spectators to reconcile, consciously or not, profound questions of ethnicity and nationality. Linked to the idea of the Creole was antimodernism, whereby a (nostalgic) view of the past was juxtaposed with what some considered the overly rapid pace of modern life. Paradoxically, the narratives of antimodern heroes allowed for people to engage with the modern.

Last, though not reducible to a single term, we must underscore the transmission of lessons and social values via forms of collective or public entertainment, in particular performance. Here the takeaway lies in the impact theatrical or other types of symbolic representation can have on individual and collective behavior. Levine puts a finer point on the idea. "When the representations become embodied in theater, tales, radio, movies, they become forms of reality themselves . . . in which many essential things are realized: lessons are learned, values enunciated and repeated, modes of behavior scrutinized, social institutions and their effects explored, fantasies indulged."[5] The ability of representational meaning to become fused with daily life, ideas of authenticity, and notions of truth was in part what allowed for fantastical frontiers onstage and popular culture writ large to be at once heterogenous, mundane, and transformative.

But don't take my word for it. Take those of the Uruguayan lawyer and occasional playwright Víctor Pérez Petit, who cut his dramatic teeth in the era of the Creole Circus. For all the rudeness of Creole dramas, he wrote in his "defense" of these plays, they leave the impression of "something great."[6] Let's see what that something great was all about, why it was such a force of attraction, and how its legacy lingered long after the excitement that characterized that March evening at the Jardín Florida had become a distant, dim flicker of the region's history.

PART 1

A Cultural History of Popular Entertainment (1780s–1880s)

CHAPTER 1

Royal Impressions and Patriotic Diversions

The Social World of Entertainment

✦ "THERE WAS A POOR, LITTLE THEATER, WITH A THATCH ROOF. THERE
were poor actors and a sad orchestra. And there were moralists, mainly
priests, always lambasting this place." So wrote Mariquita Sánchez, socialite
and matron of patriot gatherings during the independence era of the 1810s,
in her prolific reflections on colonial Buenos Aires and its first theater. An
anonymous Englishman who compiled a narrative of his residence in the city
during the early 1820s complained similarly about the town's second theater.
"The theatre, as an edifice, has nothing to boast," he wrote. "The exterior
looks like a stable"—a fitting description for a place where just about everything related to daily life seemed to occur on horseback. On the interior,
there was nothing very noteworthy either, save the *cazuela*, or upper gallery,
where women gathered to watch the show, gossip, and arrange amorous ren-
dezvous. This visitor pointed out an aspect of the shows that bothered other
observers as well—the unwanted stereo effect of the prompter, who called out
lines from his "tub" set in the middle of the stage, "destroying all illusions of
the scene." Actors then repeated these, taking care not to fall into the
prompter's box. Looking beyond these flaws, the Englishman noted with a
bit of surprise that the residents are "a people so theatrically inclined."[1]

Some 120 miles east, across the Río de la Plata, another Englishman by the
name of Alexander Caldcleugh made a stop in Montevideo on his trip from
Rio de Janeiro to Buenos Aires in early 1821. The governor's office received

him well, and the evening of his arrival he attended the city's sole theater. Despite the good food he was served and the conversation with "all the most celebrated beauties of the city, who were extremely polite," he described the theater itself as "small and ill arranged; the actors, it may be supposed, not of the best." And even though the "well dressed women in the streets" and at the theater left a more positive impression on Caldcleugh, he held firm in his higher opinion of theaters in London and Paris.[2]

Aside from scoffing at the theater, such accounts point to a simple fact: prior to the 1830s formal entertainment options in the region were limited. A handful of theaters offered inhabitants—particularly the more well-off—a place to see and be seen, as well as a small number of fairly poorly presented plays, if we are to believe Sánchez and the Englishmen. Plazas de Toros were another formal performance space on both sides of the Plata river, though bullfights were much less common than in Spain, New Spain, or other parts of the Spanish empire in America. Despite the scarcity of formal venues, there was an increasing environment of popular spectacle that developed between the late 1700s and the 1820s, revolving initially around religious and royal celebrations, and then gathering force with the wars of independence, patriotic commemorations, and entertainment in public spaces.

If one were to live long enough to be able to tour the social world of entertainment from roughly 1780 to 1830, the half century corresponding to the transition of the Río de la Plata region from its colonial frontier days to an emerging commercial area comprising two independent republican nations, several stops would be imperative. The first of these would allow for vivid observation of royal ostentation and the presentation of religious zeal, forms of spectacle that more often than not went hand in hand until the crisis of the Spanish monarchy shook the colonial order in the early 1800s. A second extended stop would reveal nativist undercurrents that begin to permeate forms of entertainment both inside and outside of the theater as early as the decade of 1780. More precisely, such undercurrents materialized in the first examples of gauchesque drama, and they remained an important vehicle of communication during the wars of the 1810s. This nativist spirit meshed with the patriotic messaging of independence. A final, overlapping vista comes from the back and forth between the silly and the serious. That is, serious representations of political, military, and religious power often found expression through or alongside more silly acts. This abstract concept was on the minds of the first theater entrepreneurs. Thus, Manuel Cipriano de Melo, who financed Montevideo's Casa de Comedias, had the slogan "Through laughter and song, theater improves behaviour" embroidered onto his theater curtain. Gauchesque poet and theater director Bartolomé Hidalgo fused humor and country wit together in his dialogue between two gauchos who paint a seriously patriotic portrait of the 1822 *fiestas mayas*, or civic celebrations, honoring May 1810 when the push for independence got its start in the region.[3] Finally, a game of *sortija*, which was basically horseplay (more on this below), was never temporally or geographically far from the more solemn masses or military parades that took place on a regular basis throughout this period.

In this chapter we will undertake this tour as a point of departure for understanding the emergence of popular spectacle in the region during the half century in focus. The stops highlight transformations in forms of spectacle as well as their rules of social engagement. The transition from religious to secular entertainment resulted in not only a proliferation of the types of entertainment activities but also modified forms of sociability associated with these. Before the 1810s, the theater was one of the few public diversions for women, whereas men had other sites they frequented, such as cockfights and horse races. In Montevideo, so common was it to see women and their children at the theater that complaints of screaming kids are frequent in local press reviews of the performances. Of course, women and men in Montevideo, Buenos Aires, and in sleepier towns of the interior yearned for ways to escape the boredom of daily routine. Entertainment provided this escape.[4]

Before beginning our tour of the early social world of entertainment, one caveat bears underscoring. The goals and nature of entertainment no doubt underwent substantial transformation as political representation and forms of power shifted from monarchical control to republican institutions. Royal authority gave way to incipient republican, state oversight and appropriation of forms of popular spectacle. At the same time, the shifting political character of entertainment started to evidence growing distance between a formal state connection and the world of entertainment. This point is critical to bear in mind. Moreover, participation in the social world of entertainment brought people together in more and different ways. However, this burgeoning atmosphere of popular spectacle did not usher in a radical reshaping of the social hierarchy in the region. Men, women, free blacks, slaves, children, and peasants did mingle more thanks to entertainment options. But these people also "knew their place," even if that place was increasingly less fixed.

Royal Ostentation and Religious Zeal

When the Bourbon reforms led to the creation in 1776 of the Viceroyalty of the Río de la Plata, encompassing today's Argentina, Bolivia, Paraguay, and Uruguay, as part of the Spanish crown's effort to shore up control in the Southern Hemisphere, Buenos Aires and Montevideo were just sparsely populated frontier contraband ports.[5] The official census of Buenos Aires in 1778 reported a population of around twenty-five thousand, though as Lyman Johnson has shown, the real number of inhabitants was higher. Even as the region's most populous city, Johnson points out that "in 1780 Buenos Aires was the least distinguished viceregal capital in Spain's American empire."[6] However, the decision to make Buenos Aires the capital of the new viceroyalty changed the trajectory of the city and the region.

From roughly 1780 to 1810, there was significant demographic growth, construction, and an uptick in economic activity. By the 1810 census, the population of Buenos Aires had swelled to more than forty thousand. A broad mixture of groups, including startling numbers of African slaves and their descendants, recently arrived European immigrants, and migrants from the region's countryside, contributed to the new social architecture, as well as to the expanding urban infrastructure.[7] The hub of this urban expansion was the Plaza Mayor (today's Plaza de Mayo), the political, religious, and military center of Buenos Aires, as well as the epicenter of the city's ceremonial activity. There the whitewashed Cabildo looked east across the Plaza to the fortress. On the north side of the Plaza the new cathedral was under construction. And in the Plaza itself, a makeshift market formed daily with foodstuffs and artisans' wares for sale. Travelers complained of the marketplace becoming a central swamp when it rained, while Cabildo members harped about butchers moving their products into the halls of the government building.[8]

By the end of the 1700s, the city center had started to experience a facelift, with new homes constructed of sturdier materials, and some brick- or stone-paved streets, though these were the exception.[9] Parish church steeples pierced the skyline.[10] A visitor from the United States commented on these features, noting that from the river the city's "domes and steeples, and heavy masses of buildings give it an imposing, but somewhat gloomy aspect."[11] At night most of the city's buildings and streets were dark. The Teatro de la Ranchería, thought of as a temporary locale that would help fund an orphanage, opened for performances at the end of the 1770s as the city's first formal theater. It was located at the intersection of Perú and Alsina Streets, about two blocks from the Cabildo and the Plaza Mayor. The viceroy asked the theater's neighbors to place a light in their doorway so that spectators would feel comfortable when leaving the show after nightfall.[12] The Ranchería offered denizens a new entertainment outlet, but its spectacles did not compete with either royal or religious pomp and circumstance.

Montevideo at the turn of the nineteenth century shared many of the same characteristics as Buenos Aires, though on a smaller scale. The town's population numbered less than half that of Buenos Aires on the eve of the nineteenth century, though its growth kept pace with the expansion of Buenos Aires, and it was the most populated area of the Banda Oriental, the territory that would become Uruguay.[13] The demographic makeup was similar, too: Afro-descendants constituted close to 30 percent of the population, substantial numbers of Spanish and Portuguese migrants settled in the city as economic opportunities opened up, and migrants from the countryside relocated to the port town in search of work.[14] The core of the city (today's Ciudad Vieja) was compact, with an urban layout similar to Buenos Aires: Cabildo and Cathedral faced each other across the newly designed Plaza Mayor—the town's nerve center—set roughly in the middle of a tight grid layout, and parish churches marked other distinct points of the cityscape. The Casa de Comedias, which opened in 1793, was a couple of blocks south within the city's fortified walls. While both Buenos Aires and Montevideo were perched on edges of seemingly endless plains, Montevideo was erected on a peninsula that jutted out into the river. The advantage was that it sat on a natural harbor that was deeper than Buenos Aires's, accommodating larger ships and making unloading at the shore possible.[15] The smaller town was also more strategically located vis à vis the entrance to the Río de la Plata, which made it a crown jewel in the control over access to South America from the South Atlantic.

Though the strategic allure of Montevideo and the region's commercial prospects were not lost on the British navy, which invaded the region twice (1806 and 1807), travelers were more ambiguous about their impression of the city. In a series of letters fit for a soap-opera tale, the Englishman John Constance Davie wrote about his forced arrival in South America in 1797, en route to Australia. He landed at Montevideo and was curious to see the town, "though, God knows, besides the river and the mountain there is but little to excite the traveller's curiosity."[16] Twenty years later, at the beginning of the Luso-Brazilian occupation of the Banda Oriental, Henry Brackenridge dashed a similar appraisal of Montevideo, writing that from the bay the town gave "no mean appearance." Once on land, though, he expressed surprise at the devastation war had caused. There was an eerie quiet in the city center, with rough-looking types sleeping on thresholds—though he admits this may be due to the hour of his stroll, during the siesta. Brackenridge attributed the decline of the city's activity to the "barbarian" José Artigas, who led a series of sieges of the city in a bid to overthrow Spanish control.[17]

That most of the region's population was concentrated in Buenos Aires and Montevideo helps explain why interior towns were less central to the performance scene that emerged, and why documentation is scarce for interior cities, except places like Córdoba or Colonia del Sacramento. Moreover, this sketch of the population distribution and the cityscapes of Buenos Aires and Montevideo at the turn of the century makes it easy to see how these cities could feel like frontier towns where boredom could easily settle in prior to the construction of their first theaters or the more frequent performances in public spaces of the early 1800s. The performances of royal power, however, were anything but boring.

By nature, representations of monarchy had to be ostentatious, and there were plenty of occasions for conveying, through show, royal authority and the Spanish empire's reach. As in other Spanish American colonies, the coronation of new kings occasioned lavish ceremonies.[18] In addition to the hierarchical and ordered marches of colonial officials, the Cabildo, churches, and the houses of the most distinguished residents were illuminated; there were bullfights and marching bands; acrobats performed their tricks; and usually the activities carried into the night with fireworks, dancing, and theatrical performances.[19] Thus, in 1747 the new king, Fernando VI, was honored with plays by the acclaimed Spanish author Calderón de la Barca. Twelve years later dramatic representations were again central to Carlos III's coronation. Of course, in the commotion there was a distinct order on display, and participants saw reminders of this order in what is often termed the *verticality* of the ceremony. The sequence of procession marchers, the organization of the ceremony, the path the procession followed, and so on, all embodied this verticality, guiding participants to revere the new monarch. Portraits of the king were also important elements that made concrete the presence of the distant father figure.[20] A final example comes from November 1789, when the governor of Montevideo documented that the city's residents and artisan guilds welcomed the new king with four days of "wonderfully expressive demonstrations of jubilation . . . that serve as proof of their love and loyalty to the Sovereign."[21] During these festivities authorities distributed food, and fountains of water, milk, wine, and brandy spouted their juices for a week.[22]

Reinforcement of the colonial social hierarchy through royal ostentation was manifest on other occasions, too. Take for instance the *paseo del estandarte*, or parade of the royal banner, which was part of coronation festivities as well as royal birthdays, Patron Saint days, appointments and welcoming events for colonial authorities, and Corpus Christi processions (we will return to Corpus shortly).[23] Royal marriages similarly entailed a display of royal power and merriment. Such was the case with the first plays staged in the Banda Oriental, which took place in Colonia del Sacramento in 1729 as part of the festivities surrounding the wedding of the prince of Brazil. The "actors" were soldiers and they ironically (given Portugal's control of the city in this year) performed plays by Calderón de la Barca.[24] In all of these instances the role of theatricality was to highlight the pedestal on which subjects were supposed to view colonial authority, even when the highest representative of such authority was thousands of miles away. Thus, at the bullfighting events that took place during coronation celebrations and on other select days throughout the year, royal authorities enjoyed their box seats, centrally located for all to see.[25] Despite the lower number of bullfights in Buenos Aires and Montevideo, not to mention smaller towns of the region, as Juan Pedro Viqueira Albán has illustrated for eighteenth-century New Spain, these spectacles were held in large measure to preserve a certain order and to promote the awe of authority.[26]

Awe was central to the expression of religious zeal, too. This zeal was on display at religious processions, which were intimately linked to the social life of the region's residents. Recalling her childhood Buenos Aires, Mariquita Sánchez tells us that "events organized by the church constituted the principal social activities of the city. Basically, praying and eating (on days not designated for a fast) is what we did."[27] Sánchez is quick to point out that these activities did not necessarily translate into a lackluster social life: "When a parish organized a procession, everybody in the neighborhood participated." Parishes competed to outdo each other in the scale and magnificence of their processions and related activities. She cites the example of the Merced Church, where one year the congregation was treated to the sight of a giant sky blue and white cotton cloud hanging from inside the church. Inside the cloud there was a young boy who sang during the service—the voice of an angel. As the cloud was lowered and then raised again, the angel threw out flowers to the parishioners below.[28]

The most elaborate religious entertainment occurred during the Lenten season and the feast of Corpus Christi. Throughout Lent, Buenos Aires priests pronounced fiery sermons in public squares; penitents marched seeking forgiveness; young girls dressed as angels and paraded in each of the city's seven parishes; effigies of Judas, filled with explosives, were set off at the end of Holy Week; and, of course, there were highly symbolic processions on Easter Sunday.[29] Corpus Christi likewise called for dazzling processions that provided entertainment in which thousands participated, and thousands more watched. One historian described the general pattern of the beginning of the Corpus festivities in colonial Montevideo: black dancers and drummers led the procession, which made for a thunderous, theatrical display, followed by city dwellers and then church and city officials.[30] Expenses for the 1777 feast of Corpus Christi in Montevideo illustrate the fanfare associated with the event. Costs include payment for whale fat and tallow to illuminate the Plaza Mayor at night, carpenters to build decorative arches, food for soldiers, a few pesos for the street sweepers who cleaned the square after the events ended, compensation for "the Black residents who, in their costumes, danced at the head of the procession," and a meager amount for the musicians who enlivened every moment.[31]

John Davie, whom we met earlier, wrote about his joy of participating in the festival of Corpus Christi in Buenos Aires in 1797. After disembarking in the region in February he was "seized" with an illness that purportedly "usually attacks Europeans upon their first landing."[32] For the next three months Davie convalesced in the Convent of Santo Domingo and pretended to be a devout Catholic. So when the festival of Corpus came that June, he had a unique vantage point, one that ended up surprising his previous thoughts about Catholicism. "The holy festival was celebrated yesterday, with a degree of pomp of which I had not entertained the smallest idea." He notes the sounds of bells and cannon fire, song, and musket salutes, and then describes decorations and other elements prepared for the procession.[33] "All the sweets of nature," continues Davie, "seemed collected in one spot, to honour the sacred festival; and a greater assemblage of people of all ranks, ages, and conditions, I never witnessed, even in the most populous city in Europe."[34] Davie concedes that such a show of religious zeal may appear strange to protestant English readers. But he argues that the festivities were necessary for attracting new converts. "By witnessing the grandeur and solemnity of the spectacle they [those who are not yet devout Catholics] might form a wish to become members of a church which, to all outward appearance, is so extremely fascinating."[35] Davie's account does contain its share of disparaging remarks, especially when claiming that the only way to reach "an ignorant people" is via the senses. Yet even this skeptical Englishman was dazzled by the theatricality of it all. And as Viqueira Albán maintains, "Corpus was the theatrical festival par excellence; in it, the spiritual, the infinite, the invisible were materialized physically, in the finite and the visible."[36]

The Patron Saint days of Buenos Aires and Montevideo rivaled Corpus Christi with their displays of zeal and often surpassed the Corpus feast in their offerings of entertaining diversions. Buenos Aires's *fiesta patronal* began October 12, honoring Nuestra Señora del Pilar and usually lasted at least a week. Everything took place in the Plaza de la Recoleta, in front of the Church of Nuestra Señora del Pilar and the attached convent (next to the now famous Recoleta Cemetery). In his memoirs, José Antonio Wilde recalled that "people of every class and condition came and went on foot" to the festivities.[37] There were acrobatic performances, food and drink, dancing and music, horse races, and bullfights, as well as the expected masses and processions, all in the name of the Patron Saint. Similar expressions of faith and entertainment characterized the May 1 Patron Saint festival in Montevideo. There, as in Buenos Aires, inhabitants wore their nicest clothes and—perhaps more important—saddled their horses with their most ornate riding gear for show and for sortija games, where riders at full gallop attempted to snag a dangling ring. For their part, royal and religious figures dressed in their impressive garb and marched the royal banner into the cathedral in a synthesis of royal ostentation and religious zeal.[38]

By the early 1820s the spirit of this celebration had started to lag. An English resident complained that "the amusements are not very great; there are a few booths for eating and drinking, swings, two or three sullen clowns running about, and a military band." But one could still enjoy watching "country people dance till a late hour in the booths."[39]

A final example of a site where the theatricality of religious zeal was manifest comes from the *candombes*, or ceremonial, musical, religious gatherings, of black "nations" in Buenos Aires and Montevideo. These nations were ethnic and linguistic groups of Africans and their descendants. In addition to providing a sense of community, black nations functioned as aid societies for their members, petitioning officials for protection, to redress wrong doing, or for permission to gather on Sundays and holidays, like the Day of Kings, to play music and celebrate their faith.[40] It was precisely on these days that candombe became part of the early social world of entertainment, for the music and dance events attracted spectators from all points of the city. Take for example the colorful (and perhaps exaggerated, though still worthwhile) description Isidoro de María makes of candombe in Montevideo. De María sketches the scene on the south side of town during summer holidays and Sundays: "Not a single old storekeeper, no head of family or midwife, not a sole young woman missed it. Along with the *decent people*, they all made their way to the popular candombe of the African race." The Day of Kings offered the most elaborate and perhaps intense celebrations among black nations. In addition to the music, elegant clothing, and sizable crowds, each nation's members presented an altar to San Antonio or San Balthasar, the black king.[41]

While candombes remained a critical entertainment and social space for Afro-descendants and the broader population in the region well into the 1840s, religious entertainment and the performance of royal power entered a rapid phase of transition to wartime festivities and more secular forms of spectacle at the outset of the nineteenth century. The writing was on the wall or, rather, the ceiling. In August 1792, the Teatro de la Ranchería, located just a few paces from the heart of viceregal and religious power, burned down after its thatch roof caught fire. The apparent cause of the conflagration was a series of fireworks launched from the nearby, newly inaugurated church of San Juan Bautista. The contemporary man of letters Juan María Gutiérrez related that the church's priests and nuns spoke of a sign of heaven in the fire, ridding the city of "the house of wrong and worldly pleasures."[42] What is certain is that there was a brewing tension between supposed divine reverence and its representation on the one hand and, on the other, perceived lasciviousness in the world of "secular" entertainment. The cityscapes of both Buenos Aires and Montevideo bespoke the new position the theater was thought to occupy. Both the Teatro de la Ranchería and Montevideo's Casa de Comedias were centrally located. That location at the center of power (along with the church and the Cabildo) was meaningful in terms of urban geography and how residents conceived of the theater in their visual schema of society going forward.[43]

There were other signs of the tension, too. In 1809, following the Napoleonic invasion of the Iberian Peninsula, the parade of the royal banner was temporarily suspended in Montevideo.[44] Three years later, in May 1812, the revolutionary government of the United Provinces—which would soon form Argentina—decreed the practice offensive, signaling the end to the performance of royal power associated with its display, in line with a broader transformation underway of royal symbols.[45] The decree itself is telling: "Considering that the parade of the royal banner in towns across Spanish America is a humiliating ceremony introduced by tyranny and incompatible with the prerogatives of liberty, this government has reached the following resolution on this 11th day of May: that the aforementioned ceremony is hereby suspended . . . and should be substituted with a more dignified demonstration analogous to our civil regeneration."[46] Clearly, royal ostentation and religious zeal were in decline and then under outright attack.

The results of this process were visible in the social world of entertainment. Soon after the inauguration of the Casa de Comedias in Montevideo, it became a symbolic place where conflicts between local officials (Cabildo members) and royally appointed authorities (like military leaders and the governor) played out, literally, with one group barring the other's access to the private seating areas in the theater.[47] Similarly, the new forms of sociability that the venue allowed initially bumped up against more deeply ingrained representations of social hierarchy. In addition to *gente decente* who frequented the shows, the Casa de Comedias attracted people "from other walks that were less than flattering, but who were crazy about buying their way up the social ladder." Socialites did not let the issue go unnoticed. "The principal matrons of the city" complained to authorities that "the best seats were taken 'by women of ill repute'." The governor called a reunion with his enemies at the Cabildo in which they resolved that the Cabildo would oversee ticket distribution for these seating areas. They would offer tickets first to "distinguished" residents; leftover tickets would then be made available to those of lesser social standing.[48]

Around the dawn of the nineteenth century, then, the entertainment geography in the region started to experience significant changes. The wars of independence exacerbated these developments and catapulted patriotic messages to the forefront of entertainment. By the time the anonymous author of *A Five Years' Residence in Buenos Aires* recorded his experiences in the early 1820s, the power of Catholicism in the public sphere was clearly in decline. A January 1824 visit of the archbishop, for example, generated little interest. Few residents came to greet him, and the government's response "was anything but cordial."[49] Such a muted ceremony would have been unthinkable two decades earlier.

Nativist Undercurrents and Patriotic Messaging

The waning sway of religious spectacle was clearly manifest in a new form of theatrical representation materializing at the end of the 1700s and gathering momentum during the first third of the nineteenth century: gauchesque drama. Dramas in this sort of popular theater cycle were written and initially performed between the decades of 1780 and 1830.[50] Their resonance was particularly strong during the crisis of the independence wars beginning in 1810, when the voice of the countryside was deployed in popular verse as well as in entertainment venues to recruit adherents to the patriot cause. It was during the decade of 1810, too, when such nativist undercurrents combined with patriotic messaging of the new *fiestas cívicas* and fiestas mayas—multiday public festivals commemorating events of the wars for independence, most notably the May 25, 1810, "revolution," when a junta at Buenos Aires declared self-rule in the absence of the Spanish king. Though Catholicism retained an important public presence following independence, by the 1820s civic pride had replaced religious passion in the realm of spectacle, while acrobats, horsemen, and an increasing repertoire of gauchesque and other dramas at theaters entertained both city and rural inhabitants.

Long before Estanislao del Campo made readers laugh with his presentation of gauchos at the operatic performance of *Faust*, and decades before the best-selling authors José Hernández, Eduardo Gutiérrez, or Antonio Lussich celebrated the countryside and warned against the abuse of its inhabitants, the Rioplatense rural experience acquired political value in a handful of short plays—*sainetes*, to be exact. These sainetes made their debut on the eve of and during independence. Though such plays were contemporary with Bartolomé Hidalgo's *cielitos* and *diálogos*, deploying gaucho speak in print, they have garnered less attention from scholars, no doubt because of the scant evidence surrounding their reception. However, these short plays reveal much about the shifting focus on the entertainment horizon.

The first of these sainetes, *El amor de la estanciera* (The Ranch Girl's Heart), dating most likely from around 1790, established a framework on which the others would elaborate. The scene is the ranch of Cancho and Pancha, with references to daily life in the countryside—milking cows, branding animals, the open plains. The couple is close to giving their daughter Chepa in marriage to Marcos Filgueira, an apparently wealthy Portuguese immigrant. There is another pretender, though: Juancho, a noble native son. Chepa is inclined to accept Marcos's proposition, even disparaging Juancho as a "dark-skinned, brute pig."[51] But the foreigner's arrogance turns the family against him, and Chepa and Juancho join hands happily. Every aspect of the show breathes country life. The virtues of Chepa are that she milks cows well and can make good cheese, while Juancho himself is a strong herdsman with abundant cattle. Marcos is not only an intruder from Portugal, illustrating longstanding tensions between residents of the two empires vying for control in the region; he is also a caricature of an urban charlatan whose lofty speech masks his cowardice. The entertainment quality of the sainete is clear, and most residents of Buenos Aires, where it debuted, would have found the language accessible and familiar. Protecting family honor, the value of hard work, and the family structure as a critical force of social relations all stand out as key themes in the piece.

Two other sainetes, intended to function together, picked up the same themes some twenty years later: *El valiente fanfarrón y criollo socarrón, o El gaucho* (The Show-Off and Creole Smart Aleck, or The Gaucho) and *Las bodas de Chivico y Pancha* (The Marriage of Chivico and Pancha). Both plays drew on the earlier example, staging many of the same characters in the setting of a ranch with all its usual accoutrements: cattle skulls; a horn flask full of brandy; animal haunches to serve as seats; and a fire heating a kettle for the extra character, the ubiquitous *mate*. A dispute over the hand of a daughter is the source of conflict. The difference in these plays is that the conniving charlatan characters are not foreigners but two buffoon doctors—a sacristan and his sidekick—who make fools of themselves reciting passages in Latin that they believe will heighten their attractiveness. The wedding works out in the end, though not before humorous descriptions of women socializing in the upper balcony of Buenos Aires's new Casa de Comedias.[52] Little is known about the performance history of these sainetes. But theater historians argue that *El valiente fanfarrón* and *Las bodas* must have attracted audiences given that the story line and characters carried over the two plays (a sign of decent reception), and in light of the fact that they enjoyed success on the stage throughout the 1830s and 1840s, with modifications to accommodate political expediency.[53] Like the earlier sainete mentioned, the native son is the hero in both of these, too.

The last known sainete from these years pairs native-son heroes with news from independence battles. *El detalle de la acción de Maipú* (The News from Maipú), from 1818, relates the victory of José de San Martín's forces in Chile on April 5 of that year. News of the success gave residents in the Plata reason to hope that the patriot cause was not lost. The scene again is the countryside, where family members of Juan José—a soldier who had accompanied San Martín—gathered round a fire, awaiting news of the army's progress. The play is full of colorful language and anti-Spanish slurs. Juan José tells of the trials of the battlefield and how he and other patriots really gave it to the *Godos*. After the news, the local mayor brings a guitar, which leads to payadas, or improvised singing, and all dance a *cielo*, or folk dance not unlike a form of square dancing from the Argentine countryside, which is important for the incorporation of popular dance into the more formal space of the theater.[54] Following the scene of music and dance, the sainete ends on a metatheatrical note: all the actors gather onstage to give Spaniards a warning of American strength, and to proclaim that soon Montevideo will be free, too. The final lines admonish spectators to obey the new Buenos Aires government that will lead to unity.[55] Clearly, a new kind of politics that blended nativism and the patriot cause infused these plays.

Gauchesque dramas constitute one example of an expanding variety of entertainment forms in the region at the dawn of the nineteenth century. There were other types of plays that, while more conservative in their use of language and with more formal settings, still explored contemporary regional political circumstances. One of these dramatized the defeat of the British by residents of Buenos Aires. Another, titled *Sentimientos de un patriota* (Feelings of a Patriot), was part of the 1816 fiestas mayas in Montevideo.[56] In effect, the patriotic celebrations that took place with regularity beginning in 1811 offered a different site where the inhabitants of Buenos Aires, Montevideo, and towns across the Rioplatense countryside engaged in new ways the early world of entertainment with its patriotic messaging.

Both fiestas mayas and fiestas cívicas were multiday events where all social sectors came together to honor the new idea of the republic, soldiers fighting in the wars, and major victories against Spanish forces. A sample of the abundant documentation of these parties in the region gives a sense of the types of entertainment activities that attracted so many people day after day and that encouraged participants to socialize. The May festivities usually began on May 24 and lasted anywhere from three days to a week. The first fiestas mayas in 1811 in Buenos Aires set the tone and the stage (literally) for future years. Already on day 1 there were artillery salutes, music, and fireworks in the evening. For the next four days, relates Juan Manuel Beruti, there were "infinite amusements"—dancing, people in costumes, and masked balls, all kept orderly thanks to a ban on the sale of "the stronger sort of drink" during the festivities.[57] Two years later a dramatic version of *Julius Caesar* was performed at the Casa de Comedias on the opening day of May 24, "instructing viewers to cultivate an eternal grudge against tyranny."[58] The anonymous chronicler of this year's event noted that it lasted a week, and that on May 25 a huge crowd of all ages gathered in the Plaza Mayor to usher in a new year of liberty. Against the backdrop of canons firing, and along with representatives of the new government who wore Phrygian caps, the crowd cheered "with such delight and emotion whose real meaning can only be felt, not described by words."[59] Cabildo members doled out monetary gifts to artisans, poor residents, and to orphans. A unique spectacle was the burning of tools and a torture chair of sorts that colonial officials used to extract information or force confessions.[60] Isidoro de María as well as the anonymous author who chronicled the Banda Oriental's first fiestas mayas in 1816 describe them in similar terms to the events in Buenos Aires. Activities took place in the Plaza Matriz; schoolchildren sang hymns beside a patriotic pyramid; women distributed patriotically colored hats and flags to children; and people enjoyed the merriment while it lasted. That year the public library was inaugurated as part of the festivities.[61]

Fiestas cívicas shared much in common with the May celebrations; they just took place on other dates throughout the year. Consider Henry Brackenridge's reaction to the festivities in Buenos Aires honoring Chilean independence in 1818. He writes that some six to eight hundred school children marched in the Plaza Mayor, sang hymns, and dedicated short speeches to republicanism. "There is no doubt," stresses Brackenridge, "that these exhibitions must have a powerful effect on all classes of society, and, with the youth, they give rise to sentiments and feelings inseparable from their very existence."[62] Beruti recorded details of the February 1825 celebration of the favorable outcome to Simón Bolívar in the Battle of Ayacucho. Upon hearing the news, patriot soldiers and civilians literally carted a portrait of Bolívar through the streets of Buenos Aires in what was a grand parade of Spanish American independence.[63] The end of the hostilities among Brazil, the Provinces of the Río de la Plata, and England, resulting in the independence of Uruguay, were celebrated with fiestas mayas–like events during the entire month of October 1828. Similarly, the July 1830 swearing-in of the new Uruguayan constitution was another occasion of public, political theater, with a high level of citizen participation.[64]

In addition to all of these forms of commemorative entertainment, there was a constant presence of spectacle related to war and news from the battlefield that echoed throughout the region's cities from 1810 through the end of the 1820s. On the first Sunday Henry Brackenridge spent in Buenos Aires, he observed a parade of troops in the city center. "The black regiments made an uncommonly fine appearance," he writes. "I saw very fine bands of music. A battalion of slaves, consisting of five or six hundred men, was also mustered, and then marched to one of the churches." These sights clearly marked his experience that day, which he finished describing as full of "the most animating scenes I had ever witnessed." [65] Beruti's diary recounts hundreds of such episodes—let us call them low-grade everyday symbolic spectacles—where soldiers marched, enemies faced firing squads or were hanged, cannons were fired, artillery salutes were carried out, outcomes of entanglements were posted in print or read aloud. Such symbolic acts were not meant for entertainment purposes, although they often featured in the public festivities held on holidays. Yet they seasoned public spaces and were a critical part of performance tapestry that inhabitants experienced on a regular, oftentimes daily, basis.

Then there were grandiose public ceremonies held for the transfer or repatriation of the remains of newly minted heroes. Such was the case with Manuel Dorrego in December 1829. His remains were brought from Navarro, where he was initially interred, to Buenos Aires, providing a source of solemn entertainment and collective mourning. Somber masses were held over multiple days while torches illuminated the casket. Soldiers and citizens accompanied the procession of the funeral carriage from the church of Nuestra Señora de Piedad on the outskirts of the city to the government palace. Cannon fire from both the fortress and a set of ships in the port marked every half hour of the procession. One account mentions that the adornments of the cathedral as well as the music were of "inexpressible magnificence, like the immense crowd that was present and that overflowed from the temple." [66] A similar spectacle took place in both Montevideo and Buenos Aires a little more than twenty years later when Carlos de Alvear's remains were repatriated from the United States, where he was serving a diplomatic mission.[67] In sum, bodies had been at the center of symbolic exchange during the colonial period, and public show of such state fanfare only intensified in the postindependence years.

These glimpses into the character of gauchesque dramas and patriotic and civic celebrations point to their place in the early social world of entertainment. While many of the practices that were part of colonial religious and royal ceremonies—the Te Deum, hierarchical processions of officials, cannon fire, or artillery salutes—continued at patriotic gatherings, there were also marked differences. As Juan Carlos Garavaglia has shown, fiestas mayas and cívicas introduced the individual as a political actor. Individuals swore loyalty to the notion of the republic, and this personal allegiance, displayed publicly, was distinct from the previous staging of religious and royal power.[68] In effect, public display of private sensibilities and sociability became an important feature of independence-era entertainment, from increased number of *tertulias,* or the social and political gatherings usually held in elite homes, to café conversations and making an obliged social appearance at theater functions.[69] The combination of the solemn and the playful evident in both nativist dramas and patriot festivities increasingly reflected changes in rules of social engagement. Where these changes come into greater focus is in the back and forth between the silly and the serious that permeated forms of spectacle and audience participation from the outset of the nineteenth century.

From the Silly to the Serious, and Back

The juxtaposition of the silly and the serious at patriotic celebrations no doubt made the patriotic jingoism more palatable, even more effective. At the same time, silly acts or lighthearted diversions decoupled from the Church and the political atmosphere of independence were also attracting crowds in the early 1800s. In stark contrast during the same years were shows of public punishment, which were anything but humorous. What this last stop in our tour evidences is the pendulum that swung between the silly and the serious as forms of entertainment spread during the first third of the nineteenth century.

Of course not everything at fiestas mayas and fiestas cívicas was solemnly centered on paying homage to the patria. Horseplay, both figurative and literal, was a prominent activity. Bartolomé Hidalgo crafted one of his gauchesque dialogues on the subject of the 1822 May fiestas that the *paisano* Contreras had seen in Buenos Aires. Contreras relates a colorful tale of the usual activities and then adds humor. So, while watching the customary fireworks Contreras notes that he got burned when getting too close to them. One afternoon he left the Plaza Mayor to go down to the river to play sortija, where there were "as many people, friend, as blades of grass." He was back at the square later, where he watched an Englishman scurry up the greased pole to grab a handful of coins at the top. Contreras tried his

Figure 1.1. Carlos Enrique Pellegrini's lithographic representation of the *fiestas mayas* in Buenos Aires. The cathedral appears just to the right of center, and the Cabildo to the left. Different groups have gathered for the festivities—some on horseback, others chatting casually with children playing. On the far left participants cheer the "greased pole" competition. Circa 1841. Lámina 76 in Bonifacio del Carril, *Monumenta iconográphica: paisajes, ciudades, tipos, usos y costumbres de la Argentina, 1556–1860* (Buenos Aires: Emecé Editores, 1964).

luck on the *rompecabezas* (a balance beam of sorts) and landed flat on his rear, as did most contestants.[70] The greased pole, as illustrated in the image above, was one of the most popular games at patriotic celebrations. Contenders tried to make it to the top to grab "shawls, watches, and purses of money," but few were successful.[71] At the 1828 fiestas mayas celebrated by the Uruguayan army in the town of Cerro Largo, officials danced on a tightrope, which must have been a laughable sight, while black soldiers danced according to nation (i.e., ethnic community); one battalion staged a bullfight; and one evening there was a grand ball with soldiers and local women residents. These events apparently permitted "the army a short rest from its difficult work and many obligations."[72] The idea was that fun was as much a part of the patriotic gatherings as were the more austere elements.

Another example, albeit from several decades later, helps make the point. Thomas Woodbine Hinchliff wrote about the fun he saw at the 1861 fiestas mayas in Buenos Aires. There, "rope-dancers, tumblers, and jugglers were to perform in the open air for the amusement of the people." It was the clown, though, who stole the show. "Nothing . . . seemed to delight the mob so much as the production of a man apparently suffering from the agonies of swelled face and toothache; the clown took him in hand with a crowbar, and, after the fashion of our pantomimes, very skillfully extracted a wooden tooth about six inches long, and wide in proportion." [73] Silliness not only provided gatherers a break from the serious, it also kept their attention and helped the solemn moments sink in more.

Almost two decades prior to the outbreak of the wars for independence, playful attractions from puppetry to circuses were growing in appeal in the region. As early as the mid-1780s Francisco Velarde, the impresario who was running the Teatro de la Ranchería in Buenos Aires, complained about low audience turnout due to competition from cockfights, the occasional bull run, and acrobatic shows. [74] Traveling acrobats or *volatines* had circulated throughout the region since midcentury, aiming to score enough success to settle in a town, if only for a short while. This was the hope of Antonio Verdún, who arrived in Buenos Aires via Santa Fe in 1758. He spent six months performing before leaving for a multiyear tour of Brazil. In the 1790s the volatín Joaquín Oláez and his son offered shows for several years in Buenos Aires before having to leave for Brazil and Chile to make a living. [75] After the turn of the century, acrobats like Fernando García, with his family and his slave José, and José Cortés regularly mounted events in Buenos Aires. In Montevideo, which was the center of the region's theatrical activity in the late 1790s and early 1800s following the conflagration that destroyed the Teatro de la Ranchería, the puppet master Juan Camacho held regular events in the Plaza Mayor. [76] A handful of other names of volatines or directors of groups of acrobats crop up in records between 1786 and 1806, with mentions of puppet shows, exhibitions of *saltimbanquis* (acrobats), and shadow theater called *sombras chinescas*. [77]

These accounts point to a clear space for silly attractions, though limited in number (in part due to the size of populations where the shows were held), orchestrated by itinerant performers. With the May revolution such entertainment took on political colors, either as part of patriotic celebrations or to raise funds for the war effort. [78] It was in the 1810s, too, when playfulness stood in distinct contrast to public demonstrations of punishment. The idea of doling out punishment in public was, of course, nothing new. Royal authorities in the American colonies, as well as throughout Europe, had hoped that such spectacles would inculcate discipline through fear among subjects. And while instruments of torture had been burned at the 1813 fiestas mayas, wartime of the 1810s was no time for radically altering the long-held belief that some public good could come from the exercise of public punishment. At least this was the thinking of revolutionary leaders in the region and throughout Spanish America; threats to the patriot cause must not got unnoticed. Thus, the diarist Beruti records time and again the public hanging and exposition of the bodies of "traitors" and thieves.[79] Political enemies and other criminals were executed, their bodies often left to rot in town squares.[80] These few examples point to grim uses of spectacle that were part of the socialscapes citizens took in during these years.

"Pure fun" and plain silliness returned to the region in the 1820s, before civil war would alter the entertainment world yet again beginning the following decade. At the Parque Argentino, erected between Córdoba, Uruguay, Paraguay, and Viamonte streets in Buenos Aires, there was a circus that seated 1,500 spectators for shows by local performers and troupes from abroad.[81] In both Buenos Aires and Montevideo folk dances from the countryside like the *cielito* and the *media caña* as well as the African-descended *lundú*, performed by star actors like Fernando Quijano and Petronila Serrano, were all onstage beginning during the decade of 1820.[82] Variety entertainments likewise made their way into both cities in this decade, adding more layers to the shows residents watched or in which they participated. Consider for a moment an early one-eyed viewfinder of sorts that displayed battle scenes and panoramas in Buenos Aires. Those peering into the object were treated to live audio with an announcer who related or, more often, shouted stories about the images.[83] And then there was the magnificent Stanislas, a Franco-North American who was a beloved illusionist and "Professor of Experimental Physics." He captivated audiences on both sides of the river in 1824 and 1825 with his new-fangled stunts that ranged from mechanical displays to prestidigitation. One of these tricks stood out particularly. An English chronicler who attended Stanlislas's presentations in Buenos Aires wrote that the showman "has given several exhibitions at the theatre . . . the best I have seen of the sort. . . . The natives declared he must have dealings with the devil, or how could he transport handkerchiefs from the pockets of individuals in the theatre to the lofty towers of the Cabildo, in the Plaza?"[84] The parade of handkerchiefs across the Plaza Mayor must have been an exhilarating, albeit puzzling, sight.

Stanislas was not alone in offering playful shows alongside the more serious fare. The 1820s saw the leading edge of the arrival to the region of a steady stream of international performers. As we will see in the following chapter, these not only attracted spectators to new performance venues but also expanded entertainment options and inaugurated a period that would see a growing presence of hemispheric travelers who shaped the next phase of entertainment in the Río de la Plata.

The social meanings of entertainment covered in this chapter have ranged wide, from illustrations of religious zeal to promotion of nativist pride to simple humorous escape, juxtaposed with public punishment. As our tour guide would have experienced, and as Victor Turner has argued broadly for ritual and performance, in each instance the forms of entertainment modified the experience of time and the rules governing daily life. They constituted a liminal experience, separated from the tasks of work or the chores of home. These moments out of time brought people together, across social frontiers, at the height of the process of decolonization, and they were part of making meaning out of political culture and societal structures in constant flux.[85]

Entertainment and theatricality from the late 1700s up through the 1820s often put people in touch with the forces that organized society, especially as independence leaders were attempting to repurpose royal symbols with republican meaning.[86] These forces were expressed partly in the slogans that appeared about the ragged Teatro de la Ranchería (Entertainment shapes mores) and on the ornate imported stage curtain of Montevideo's Casa de Comedias (Through laughter and song, theater improves behavior). Colonial and republican officials valued these venues as important learning spaces. Yet, from all accounts, the theater in its first fifty years rarely lived up to its lofty educational goals, at least in the ideal ways officials and early financial backers of these spaces had hoped. This is not to say that the enlightenment goal of educating theater audiences was a spectacular failure; rather, more abundant amusements such as processions, horse races, or greased pole competitions vied for audience attention and participation. More in line with the reality of the early world of entertainment, then, was the inscription above the stage of the new Coliseo Provisional in Buenos Aires (erected in 1804): "Theater is the Mirror of Life."[87] As we have seen, there were plenty of other sites for entertainment to "mirror life," some more educational than others, where people mingled and where religious, military, and state power were represented.

Over the years our tour has covered, there was a shift in the political character of entertainment. Royal and Church authority over spectacles gave way to incipient republican state oversight and appropriation of popular amusements. The new governing institutions cashed in on the political value of entertainment at patriotic ceremonies or more solemn public displays. And the individual as a political actor who displayed publicly personal loyalty to the state was a central element of independence-era entertainment. But perhaps most remarkable in this changing political character of the world of entertainment was the decoupling of its offerings, especially playful acts, from sources of power (Church or state) and their celebration. By the 1820s awe and ostentation were no longer required features of spectacles or their experience. In their place came abundant varieties of play brought by hemispheric travelers who transformed the world of popular entertainment.

CHAPTER 2

Hemispheric Travelers

✦ LONG BEFORE SARAH BERNHARDT SET FOOT IN SOUTH AMERICA, SHE had been preparing, albeit unknowingly, for her meeting with *Juan Moreira*. The French diva had a fierce frontier spirit and an independent streak that her biographers trace back to her childhood. One example of these traits in her youth was her idea of becoming a goatherd.[1] She quickly scrapped this plan, though, when one of her mother's lovers arranged for her to enter the conservatory and later the Comédie Française. From there she set off on crafting her life's story, which one biographer summed up in the following way: "wherever she went she was first and foremost an Event."[2]

She was as daring in life as she was bold in her professional moves. When she left Europe for her first American tour in 1880–1881, much was already known and imagined about her. Her voracious sexuality, her taste for extravagance, her mischievousness, her disobedience of authority figures, and some of her secrets, all contributed to the aura of excitement that accompanied her visit. She was even rumored to be the mother of four illegitimate children, one to the pope.[3] Like many of her compatriots who had explored the Americas earlier, and as was the case with so many immigrants who yearned to "hacer la América," Bernhardt traveled through North and, later, South America to make a profit from the sale of her labors. She was a pioneer in her own right, writing her own rules as she went along. She took on masculine roles with grace and shrewdness, like a good gaucho. She purchased a small rifle in advance of her tour of the Western United States.[4] And somewhere along the way she had learned to wield a blade quite adeptly. When she embarked on her trip to South America in 1886 she was at the very height of her career. It is no wonder, then, that news of this cultural intermediary's visit to the Río de la Plata generated such excitement.

In June 1886 Bernhardt landed in Rio de Janeiro, where she began a thirteen-month tour of the Americas. Thousands, including Emperor Pedro II, greeted her at the port. The impresario César Ciacchi (a name to remember) soon met up with Sarah in Rio, too, where he arranged the final details of her trip to the Plata.[5] In July, she set off toward the south via a short stop in Montevideo. There someone commented to her that Montevideans were distraught because of many years of revolution. The actress lamented that "she had arrived too late, for she was curious to see a revolution." And true to her form, she asked, "Could they whip up one for her?" Finally, in mid-July she arrived in Buenos Aires where residents eagerly awaited her presence at a limited number of functions.[6] As could be expected, newspaper coverage of her arrival was intense and detailed. Her first night in Buenos Aires produced reports like this one: she woke at 6 a.m., after having snored seventeen times, and coughed three. Once she disembarked and made her way to the hotel, lunch was served, with all plates prepared "a la Sarah Bernhardt."[7] There were disdaining voices, too. A columnist for El Fígaro wrote that "Ciacchi was trying to make up for a bad opera season by bringing the 'flaca' Sarah, whose great accomplishment has been that she is more of a woman than an artist."[8] The major newspapers reported the sickly, cadaver-like appearance of Bernhardt.[9] But such comments did more to inspire curiosity than temper it. And for most denizens the carrot-colored hair, the elegance, and even the airs of superiority were simply magnetic.

She attracted thousands of spectators to the Politeama Argentino each night she took to the stage. Woodcuts of her portrait accompanied write-ups of her shows. Photographs of her were on display throughout the burgeoning Buenos Aires. And the press could not get enough of Sarah. One reviewer noted, "Sarah Bernhardt was a name that was on everyone's tongue. Her costumes, her movements, the excitement was the topic of all conversations, from the snootiest salon to the most disheveled room for rent."[10] There was a mix of both high society folks and less opulent spectators at the Politeama.[11] The only complaint of the high society consort was the selection of venue. They just could not "pardon the Politeama, for it had the indelible stain of serving as a site of circus performances."[12] But they continued to attend the functions.

Sarah mania spilled out of the theater into the world of fashion, with commentaries on her wardrobes complementing the standard press notes on who wore what among the theatergoing high life. Even though "some of the initial enthusiasm for Sarah seemed to ebb" toward the end of the month, one hat maker tried to capitalize on the fascination with the actress by introducing his "magnificent sombreros Sarah."[13] Sarah's "daring" behavior also kept everyone's attention. The Uruguayan chronicler Sansón Carrasco related that one of the first things she inquired about upon her arrival to Buenos Aires was a place where she could practice her hand at fencing. When she ended up at the city's Fencing Club, all were dumbfounded to see the Parisian goddess. And their jaws dropped when she defeated deftly her challenger.

Bernhardt had just missed the debut of the Creole drama *Juan Moreira* (based on Eduardo Gutiérrez's narrative of the same title), previously presented as a pantomime and now enhanced with talking characters. Yet for the next month and a half, news of both Bernhardt and *Moreira* appeared together in the Buenos Aires press. It is easy to see the prima donna attending any number of forms of popular entertainment during her stay, for her arrival coincided with the new spectacles of the Carlo Brothers (a US circus family) and Frank Brown (an English clown), while the Italian showman Pablo Raffetto put on an "unauthorized" version of *Moreira* every day! On her rest days she could have attended a Spanish zarzuela, a type of light opera, at the Teatro Nacional or strolled through the Plaza San Martín to glimpse a Gran Panorama.

But this was Sarah Bernhardt, the woman with an unquenchable thirst for adventure. *Moreira* was more her style. After all, she was performing in a space that had been home to circus shows, including the *Moreira* pantomime that the Carlo Brothers staged with such success in 1884—Ciacchi had been the impresario for that event, too. In the paper *El Orden*, Eduardo Gutiérrez's latest saga—this time about the criminal Ignacio Monges—figured below every story about Sarah, making visually concrete her connections to the world of local toughs. Just picture the chic Bernhardt (and her entourage) rubbing shoulders with local ranch hands as they watched the story of the mythic Moreira unfold—a good gaucho gone bad, bent on avenging the wrongs committed against him and his beloved family. How did she react, though, when Moreira's sweetheart realized she had been deceived to believe that he was dead, or when the play's hero was cowardly stabbed in the back in the final scene, prompting several in the crowd to charge the "stage?" This was surely a show melodramatic enough to be part of her repertoire. Bernhardt, of course, would play Moreira.

In early August, after nearly a month of sold-out performances in Buenos Aires, she traveled north to Rosario for a set of shows, then down to La Plata for a quick appearance. She returned to Buenos Aires for a benefit show, where she met Argentina's most famous nineteenth-century statesman and ardent Francophile Domingo Sarmiento (they spoke in French), and where *El Orden* was then publishing a new scathing serial story about Bernhardt that her former friend and new arch enemy Marie Colombier had written.[14] At the beginning of September, she returned to Montevideo, where suspense surrounding her arrival had been building. She gave a dozen performances, again arranged by Ciacchi, at the Teatro Solís, all subjected to detailed description in the local press. Then, just as swiftly as she had landed, she departed, having cast her spell over audiences who had long awaited the chance to see her in real life.

Bernhardt's South American tour obviously tells us something about her fearlessness to brave transatlantic travel, which she did numerous times. But beyond this quality of her character, her time in the Plata river region reveals a rich entertainment market whose performers followed a circuit that was centered in Buenos Aires and Montevideo, included smaller towns along the tributary rivers leading to the Río de la Plata, and stretched as far north as Rio de Janeiro, which was often the connecting point for ships coming from Europe and the eastern United States. By this time, however, this circuit and its corresponding entertainment market had been expanding for more than half a century.

More specifically, from the 1820s up through the 1880s, an increasingly widespread presence of Italian, French, and North American entertainers in Argentina and Uruguay offered musical and opera shows, engaged in the extravagant and the bizarre, and staged circus and equestrian spectacles that were especially successful in attracting crowds. But what explains this growing presence?

While hemispheric travelers tried their luck throughout Latin America, the population concentration in the port capitals of Buenos Aires and Montevideo, as well as their relative proximity to each other and smaller towns, linked by an easily navigable river system, made this particular region an attractive destination. Performers could easily give shows in a dozen or more towns without having to travel very far at all. By the time they had finished a cycle—which could last from several months to a year—they could start over again with new offerings. Moreover, massive immigration to this area during the second half of the century resulted in rapid population growth. For hemispheric travelers this meant new potential audiences and chances for turning a profit, which was the logic that governed their movement. As this performance circuit took shape, with growing numbers of travelers, spectacles, and spectators, the scale of the entertainment marketplace grew impressively large.

Bernhardt's short stint in the region also points to the importance of hemispheric travelers as cultural intermediaries (to borrow a term from Pierre Bourdieu).[15] In contrast to other types of travelers who chose to observe from a distance or who had little contact with local populations, the entertainers who traveled to the Southern Hemisphere were invested in connecting with their audiences. Most tried to exploit such connections for as long as possible, for their earnings and livelihoods depended on those bonds. Thus, the Italians Pablo Raffetto and Giuseppe Chiarini, both international ring leaders of sorts who contracted circus artists from three continents, performed in the region for decades on end. The more cosmopolitan acts of illusionists, opera stars, and theater icons like Bernhardt likewise served as the very interface between new cultural spectators in the Río de la Plata and trends and fashions from afar. When such cultural intermediaries landed at a border post like Monte Caseros, Argentina, or the quiet Mercedes, Uruguay, the world literally came to town. For most of the residents in similar sleepy interior towns, a ticket to see a hemispheric traveler was a ticket to see the world. Even in the more urban Buenos Aires or Montevideo, the force of attraction cultural intermediaries exercised was powerful, as displayed with the crowds who clamored to glimpse that elegant embodiment of cosmopolitanism, Bernhardt. Our hemispheric travelers did not make up any defined class, but they devoted their lives to mediating between the production and consumption of culture and they drove the expansion of an entertainment economy.

While there are multiple layers of politics at work in this marketplace, state involvement is remarkably absent, with the exception of a couple decades. During the 1830s and 1840s we can detect direct connections between the governments of Juan Manuel de Rosas in Argentina, his Uruguayan counterpart Manuel Oribe, and popular (or populist) spectacles, most especially the circus. Yet for most of this half century in question, politics were much more local and personal, as well as practical. Performers offered benefit shows to bolster relationships with local authorities or remain in the good graces of impresarios. And while hemispheric travelers may have been aware of local politics, their opinions on these or ideological positions are far from clear, although many of the acts had political ramifications. More than ideology, a sort of "practical capitalism" motivated performers to keep audiences coming for as long as possible. What we can observe during these years, then, is an unintentional, or at the very least, an unstructured depoliticization of the popular entertainment experience. This process of depoliticization carried over from the decoupling of entertainment offerings from sources of power seen in chapter 1.

Finally, as we make our way into the cultural geography of entertainment options that grew more dense by the decade, it will be crucial to keep in mind that hemispheric travelers ultimately did much more than entertain. They unwittingly anchored the Río de la Plata in a broader Atlantic world of entertainment flows.[16] Our travelers also ushered in a new emphasis on spectatorship. This feature of the half century in focus in this chapter stands in marked contrast to the forms of royal ostentation, religious ceremony, and patriotic celebrations we covered in chapter 1, all of which were highly participatory spectacles. Audiences continued to participate on occasion in performances after 1830—sometimes wrestling an Italian Hercules, at others engaging in horse races with traveling equestrian artists, for example. Yet being a spectator became a defining element of this moment in the history of entertainment in the region.

Diversiones Públicas

The last weekend of May 1878 in Montevideo was a busy one. Those looking to go out could choose from quite a variety of *diversiones públicas*, as papers by this time titled their sections announcing pastimes and public amusements. The city's new main theater venue, the Teatro Solís, was offering a fairly standard group of operas—*El Trovador* and *Faust*—by the recently arrived Compañía Lírica Italiana. Those in a dancing mood could attend a ball from 10 p.m. to 3 a.m., where señoras and señoritas had free admission. Somewhat more extravagant was the show at the Optical Museum and Magic Castle. Visitors took in new diversions with titles like "Evangelical Visions"; "Purgatory"; "The Terrible Last Day"; "Horrific Hell"; and "Glories of Heaven." Most outstanding among the choices, though, were two spectacles of a bizarre nature. One was the "Microscopic Woman," billed as a "great marvel." Twelve-year-old Marcelina Ribeiro was from Corrientes, Argentina, and she weighed a meager twelve pounds; 17,940 people had visited the charming Marcelina somewhere in southern Brazil, and she was only going to be in town four days. And then, there was Fish Man. That's right. "HE'S HERE! The celebrity of our time! The fixation of every audience! The inimitable FISH MAN!" Otherwise known as Mr. Watson, Fish Man acted with his sidekick siren and a handful of other guest artists as part of the English Hadwin and Williams Equestrian show, successful across the region.[17] Who would want to miss Fish Man and his aqua show?

The choices open to Montevideans that weekend reveal several characteristics about the diversiones públicas in the Río de la Plata. To begin, the variety of options was impressive for a city of just over one hundred thousand. Yet similar lists can be found for Montevideo as well as Buenos Aires throughout the 1870s and, to a slightly lesser extent, 1860s, when the category of diversiones públicas began appearing with frequency in the region's press. Prior to 1860, "theater" served regularly as a rubric for opera, zarzuela, and drama, while the more general "avisos," or "ads," also commonly announced these pastimes and others, like circus troupes or prestidigitators. As entertainment options multiplied during the second half of the century, there was a need to establish a separate publicity space in the press that corresponded to the growing place entertainment had in people's lives and local economies. Second, hemispheric travelers are the driving force behind these public diversions. Two types of these—opera and formal theater, on one hand, and what we can call the extravagant or bizarre spectacle on the other—are especially illustrative in this regard, and both gained a foothold in the region around 1830. Let's consider some of these travelers and their stories.

The first opera "stars" (perhaps too generous a term for the moment) arrived in the 1820s. Though their functions were publicized, the quality of opera performances was far from uniform, with many missed notes being a hallmark especially of the earlier years. Opera shows took place in Montevideo's Casa de Comedias and the Coliseo Provisional in Buenos Aires, though often crowds went more to engage in the favorite pastime of social gazing than to enjoy the musical drama. And while opera numbers were geared for small, more well-off sectors of the region's population, popular classes were also occasionally in attendance, as complaints about the "excess of people of color" and others on foot occupying the doorways and halls of the Casa de Comedias attest.[18] That said, opera was a natural source of hemispheric travelers to the region and helped fill an entertainment gap that was left by a decline in bullfights in the late 1810s and 1820s.[19]

Prior to steamship travel in the mid-1800s few opera singers ventured as far south as the Río de la Plata. Many of those who did brave the voyage were unable to land lead roles in Europe and decided to try their luck abroad.[20] Others came as guests of the Brazilian emperor to Rio de Janeiro and then took advantage of the relative proximity to Buenos Aires and Montevideo.[21] Julieta Anselmi and her daughter, for example, arrived in early 1823 to Buenos Aires from Rio de Janeiro and joined with musicians to put on shows through Lent.[22] The chronicler Manuel Bilbao wrote about the *Barber of Seville* being performed at the Coliseo Provisional in Buenos Aires in 1825 and a mix of local performers teaming up with European artists to stage opera or lyrical numbers during the late 1820s.[23] The ubiquitous Isidoro de María likewise wrote of celebrated Italian and Spanish singers who gave several monthly performances at Montevideo's theater around 1830, of acts from plays like *Othello*, and of pantomimes and sainetes (short one-act plays) that added life to intermissions or bid farewell to audiences. De María also commented that these performers enjoyed success on both sides of the Plata River.[24] A handful of local theater favorites even emerged in these early years—Trinidad Guevara, the Afro-descendant Luis Ambrosio Morante, Felipe David, Fernando Quijano, and Juan José Casacuberta.[25]

As we learned in chapter 1, both local as well as European dance styles that performers from abroad introduced helped early opera and theater reach a broader public.[26] Yet from the late 1820s through the 1850s, consistent success at the box office was not a regular feature of the theater or opera in the entertainment market.[27] Limited infrastructure was in part to blame, but the slow start of such entertainment owed as well to the political climate of the 1830s and 1840s and, as we will see below, state support for circus activity.

Travel narratives from these years register complaints about the limited fare. One Englishman told his readers, "The theatre at Buenos Ayres is a neat building, but I only visited it once, as I did not understand the language; it then appeared well-attended. Horse-racing and cock-fighting were . . . the most prevalent diversions amongst the natives . . . Near the doors of the poorer classes there is always standing a game-cock, tied by the leg."[28] That onlooker's more linguistically capable compatriot William Parish Robertson was thoroughly unimpressed with the theater's design. The cast—save the European members—and interior décor left much to be desired in his mind, too, especially compared to London's offerings. But, he admitted, some of the locals thought very highly of their theater.[29] Uruguayan author Antonio Pereira noted that French and Italian opera companies—the same ones who made occasional appearances across the river—played in Montevideo's theater, despite the siege of the city throughout the 1840s. These traveling performers only offered opera fragments or abbreviated concerts during the 1840s, plagued by political infighting that erupted into full-blown civil war.[30] Yet such shows provided the city's residents sporadic solace. A Chilean visitor to Buenos Aires in 1855 continued to complain about the lack of variety at the theater. There is an "okay" company, but all they really do, he lamented, is put on sainetes. So most of the time he chose instead to attend opera to flirt with *porteñas* chattering in the upper-most gallery.[31]

In the 1850s, however, after the end to two decades of civil war that had gripped the region, opera and formal theater productions slowly began to gain momentum. New performance venues that had been designed, but whose construction was on hold due to the conflict, came to fruition. The Teatro Solís in Montevideo opened its doors in 1856, with Buenos Aires's first Colón Theater following suit the next year, both with full-scale operas and star power. Hemispheric travelers, from Italy to be precise, gave the

Figure 2.1. Lithographic portrait of the new premier theater venue in Montevideo, the Teatro Solís, circa 1860. The variety of wardrobes and diverse demographic groups milling in front of the theater showcase it as a place to socialize. MHN Giró.

Figure 2.2. Attending the theater to see and be seen. Here we see theatergoers catching up on the latest gossip, while others lock eyes in flirtatious glances. Juan León Pallière, *Cazuela del Teatro Colón*. Watercolor, circa 1858. Lámina 123 in Bonifacio del Carril, *Monumenta iconográphica: paisajes, ciudades, tipos, usos y costumbres de la Argentina, 1556–1860* (Buenos Aires: Emecé Editores, 1964).

inaugural performances. In fact, the headlining soprano in Montevideo took the same role in Buenos Aires.[32] Investors and politicians who supported the building of these premier spaces subscribed to the old idea of the theater being an educational site, one that would reflect the "enlightened stature" of their society, or help citizens achieve that state. What supporters recognized as perhaps more important than the educational character was the function of these new venues to promote a "strong sense of association."[33] That the Solís and Colón were built as part of each city's central core was crucial to promoting them as social gathering places.

The increase in the number of shows as well as the development of additional performance spaces in the 1860s and 1870s helped in this respect. This was especially true after the end of the gruesome Paraguayan War (1865–1870), which had involved Argentina, Uruguay, and Brazil in an alliance facing an isolated Paraguay. These two decades saw provocative shows like a dramatic rendition of *Uncle Tom's Cabin* and visits of prominent figures like the pianist Louis Gottschalk, the Italian artists Adelaide Ristori, Ernesto Rossi, and Eleonora Duse, one of Sarah Bernhardt's rivals who performed at the Politeama before Sarah.[34]

Audience reactions were seemingly positive to the surge in these sorts of performance groups from abroad. Gottschalk gloated of being "everywhere successful, everywhere fêted . . . making his life a complete ovation" while touring Buenos Aires, Montevideo, and other points in South America in the late 1860s.[35] Similarly, Ristori wrote in her autobiography of her second trip to the Americas, arriving in Rio de Janeiro in June 1869. She related that crowds loved her in Rio, and that the emperor honored her with a "special" friendship (she doesn't provide any further detail on this). By September Ristori was performing in Buenos Aires. "Fresh joys awaited me in that pleasant land, where the numerous Italian colony . . . gave me a truly royal welcome." Her stay in Buenos Aires was profitable enough for her to remain through the end of October, before heading to Montevideo and "obtaining the same results."[36] In 1874 Ristori took a more extended tour of South America as part of her journey around the world. The beginning of her itinerary was the same: first Rio de Janeiro, then Buenos Aires and Montevideo, before moving on to Chile and beyond. One reviewer of Ristori celebrated her role in *Giaconda*, for it left impressions that "won't disappear from the memory of the Buenos Aires public."[37] Manuel Bilbao remembers that Ristori "moved her audience to laughter and tears."[38] In Montevideo she had a similar effect. Antonio Pereira, who attended all of her shows, praised her "perfection" and that of similar performers from France and Italy.[39]

So while crowds attending theater and opera performances may or may not have understood their experience as educational, they appreciated the entertainment and, as will become clearer with other amusements we'll survey, the social value of being there. Impresarios like Ciacchi wanted to capitalize on this appreciation in addition to marketing the latest European artists who, in the words of the contemporary cultural commentator Santiago Estrada, were "raising the stages of Buenos Aires [and Montevideo] to the same level as the best theaters of the Old World."[40] Estrada was talking about one of the desired impacts of cultural intermediaries.

The scope of the entertainment market was closely tied to the demographic revolution that the region experienced in the second half of the 1800s. Massive waves of immigrants, with Italians and Spaniards being the most numerous, doubled, tripled, and quadrupled populations in short time spans. Newcomers fueled the urbanization of Buenos Aires, Montevideo, and smaller cities located nearby. They also constituted a new group of entertainment consumers or, more precisely, spectators. A few municipal and national census numbers put this population growth in perspective. In Buenos Aires Province, which ultimately received the largest influx of immigrants, their numbers rose from around 150,000 in 1869 to some 284,000 in 1895, accounting for roughly 30 percent of the provincial population. In the city of Buenos Aires, which was tallied separately in the second national census (1895), immigrants made up more than half the population of 664,000. Similarly, in the department of Montevideo, the immigrant population swelled from 27,000 in 1860 to more than 100,000 in 1889, hovering between 40–50 percent of the total number of departmental residents.[41]

In short, then, cheaper and faster transatlantic travel, rising numbers of potential spectators, including large immigrant communities, and a rapidly changing urban landscape with new performance venues made the Río de la Plata a smart destination for hemispheric travelers. This rang as true for curators of the extravagant and the bizarre as it did for opera and theater performers.[42]

From the 1830s through the 1880s, there was a growing stream of travelers who presented optical illusions, constant surprise, and exaggeration. Shows of this nature often involved a dose of swindling or craftiness, in addition to genuine creativity. They enjoyed high audience turnout and overlapped regularly with opera and theater offerings, occasionally peeling away spectators from these. Similar to the world of opera, prestidigitators, illusionists, "professors" of occult sciences, and other stunt artists or practitioners of the bizarre who ended up in the Río de la Plata were primarily European. While their shows did include audience participation, they were largely spectacles meant to be watched—preferably with amazement. And like Bernhardt and so many others, these practitioners of the extravagant set out on international tours in hopes of making a buck.[43] Some did strike it rich and return home. Others stayed for years, working the performance circuit. Still others wandered around South America in search of new audiences or fleeing from accusations of being hack artists or thieving charlatans. As with opera and formal theatrical productions, the number of these more popular forms of entertainment increased dramatically after 1860. Across the chronological board their shows were enthralling, for they promised to introduce viewers to the never-before-seen.

Readers will recall from chapter 1 the famous Stanislas, the Franco-North American master of tricks and prestidigitation who roused audiences in the region in 1824–1825. Many others were soon to follow, and with similar success, long before the Great Hermann would make prestidigitation a household word. Take the Swiss "professor of physics" and self-proclaimed magician Pedro Latzon, who also went by the name Mr. Nelson. Latzon had given his most provocative number in Montevideo in 1829 before taking it to Buenos Aires. It was the classic decapitating act, with the subsequent resurrection of the victim, which he and others repeated in the following decades.[44] In the early 1840s, another "professor of physics and ventriloquism," George Sutton, attempted to impress audiences in Montevideo and Buenos Aires. Members of the press covering this English prestidigitator's shows accused him of "promising much, but making good on very little."[45] Sutton was an early representative of a type of hustling trickster about which we will learn more in a minute.

More warmly received was a company led by Monsieur Robert and his wife, from France, who remained active in the region for close to twenty years. An advertisement for one of their performances in November 1842 gives a sense of what made their shows appealing. The evening opened at 8 p.m. with a performance of a full orchestra, which gave way to the show's three main parts. Part 1: a short comical act. Part 2: an "hour of magic" with Monsieur Robert himself headlining the act. He wowed the crowd with his "*creative physics*, sleight of hand, disappearances," and the like. The third part of the evening's show, however, was the most action packed. Robert was again on center stage, juggling china. He followed this with a knife wielding display (always a crowd pleaser in the Plata) and "various tricks that words cannot express." Next came a dance where dancers launched fireworks from their fingers and toes. Spectators then laughed at two dogs dressed in royal attire who walked around on their hind legs, and marveled at Robert's balancing of "five rifles stacked in a pyramid whose weight rested on one bayonet poised on Robert's teeth." The show concluded with the patriotic hoisting of the national flag, with a young boy perched on top of the flagpole for comic relief.[46] The local paper *The British Packet* commented that the show was sold out despite ticket prices that went for double the normal rate.[47]

With music, dance, magic, and a touch of the bizarre, the Robert Company attempted to pack in something for everyone. Similar shows could be seen at new venues in the 1830s and 1840s, such as the Jardín del Retiro, the Teatro de la Victoria, the Jardín Florida, and the Teatro de la Federación in Buenos Aires, plus outdoor spaces across the region where performers threw up

Figure 2.3. An advertisement for Monsieur Robert, depicting the thrilling "rifle balancing act," 1842. AGN, Ar, Fondo y Colección José Juan Biedma 1126.

tents. Not all, however, were as beloved as the Roberts. The Cañete husband and wife duo were jeered repeatedly. There was the example of Antonio Leroux, another French prestidigitator, who was far from impressive. Audience members demonstrated regularly their dissatisfaction with his shows. Rather than trying to address the complaints by modifying his numbers, one night in April 1845 Leroux stopped his show to insult the public and was subsequently imprisoned.[48]

Aside from becoming more numerous in the last third of the century, spectacles of this nature grew increasingly extravagant. Rafael Scalli, a.k.a. the *Italian Hercules* (a stage name several such figures adopted), spent a month in Montevideo in 1863. He set up in a tent in front of the Teatro Solís, where ticket holders attended a multipart show. There were displays of human strength, with Scalli lifting enormous weight or gripping a ladder while two horses tried to pull him free. There were arias from Italian operas. And then the main event had Scalli wrestling foes, initially from his company, followed by invitations to members among the crowd.[49] Prestidigitators traveled from town to town, staying as long as they could maintain a following. Some of these were amateurs, like a fifteen-year-old in Buenos Aires or disciples of renowned figures in the field. Such was the case of Teodoro Trua, the African prestidigitator who delighted his public in spite of excessive summer heat in the town of Monte Caseros, Argentina, located on the Argentina–Uruguay–Brazil border. Trua had previously been in Asunción, Rio de Janeiro, Buenos Aires, Montevideo, and somewhere in Bolivia. A review of one of his benefit shows for the town's public school underscored audience enthusiasm. The ballroom where he performed filled initially with "families, respectable matriarchs, and distinguished young women of our society. Then, all of a sudden, a wave of rough-looking bearded guys took over the remaining seats."[50] As much should have been expected, though, given that Trua was the only cultural intermediary, not to mention the only show, in town at the moment.

The masters themselves came, too, like the French duo Carl and Alexander Hermann (the Great Hermann), who enjoyed repeated success in Brazil, Argentina, and Uruguay in the 1870s and 1880s.[51] One observer of the Great Hermann put his finger on a source of success for these entertainers: the metaphysical character of the shows. "Hermann is a sort of symbol, a living representation of something that has many names. Modern reason; modern philosophy; modern law. Prestidigitation." This viewer went on to note that Hermann's and other prestidigitators' handy work provoked deep thinking at the same time it elicited uproarious laughter or great gasps.[52] After all, these performers were defying logic, playing with sight and memory, and challenging viewers to make sense of acts that defied reason.

In effect, the incorporation of "modern technology" and "science," in addition to making sense of the new, were other ways to give performances a competitive edge. Thus "Fly Man" performed a "scientific" trick consisting of walking on a ceiling without any form of suspension or assistance. The publicity for the stunt in Montevideo announced that it had already garnered admiration among the "most scientific men" of London, Paris, New York, Havana, San Francisco, and, most recently, Buenos Aires.[53] Constantino Siciliani, another traveling prestidigitator, offered audiences of Salto, in northwestern Uruguay, his wildly innovative RATAS SABIAS show in which "500 trained rats exhibit difficult tricks that confirm the advances of modern science and that have caused admiration in theaters of Europe, Argentina, and Brazil." Siciliani and his "troupe" held functions for more than a month in early 1889. And though it might sound like quite a gimmick, people went, according to the local press. But they were prohibited from taking any pets to the show for the "safety of the company's *artists*." [54] All of these shows, from Scalli to Siciliani, appealed to crowds by defying logic and selling the never-before-seen, often at a bargain for families—children usually benefited from half-price admission.

An extensive list of others defied gravity. The Great Spalding and Rogers Oceanic Circus were early innovators in this regard. At the end of March 1863, they announced that, while most of the company would leave Montevideo for Rio Grande do Sul, guest actors from France—the Buislay family—and other company members had prepared a few special events at the Teatro San Felipe. There spectators could enjoy the Zampillaerostation— or flying trapeze—new balancing acts, and the trademark Buislay stunt called the Niagara Falls jump. Writers for *El Siglo* described the move in detail.

> Picture a man plunging from the upper-most gallery of the theater, covering the distance from there to the stage, and then catching himself by his legs on a trapeze. This was José Buislay. From there, he swings up to the ceiling where he holds another trapeze with his arms of steel. Then, his brother Julio launches himself in the same manner, catching hold of the trapeze José is tending, only to let go and grab onto José's legs at the last instant as the crowd gasps with relief. They would continue were it not for the audience breaking into a wild applause and screaming "Enough!" [55]

The "intrepid" Capitán Martínez was another daredevil, proclaimed to be "without rival in Europe and America . . . the non-plus ultra in the difficult and dangerous aerostatic art." That is, he wowed spectators on the outskirts of Montevideo in the mid-1880s with short flights in a sort of hot air balloon named the Cid Campeador (he had another called La Perla de Castilla). The announcements for the Capitán's shows hailed the size of the craft (measuring some ninety feet tall) as part of the allure, though warned the public not to gather around Martínez's landing point, for the company was not going to be held liable for injury.[56] Pablo Raffetto's circus company also built in gravity-defying elements into its shows such as the young María Hatton leaping over thirty bayonets at an event in Paysandú, just south of Salto.[57] Like Martínez or the Buislay family, the Compañía Imperial Japonesa, who came from Tokyo and arrived in South America via the Brooklyn Academy of

Music, and the French tightrope walker extraordinaire Félix Hénault offered similar excitement for years on end as they circulated from Argentina and Uruguay to Brazil, and back.[58]

On the heels of prestidigitators and high flyers was a final cohort of extravagant hemispheric travelers who were crafty, often sold themselves as professors of the occult, and were skilled at modifying their identities. Such was Mr. Wallace—at times from Scotland, and at others from Brazil—who combined "great novelties in hypnotism and creative physics" with juggling, comic acts, and displays of strength.[59] In a similar vein, the illusionist and "magnetizer," that is, hypnotist, the Gran Enireb, and his wife Julia "lectured" the public of Paysandú with the "levitating somnambulist," before taking the lesson to Buenos Aires.[60] Some of these "professors" were outright swindlers. There is no better illustration of this strand than the mysterious Conde de Dás (as he was most often called), who began crisscrossing the Río de la Plata around 1890 during his multiyear stint in Latin America.

The Count had come to Buenos Aires from Spain, where he allegedly was in such debt that his return was prohibited. In Buenos Aires he and his "wife" established a "Lodge for Occult Studies." When the Lodge was denounced in the press for exploiting the good faith of porteños who had signed up for membership, Dás wrote a letter blaming everything on his hustling wife (who had, by the way, left him), and took off for somewhere in Brazil.[61] In 1895, though, Dás turned up again in Uruguay, where he and his spouse (most likely the same woman) performed shows with programs like the following. Part 1: the importance of the occult and the power of will; part 2: a demonstration of things ranging from astral perception (not to be confused with anything scientific, for the activity consisted of "painting blindfolded") to helping a plant to germinate in less than ten minutes; part 3: telepathy and other acts of "second degree occult sciences." [62] They received a warm reception in Montevideo, a harsh critique in Salto, and a weak turnout in Paysandú.[63] In the smaller town of Mercedes, though, there was a more positive showing. The Count wrote a letter in the local paper in hopes of disarming whatever preconceptions his audience may have had and to make them in part responsible for the success of his performance. Whether or not Dás's letter lowered audience expectations to the point of accepting whatever he pulled off, the local paper reported that the theater was full for both showings and that the audience was "completely satisfied" with the display of telepathy and other "most interesting phenomena." Some spectators, however, "seemed to harbor skepticism of Dás's act." [64] People began to doubt everything about the Count, including his supposed medical title and his claim to have studied in India.[65] This palpable doubt led Dás to move from venue to venue with frequency. But he continued his travels, returning to Buenos Aires again—where spectators booed, snuffed out the lights at the theater, and threw chairs onto the stage during the standard plant-growing number—before attracting attention and creating scandals elsewhere.[66]

By now a general outline of the development of the entertainment market-place should be coming into focus. Thus far we have seen the gradual growth of opera and formal theater, as well as more extravagant spectacles, thanks to cultural intermediaries who traveled to the Río de la Plata over the course of half a century. The impressive assortment of these modes of entertainment in the 1860s generated a more prominent place for diversiones públicas in daily social life. The overwhelming majority of these amusements empha-sized spectatorship; they were spectacles meant to wow, amuse, and entertain audiences, and where audience participation was limited.

Hemispheric travelers helped develop two other staple public diversions from the 1830s on through the 1880s: the circus and the equestrian show. These forms of entertainment stand out for their close relationship in com-parison to other modes of spectacle, and for the deep, sustained impact they would exercise in the region. In this world of circus fun and equestrian play another element commands attention: a blend of artists from afar with locals eager to get in on the action.

Circus and Equestrian Marvels

As we saw in chapter 1 with horse races and games of sortija, horseplay had a long history among the region's entertainment options. Generations had lived on horseback, so to say, and they respected demonstrations of horse-manship. It was in part for these reasons that circus and equestrian shows not only took horseplay to new levels of commercial success, they also reso-nated widely with audiences in the region. There was a local feel to seeing men and women show off their equestrian talents. Contributing to this local character were locals themselves. Hemispheric travelers who mounted circus and equestrian marvels no doubt fit the pattern we have been following up until now. But in contrast to opera or theater groups, traveling circus troupes readily incorporated local artists into their productions and attempted to fit in to the local social context from early on. Moreover, these groups offered variety at their shows (acrobatics, daring stunts, horseplay, and pantomime) and advertised them as something for everyone, helping to position these diversions as the most widely attended through the early 1880s. The abundance of examples of circus and equestrian performances can be overwhelming, even more so than the types of entertainment we have seen thus far. So we will just follow a handful of emblematic ones.

Touring circus and equestrian acts started arriving sporadically in the region in the 1810s, and by the mid-1820s they were already standard entertainment fare, although the frequency of performances was limited. Three groups developed a following on both sides of the river during these first decades of circus and equestrian shows. Francis Bradley led one of these groups. Bradley was an all-around circus man—clown, jockey, rope walker, and an expert with fireworks. He joined forces with other Englishmen in Buenos Aires and became the director of the city's first "Circo Olímpico," despite repeated stints in jail for daring to drop his trousers during performances and engaging in other tasteless (according to the police) shenanigans.[67] In the late 1820s Bradley formed part of other circus groups, where he made popular the pantomime *The Rustic Drunk*. The story was simple: an inebriated man tried and tried to mount a horse, with no luck—and it elicited waves of laughter.[68] What Bradley introduced to the scene, in addition to the circus-equestrian spectacle, was the multi-talented circus performer, much like Frank Brown, who would become such a beloved performer in the region sixty years later.

José Chiarini led another group in the 1820s and 1830s, the first to hold a profitable season at the new Parque Argentino in Buenos Aires, which opened in 1829, where they stayed for five months. Italians, like Chiarini and his family, and Spaniards made up most of the group, though there were a couple known Uruguayan performers, too, like Fernando Quijano.[69] Chiarini and company moved back and forth regularly between Buenos Aires and Montevideo. So after their success at the Parque Argentino, they were in Montevideo for the festivities surrounding the swearing in of the constitution on July 18, 1830. In addition to the dances, rifle salutes, and displays of dexterity on horseback, the program included Chiarini, who promised "to execute all types of maneuvers on the tightrope" spanning the square where events unfolded—the same one where royal ostentation and religious zeal had riveted crowds before.[70] Chiarini's participation in these patriotic ceremonies marked an important early instance of state recognition of the social value wrapped up in popular spectacle. As good hemispheric travelers on the move, following their time in Montevideo, the Chiarini group traveled north to Brazil, where they performed in Rio Grande, Minas Gerais, and Rio de Janeiro.[71]

The third group to develop a following in the Plata in these years was the Laforest Smith equestrian and acrobatic company, which had arrived in Montevideo from Boston. They gave performances in Uruguay from October 1833 through May 1834, and then in Buenos Aires beginning in June that year. Like Chiarini, Laforest recruited local talent to fill out his troupe. And similar to Bradley, Laforest was good at many circus numbers. He had his own special stunt horse that did all sorts of equine maneuvers, including finding objects that a clown would hide from the animal, all to the amazement of the crowds. A real delight that Laforest gave spectators was an act where he dressed and undressed himself in a variety of men's and women's outfits, all while on horseback. Occasionally he even performed this in a chair in front of a mirror, both of which he strapped to his steed. Laforest Smith stayed in the city for more than a year before apparently going bankrupt, a testament to the popular, yet vulnerable roots that circus and equestrian acts had established in these years.[72]

With the nomination of Juan Manuel de Rosas as head of the Federalist Party and governor of Buenos Aires province in 1829, the circus received a burst of state support, linking popular spectacle with populist statecraft for the next two decades. This was the period when politics were closely tied to performance, more so than at any other point through the 1880s. Theater spaces were used routinely to hold government balls and other such Federalist merriments, while the official backing of circuses helped assure audiences at these spectacles. When Rosas returned to the governorship in 1835 after a brief hiatus, his first entertainment outing was to the circus. Beginning in 1835 entertainment programs displayed as a sort of masthead with the Federalist slogan—"Long Live the Federalists! Death to the Savage Unitarians!"—that is, members of the opposing party. In 1841 one illusionist and professor of physics by the name of Mr. Nelson performed a stunt in which a Federalist slit the throat of a "savage Unitarian." A shift in audience makeup occurred in this period, too, with Unitarian families who were avid theater patrons during the early 1830s emigrating toward the end of the decade.

The result was that from the mid-1830s through the early 1850s the circus was the premier amusement in Buenos Aires, while theater underwent what some have called with obvious negative connotations a process of "plebianization." During these years theater, especially in the form of pantomimes, took an increasingly important role in circus shows, while circus acts became standard offerings alongside plays in theaters.[73] Similar politically charged details feature heavily in Uruguayan entertainment of the same period. The circus gained traction in interior towns that fell within the domain of Rosas's counterpart, Manuel Oribe. In contrast, the liberal holdout of Montevideo did not experience the same pervasive influence of these characteristics as Buenos Aires. The fall of Rosas and Oribe in 1852 led to a quick dissolution of such direct connections between the circus and state politics.

Lack of state backing did not dent the popularity of the circus, though. In fact, circus and equestrian activity gained in both momentum and stability in the decade of 1860 and flourished up through the time of Sarah Bernhardt's visit. Consider the Spalding and Rogers Great Ocean Circus, who had hosted the high-flying Buislay brothers, whose success in the early 1860s yields insight into several elements behind the circus expansion. Four principal circus troupes from the United States comprised the group. These arrived in Buenos Aires in late 1862 on the company ship (yes, the group had its own vessel refitted for its South American tour), direct from Rio de Janeiro. They were in search of peaceful places to share their art "until the political disturbances which are ensanguining their native land shall cease and again render prudent, operations of the great extent to which they have been accustomed."[74] Within a week of landing in Argentina they were advertising daily shows, with special prices and show times for families on Sundays to allow for children to be in bed early.

Everything about the Spalding and Rogers outfit heralded the expanded scale in this type of entertainment. In addition to the ship and an extensive cast, the company brought a portable amphitheater with a capacity for 1,500 (a site in itself).[75] The spectacles usually lasted several hours and packed multiple shows into one: horsemanship, gymnastics, acrobatics, pantomimes, and occasionally something the company called "Sports of the Circle," that was a sort of medieval/renaissance fest for show, replete with jousting.[76] In January 1863, before departing Buenos Aires for Montevideo, the company added a Chinese Festival to conclude each performance, apparently with Chinese performers now forming part of the cast.[77] Thus, aside from being a place to relax, chat, get away, flirt, and play, this circus was a veritable United Nations of the late 1800s.

Audiences on both sides of the river received the company's acts with great enthusiasm. According to one observer, the Spalding and Rogers circus was "the absorbing topic of the day" in Buenos Aires.[78] A chronicler for a Montevideo paper described the scene at the first show in the city in February, which opened at 9 p.m. and ended at 4 a.m.: "It's 9:30 pm, and you can't fit a needle in between the people at the circus. The President of the Republic is enjoying himself like any little kid. There have been abundant ovations. The sight is simply magnificent. . . . Our most distinguished citizens were in attendance, drawn by curiosity and the comforts of the venue, which did not become a sort of oven like most places when packed full of people."[79] The same energy flowed through crowds throughout March. These "applauded frenetically" when the Buislay family breathed new life into the company's program at the end of the month, which was "doubly significant given the presence of better known artists at the Solís." In fact, circus ticket sales in this month routinely surpassed the Solís sales.[80]

What was all the fuss about? To begin, the company selected central locations for the construction of its amphitheater. In Buenos Aires it stood on the bustling downtown corner of Córdoba and Florida streets, while in Montevideo the structure was set in the middle of the Plaza Independencia, right in front of the Teatro Solís and the Presidential Palace. Such locations were part of each city's nerve center, and thousands walked past the impressive structure each day. The Great Ocean Circus sold variety, too, which was appealing. After some complaints were registered about the monotony of the initial Montevideo shows, the Chinese contingent joined the pantomimes, acrobatics, and equestrian numbers; horse races pitted company riders against willing challengers among the audience; and the company made a clear effort to remain in the good graces of its public.[81] Cultivating relationships with city officials and players on the national political scene also served the Spalding and Rogers group well. Benefit shows with proceeds going to hospitals, orphans, the police and other authorities were a common measure for solidifying local business relationships and promoting a positive impression of the company. Pulling on local heartstrings was behind the benefit show offered for Montevideo's local jail in February 1863. The performance included equestrian scenes to commemorate July 4, 1776, and July 18, 1830, when the first Uruguayan constitution was signed into law. Communicating the two historical dates and their patriotic symbolism gave these traveling performers additional purchase with local audiences and, for us, draws attention to how they highlight hemispheric cultural flows.[82] Finally, the courteous behavior required of ticket sellers, ushers, and audiences alike (no smoking, "uncouth noises," wearing hats, or standing in the amphitheater) was mentioned repeatedly in positive terms.[83] Ironically, attending the circus in February that year gave audiences a hiatus from the "carnival game," too—that is, from the water throwing that had all of Montevideo soaking for days during carnival festivities. Launching water balloons, throwing egg-shells full of perfumed water, or the use of other projectiles was strictly prohibited at the Spalding and Rogers Amphitheater.[84]

Dozens of other internationally (or hemispherically) renowned troupes followed the Spalding and Rogers group and consisted of a similar makeup. The Lee Brothers filled the immediate gap left by the Great Ocean Circus. Then came the Nelsons, and Nathaniel Rogers and friends. Rogers had first arrived in the region as a contract performer with the Spalding and Rogers act. After separating from the company he spent several years roaming South America and living off the shows he gave. All of these performers were from the United States, where many had worked together previously, were related, or at the very least knew of the others' reputation. One of the most outstanding features in the rise to top, as it were, of circus and equestrian spectacles during these years is the enduring presence and wide circulation of US circus families. The search for more peaceful lands as the Civil War flared was one initial explanation for the stream of US performers. European groups like the English Courtney and Sanford Circus (whose debut was one calamity after another) and the Italian Circo Casali poured into the Plata, too.[85] Like the Spalding and Rogers company, these others subscribed to what would become defining features of the zenith of circus and equestrian marvels. Specifically, this meant catering to audience desires, be it through variety or repeat performances of the most lauded acts; cozying up to local officials through benefit shows; producing spectacles with increasing fanfare; and engaging in elaborate marketing such as detailed advertising in the local press, free admission for theater reviewers or people of influence, and announcing "final shows" to drum up attendance but that were rarely the last performances.

Among these participants in the heyday of circus and equestrian activity, three groups that traveled around the region the longest, that exercised the greatest impact on the course the entertainment market would take, and that made possible Bernhardt's meeting with *Moreira*, were the Carlo Brothers, Giuseppe Chiarini's Circo Italiano, and brilliant entertainment entrepreneur Pablo Raffetto and company.

The Carlos first arrived in Montevideo in June 1869 with Giuseppe Chiarini, son of the other Chiarini we met earlier. Chiarini teamed up with the Carlos regularly in San Francisco in the 1860s. After a whirlwind tour that had taken Chiarini's Circo Italiano from San Francisco to Mexico to Cuba, then down to Lima, Valparaíso, and Santiago, they arrived in Montevideo where they performed for some five thousand people at their debut show.[86] By August, this "company without rival in the Americas" was "causing a frenzy" in Buenos Aires, where they performed equestrian tricks, acrobatics, and pantomimes every day and twice on Sundays through the end of October. Chiarini's Circo Italiano was a big affair, with disciples of Chiarini such as the young English phenom Catalina Holloway and the "ebony butterfly" Belén Cuba, as well as a host of other virtuosos including the Carlos; "sumptuous uniforms" Chiarini had purchased in Mexico City that had been left behind by the Emperor Maximiliano; and dozens of horses from Spain, Italy, Cuba, Mexico, and the United States.[87] In a comical introduction of formal theatrical elements, Chiarini himself rode the horses Othello and General Grant, while Romeo and Juliette—two Brazilian mules—were regular characters, too.[88] For the next two decades, Chiarini and Carlo family members were in and out of Buenos Aires, Montevideo, and smaller towns in the interior, working together at times, as well as separately.

The Carlo family (George, Henry, Amelia, William, and Frederick) established a glowing reputation apart from the Circo Italiano. This celebrity stemmed in part from their extended performance runs in the region beginning in 1869, and lasting into the mid-1880s. In fact, all evidence points to them being the US group with the longest lasting presence on the regional performance circuit. The Carlos hired lots of local performers (other circuses later hired some of these "former Carlo Company actors" to boost ticket sales) as well as international talent.[89] The English clown Frank Brown, with whom the family had toured the United States, became a star in the Plata and definitely enhanced the group's acclaim.[90] Even more influential for their reputation, though, was the Carlos' collaboration with the young Podestá brothers who were making a name for themselves thanks largely to Pablo Raffetto.

Nicknamed the "Genoese Barnum," Raffetto had made his way to Buenos Aires at the end of 1869, too. Though his initial fame came from being a real hulk—challenging audience members to wrestling matches and always winning, or occasionally taking to his show a bear he trained to wrestle—he

Figure 2.4. Sketch of the Carlo Brothers Circus, 1882. From left to right: the Politeama theater's representative is overjoyed by the company's success; George and Frederick pose with one of their horses; the English clown Frank Brown; Amelia; and the ticket booth attendant counting "the fortunes the shows made at the Politeama." AGN, Ar, Dpto. Doc. Fotográficos, Inv. 286078; caja 1647; sobre 95; Neg. B. 244.

quickly branched out to perform all varieties of circus tricks and to direct his own companies.[91] Like Chiarini and the Carlo family, Raffetto became a sort of permanent itinerant Rioplatense entertainer, creating new content and opening theaters in Buenos Aires, Rosario, and Santa Fe well into the early 1900s. And like the Carlos, Raffetto worked with his wife and children. After all, the circus was a family industry. Raffetto hired members of an Uruguayan circus family—the Podestás—to flesh out his team at the end of the 1870s. They had met outside of Montevideo in 1877, and for the next five years they worked on and off together in both Uruguay and Argentina, before they would become competitors.[92]

It was the more immediate competition, though, from the Carlo Brothers and their employment of the Podestás in 1884 that set things in motion for Bernhardt and *Moreira* to cross paths. In March of this year the Carlo family was back in Buenos Aires following another successful run in Montevideo.[93] They gave daily shows Monday-Saturday, and two on Sundays, at the Politeama Argentino. And while crowds continued to fill the stands, the company also looked for new ways to maintain audience enthusiasm. This was especially the case after mid-April, when a competing circus set up a few blocks away at Raffetto's new space. This new circus included José Podestá in what had become his signature role up to that point, the poet-clown-*payador* (or gaucho troubadour) known as Pepino el 88.[94] The Carlos fought back.

They offered a toy lottery for children; staged pantomimes; had monkeys ride Shetland ponies in a steeplechase; held benefit shows promising all new repertoires for local authorities and organizations.[95] Then, the day after they announced their last functions at the end of June, by which time they had given more than one hundred shows in the city, and in what appears like a marketing coup, came the news of the Podestás on the Carlo Brothers' program. Little Pablo showed off his acrobatic talents on the flying trapeze; Juan and José (a.k.a. Pepino) did a type of Niagara Leap; and Pepino added his classic songs and humor. The true innovation, however, to the final shows the Carlo team staged was the theatrical adaptation of *Juan Moreira*, without words. *Moreira* succeeded in livening up the last thirteen performances in Buenos Aires, with José Podestá as Moreira.[96] After all, he could ride a horse, manage a long-bladed *facón* (a large, straight, and pointed knife), and improvise on the guitar, everything that was needed to look the part.

Three to four thousand attended each of these last shows at the Politeama, after which the Carlos and the Podestás, in the true spirit of hemispheric travelers, took their act, including *Moreira*, to Rio de Janeiro.[97]

This chapter has plunged into the dense world of opera and theater offerings, extravagant and bizarre spectacles, and circus and equestrian marvels in the Río de la Plata from the 1830s through the 1880s. From this survey of the region's cultural geography, several overarching features come into view.

To begin, a performance circuit started taking shape in the 1830s and became more standardized in the last third of the century. The hemispheric travelers who created this circuit illustrate the impressive movement of people prior to the last third of the century when advances in transportation facilitated mass migration. Our hemispheric travelers, moreover, brought frontiers and nationalities together in ways that rarely happened beyond the boundaries of their show sites. These performers were, after all, cultural intermediaries, whether they set out to be or not, and who put spectators in touch with faraway worlds and fixed the Río de la Plata firmly on the Atlantic world entertainment map. They were distinct from the Alexander von Humboldts and the Charles Darwins, who ventured to South America in the name of scientific observation. The travelers who populate this chapter differed, too, from the aristocrats who toured South America for pleasure or the "exotic" jaunt, who enjoyed extended stays engaged in business deals, or who were connected to diplomatic corps, before returning home to write their memoirs. Hemispheric performers sold their craft, however full or lacking it may have been of artistic qualities. From the lowliest gymnast or horseman to the most elegant diva, they were trying to make a living. They were in search of new audiences or, as Gottschalk put it, "tempted" by the spirit of adventure and risks of braving (and staging) frontiers in new lands.[98] The Río de la Plata was an attractive market for them given the rapid population growth, proximity of multiple performance locations, and advances in transatlantic travel.

The consolidation of this performance network and the increased number and variety of spectacles reveal the development of an entertainment market whose scale was quite dizzying by the 1880s, and in which spectatorship took the place of participation, at least when compared to the world of entertainment prior to 1830. The appeal to families, with something for everyone and show times to accommodate children, reflected the expanding marketplace, the new role of spectatorship, and the growing appreciation for public amusements.[99]

For spectators, attending the offerings of this market at times provided a respite from war or, at others, a moment of family fun. "Having fun," or the element of play cannot be underestimated here, for there was great social value in play. We saw how gossiping, flirting, and other modes of social interaction were among the most important reasons for attending early opera and theater performances. When crowds stepped into the theater to watch Monsieur Robert balance rifles on his teeth, when they stepped into the Spalding and Rogers portable amphitheater, or when they stepped into a Carlo family equestrian blowout, they stepped out of ordinary, daily time. The same was true of attending one of Bernhardt's limited performances. All of these spectacles gave viewers a Turnerian liminal experience, a time out of time, where imaginations roamed freely and greased the wheels of social interaction.[100]

Sadly, for now we have to imagine, for the most part, that playful encounter between Sarah and *Moreira*. She did share the same Politeama stage with the memory of the *Moreira* pantomime that the Carlos and the Podestás had created in 1884. And we know that her adventuresome spirit could have piqued her interest in seeing the Rioplatense frontier onstage. However, her autobiography ends before she set out on her first South American tour. And record of her attending Raffetto's unauthorized *Juan Moreira* or the Carlo Brothers' equestrian wonders has yet to surface. But—and here's the catch— as her shows and such popular performances overlapped and competed for audiences in mid-1886, the fascination of Argentines and Uruguayans with

European elegance that Bernhardt embodied met head on with an erupting local passion for all things Creole. This meeting was real beyond any doubt.

To be sure, Sarah Bernhardt was a hot ticket while in the Río de la Plata, and her visit was a commercial and artistic success for all involved. But soon the best show in town came not from glitzy hemispheric travelers, who continued to flow into the region, albeit in smaller numbers, but straight from the countryside. This triumph of the Creole, most especially the Creole drama, would lead the transformation in entertainment and its ramifications throughout Rioplatense society. Chapter 3 takes us into the heart of this process.

PART 2

Equestrian Showmen Onstage and Off (1860s–1910s)

CHAPTER 3

The Best Show in Town, Straight from the Countryside

✦ FOR LESS THAN THE PRICE OF A PACK OF CIGARETTES, A GENERAL admission ticket could be had to the Podestá-Scotti performance of *Martín Fierro* at the Jardín Florida, which started at 8:45 p.m., just as the summer night fell over the port capital of Buenos Aires. Like most other days when popular performances captured public attention, posters advertising the show that Thursday, February 25, 1892, were plastered across the city's walls.[1] And like the story of *Martín Fierro*—a noble gaucho persecuted by corrupt state officials who ends up becoming an outlaw before relinquishing violence to share life's lessons with his sons—the Podestá-Scotti Circus Company (advertised as the "original Creole drama company") was by this moment of the early 1890s a household name across the region.

As spectators arrived on foot and in carriages to the Jardín Florida, they joined with the large crowds milling around the theater enjoying the vibrant preshow atmosphere. Carriages of some wealthier attendees were double parked for blocks surrounding the venue. Street vendors hawked all sorts of goods, from inexpensive pamphlets full of gaucho heroics to roasted nuts, pastries, and other snacks. A half dozen *payadores* competed with each other in the improvisation of verses and guitar playing. They were also competing for a spare coin from passersby. And then there was the police, who came to prevent the show from being oversold and to train their watchful eye on theatergoers and Creole drama fans.

Figure 3.1. Poster for the February 25, 1892, performance of *Martín Fierro* at the Jardín Florida in Buenos Aires. INET.

Once inside the Jardín Florida the audience could make out the stage area. It was a semicircular pit, flanked at the back by a raised stage. The evening's events started with a "select equestrian-acrobatic-gymnastic program," which included high-wire acts, daring moves on horseback, displays of strength, music from a ragtag band, as well as humor provided by a clown. This first part of the show not only wowed the audience or made people laugh, it also generated suspense for the main event—the Creole drama. After a fifteen-minute intermission, the band struck up a handful of Creole airs signaling the beginning of the play's action and a change of mood in the theater. The lighting was dim, though this is what one could expect from candles strung along the theater's edges and grimy kerosene lamps. These cast their shadows on the opening scene: dawn, cocks crowing, a horse tied to a saddle post, and ranch hands sitting around a blazing fire talking about the day's work of rounding up animals for branding and the festivities that would follow.

Much stronger than the light were the smells. The burning kerosene let off its distinct scent. Perspiring audience members, mainly men, added odors to the space. After all, it was summer and the end of a long workday, at the end of a long workweek. Then there were the smells emanating from the stage area and that filled the venue—horses that stood idle or kicked up dust as they galloped across the pit; tobacco smoke drifting upward from the hands and mouths of actors towards the spectators; the tinge of burning kerosene; scents of gunpowder dissipating after performers fired blanks; and the unmistakable smell, including the smoke, of meat roasting over the hot coals of the bonfire. All part of the show.

These smells combined with the sights and sounds of Fierro's life story playing out onstage to produce the emotional charge people felt as this circus-theater whisked them away to the countryside. People were also lucky to see and hear the by-then famous Afro-Argentine payador Gabino Ezeiza, who played himself, leading spectators through his chord progressions and verse. As audience members filed out the door back into the busy night street, they exchanged or overheard comments about the Podestá-Scotti Company and themes the drama engaged. Such excitement, with its sights, sounds, and, yes, smells, made a trip to the Creole Circus that night one to remember.

The general atmosphere and program organization that February evening were characteristic of most every Creole drama, which was the heart and soul of the Creole Circus. Attending a Creole drama was an incredibly rich sensory experience. Audiences could watch on the edge of their seats a game of sortija, awaiting the clang of a steel rod snagging a dangling ring as horsemen raced across the pit; they could observe work—ranch hands lassoing a cow, branding cattle, or shearing sheep (all for real); they could stand within arm's reach of performers in the circular pit; they could stomp their feet to lively dance that animated scenes or sway with vibrations of music; they could feel the pounding hooves of horse races and hear the shrill call of roosters that were part of acts situated at dawn. And they could (and did) cheer on their heroes and jeer at their villains.

Creole dramas supplied these experiences regularly. From the July 1884 pantomime of *Juan Moreira* that the Carlo Brothers and the Podestá family staged with such success through the late 1890s, about a dozen Creole dramas turned out to be among the most widely attended forms of entertainment in the region. They were represented with increasing frequency, too, as the years went by. Traveling circus troupes who made Creole dramas their stock in trade spent months in one location performing their repertoire before moving on to their next stop. The result was forty, fifty, one hundred functions of the same set, often consisting of a handful of Creole dramas.

Figure 3.2. José Podestá looking and playing the part of Martín Fierro in Elías Regules's dramatic rendition. La Plata, 1890. AGN, Ar, Dpto. Doc. Fotográficos, Inv. 301412; caja 1409; sobre 3; neg. B. 129.567.

What made possible the multilayered sensory experience described above, and what gave Creole dramas a ritual character, was their representation of the countryside. That is, they staged the frontier for an audience who, for the most part, had to imagine that frontier from a distance. These dramas explored forces of good versus evil, the maintenance of honor, tradition, and pride, and the tensions between native sons and immigrants, to name just a few of the issues inseparable from frontiers at the time. There was no better stage for these themes than the countryside itself. When people got together to watch the countryside onstage, the collective experience allowed Creole dramas to have a far-reaching impact, so much so that staging the frontier transformed these plays from mere circus dramas into the best shows in town.

We'll explore the core elements that made these plays so meaningful for so many from varied social sectors. By focusing on content and appeal of Creole dramas, we will also gain a clearer sense how these dramas ushered in a new phase in the development of the Río de la Plata's options for going out. Finally, the proliferation and escalating popularity of these dramas and, consequently, a Creole spirit, led to the region's popular culture taking on more modern hues, manifest in the first signs of growth of a popular culture marketplace with industries churning out cultural goods.

In the Right Place, at the Right Time

The spark that lit the Creole drama fire started with the Podestá family signing on with the Carlo Brothers for the July 1884 Buenos Aires performance of *Juan Moreira*, a watershed event whose backdrop we saw in the previous chapter. Within a few years two components—the Podestás and *Juan Moreira*—were the source of inspiration for the Creole drama movement. Our first stop, then, for learning how dramas that staged the frontier became the best show in town is with the Podestás and their meandering early years as acrobats, musicians, and equestrian artists.

Circuses were (and still are) family enterprises. The Carlos, the Raffettos, the Chiarinis, the Petrays, and other hemispheric travelers who shaped the entertainment offerings in the region throughout the 1800s, especially circus and equestrian activities, worked as family units. Children often grew up with that lifestyle and took over the business once they came of age. Family circus companies that joined forces saw marriages among their members. Yet in spite of strong family networks, traveling circus life was not easy. Constant moves took their toll physically and emotionally on performers and family relations. And work, including opportunities for a big break, often depended on being in the right place, at the right time.

The Podestá brothers were *the* family who contributed most to making the Creole drama the best show in town. Ironically, though not surprisingly given the frequent participation of immigrant families in the world of popular spectacle and in generating Creole sentiment, they were children of Genoese immigrants who had arrived in Uruguay in the 1840s, spent some years in Buenos Aires, and then finally settled in Montevideo in 1851. While the parents had no connection to circus activity, most of the nine Podestá children ended up being involved in the circus. They were led by the young José, born in 1858, who encouraged the others to join his amateur equestrian, acrobatic, and musical group called Juventud Unida.[2] In his richly narrated and self-aggrandizing autobiography, José recounts his childhood preparation for a life of performance as well as the source of his interest in the circus. As a boy he spent lots of time playing in the Río de la Plata, jumping from rock to rock in the shallow waters along the shoreline and becoming a fantastic swimmer. The family house was just three blocks from Montevideo's waterfront. It was there where he built up strength and rehearsed acrobatic moves that he later incorporated into his first public performances. In 1872 José attended his first circus and equestrian spectacles in Montevideo, put on by hemispheric travelers. He was so excited that the day after the first event he and friends went to the area that is now the Parque Rodó to replicate things they had seen. For the next several years, José and Juventud Unida tried their luck at different venues around town. Some of their attempts were more successful than others.[3] But most important about these early years for the Podestá family is that they managed to be in the right place at the right time, again and again.

Hemispheric travelers inspired José and friends to perform their gymnastic and musical skills in public. They also gave the young Uruguayans their first paying contracts and took them on their first tours of the countryside. The first of these was with the Félix Hénault group and lasted six months in 1875. The Podestás worked subsequently with the Raffetto Company outside Montevideo and would cultivate this relationship over the following two decades.

It was Raffetto who took the Podestá family to Buenos Aires for their first performance at the Jardín Florida, and who contracted the Podestás to give the inaugural show at his new theater, the Politeama Humberto Primo, in 1882.[4] There, too, the fame of José Podestá's new clown character began to grow. Known as Pepino el 88 for the black circles on his costume that looked like the number 88, Pepino was no ordinary clown. He developed an extensive repertoire of songs—Creole airs—with lyrics that addressed contemporary concerns satirically and with sharp humor. He was keenly aware of the widespread interest in country motifs, song, and the tranquil way of life. And his addition of payadas to his routine as Pepino el 88, which made him a clown payador, drew on the increasing circulation of wandering songsters and musicians who strummed their guitars and sang tunes at cafés, bars, and outside performance venues.[5]

José's talent with the guitar, his ability to improvise, and his physical strength, not to mention other family members' acrobatic skill, attracted attention and a range of spectators to the Humberto Primo. Among the more famous were former Argentine president Domingo Sarmiento and Eduardo Gutiérrez, the most popular author of the day.[6] Gutiérrez was a tireless writer, filling newspaper pages on an almost daily basis with his serialized narratives. Among the more than thirty books he wrote in a ten-year span was *Juan Moreira*, the tale of a real-life outlaw that Gutiérrez published episodically in *La Patria Argentina* between late 1879 and early 1880. It quickly became a best seller. As the Carlo brothers sought an innovative component for their last shows at the Politeama Argentino in July 1884, the theater's representative, Alfredo Cattaneo, spoke with Gutiérrez about arranging the story *Juan Moreira* to add this spark of excitement. Gutiérrez hesitated and said that they needed a good criollo, a good gaucho, for the show to work. Cattaneo suggested Podestá, whose Creole spirit had impressed Gutiérrez, and the arrangement was made. A few days later the pantomime *Juan Moreira* hit the stage, with Gutiérrez and his wife in the audience for the debut. Music and a *gato* (a rural square dance led by a caller), were the only sounds that interrupted the silence of the actors.[7] Once again, José and his brothers were in the right place, at the right time.

The thirteen representations of *Juan Moreira* in Buenos Aires that July were an immediate success. Reflecting upon his memories, Podestá stressed the feel of reality the pantomime achieved: men raced across the pit on horseback, others sang or danced, while other scenes inflamed "the spirit of the public, so inclined to pay homage to bravery" and aroused in them "a special interest for the spectacle." A similar assessment appeared in the weekly *El Mosquito*: "We thought it was going to be a pale imitation of the customs of our wandering country folk. But we feel it is our duty to declare that the lead roles are perfectly developed—the gaucho payador, the gato, the country party; everything seems so real."[8] Following this short run, the Podestá family accompanied the Carlos for sixteen weeks in Brazil. In Rio the imperial family was regularly in attendance. After this stint in Brazil, the Podestás joined with longtime friend and, by then, José's brother-in-law, Alejandro Scotti to form the Podestá-Scotti Company. The newly minted Podestá-Scotti group debuted in La Plata in 1885 and then went on an extended tour of Buenos Aires province. Their stop in March 1886 in the tranquil town of Arrecifes yielded another encounter with fate that had surprising consequences.

In Arrecifes the company had set up in a shed belonging to a French immigrant named Léon Beaupuy. During rehearsal Beaupuy suggested that to make *Juan Moreira* more intelligible they should add dialogue. After all, it would not be difficult to give the characters lines since they rehearsed with a sort of dialogue already. José Podestá set to work on incorporating dialogue into Gutiérrez's dramatic rendition. Then, on April 10, 1886, seventy miles south in the town of Chivilcoy the Podestá-Scotti Company performed *Juan*

Moreira with words for the first time. According to Podestá, "Nobody imagined the impact of Beaupuy's suggestion. With the revised version of *Moreira*
we had in our hands a diamond in the rough. . . . The next day people all
around were talking about *Moreira* at the Podestá-Scotti circus."[9] Later in
the month Chivilcoy's Italian Opera Society made José Podestá and
Alejandro Scotti honorary members in recognition of *Juan Moreira*'s new
success. Gutiérrez's narrative of Moreira's trials and downfall had become
both an instant commercial sensation and a source of inspiration for similar
tales. From that point on, this Gutiérrez-Podestá dramatic rendition of the
Moreira story took the fame of this rural figure to new heights, and the
Podestá-Scotti Company would be at the center of it all.

Thus, the Creole drama craze was born, and there was no stopping it for the
next fifteen years. While most of the dramas following on the heels of *Juan
Moreira* were in dialogue and shared many themes in common, there were
some important differences, too. A brief survey of the story lines will provide
a sense of their similarities and distinctions and allow us to address the central
question of this chapter: what made Creole dramas—stories born out of a circus family being in the right place, at the right time—so appealing?

Tales of Country Life Onstage

"In these times of economic crisis that we are living," noted a writer for the
Buenos Aires paper *El Diario* at the end of December 1890, "only *Moreira* has
resulted in the notices posted recently on the Politeama's doors: 'Sold Out.'"[10]
The paper was no doubt correct in highlighting the continued box office success of *Juan Moreira*. Companies disillusioned from low audience turnouts
added *Moreira* to their program for a boost.[11] Yet *Moreira* was not alone in
bringing the countryside to life on stages both rural and urban.

From the debut of the spoken *Juan Moreira* in 1886 through the end of the
century, about a dozen dramas captured much of the ticket sales and the
attention of circus and theatergoers. These dramas explored "Creole customs" and dealt in the joys and tribulations of rural life, the daily bread of
some spectators while eye-opening material for most. Itinerant circus
troupes, with the Podestá family leading the charge, made these plays the
centerpiece of their acts, and audiences thronged to see them. Despite the
similarity of the plays, during their heyday three distinct forms developed.
A first group followed the *Moreira* model of the good-gaucho-gone-bad. A

second group that debuted in the early 1890s presented more explicitly patriotic themes, some even jingoistic. Finally, a series of introspective dramas constituted a third group that gained momentum in the mid-1890s and pointed to a shift in thematic orientation, as well as the autumn of the Creole drama movement. By this time, the Creole spirit and its representatives seemed to permeate every area of life in the region. Scanning the contours of Creole drama stories can help one understand how tales of country life onstage garnered and maintained their place as a premier form of entertainment and public culture for close to two decades.

The catalyst for the impressive reach of the Creole drama phenomenon was the story of a gaucho literally caught between "a sword and the wall," as the expression in Spanish goes. This was the story of *Juan Moreira*, the play that modeled the good-gaucho-gone-bad—an iconic figure who reappeared in a handful of Creole dramas and who determined the story line of these. Plays in this first group foreground an incident that triggers the downfall of the protagonist. Thus, in both the pantomime and spoken versions of *Juan Moreira*, as well as in Eduardo Gutiérrez's serialized narrative that inspired the play, the main character lives a simple life with his wife and son, working as a horse tamer, tending to his livestock, and transporting goods to the local rail station for export. The peace and quiet come to an end, though, when a *pulpero*, or owner of a dry-goods store, named Sardetti, who not coincidentally is an Italian immigrant, refuses to pay back a debt he owes Moreira. The refusal takes place in front of the justice of the peace, who sides with the pulpero and who is enamored of the gaucho's wife, which leads to Moreira being placed in the stocks and vowing to get his revenge. Moreira collects his due, first by stabbing the pulpero one time for every thousand of the ten thousand pesos he's owed, then by avenging his honor with the corrupt lawman. The cycle of violence continues, spiraling out of control until Moreira is cornered in a brothel by a contingent of army and police officers. There, as he tries to make his getaway, an officer wounds him in the back as he scales a patio wall—a cowardly act by gaucho standards. In this last scene of the play, which includes no specified dialogue and is left open to improvisation, Moreira sheds the outlaw aura that he had been developing. More precisely, here the protagonist becomes "good" again: a sense of honor stands out against the bass note of treachery, and Moreira the character began his leap to Moreira the mythic figure.[12]

The good-gaucho-gone-bad coming full circle likewise drove José Hernández's epic poem *Martín Fierro* and, more to the point here, Elías

Figure 3.3. Scene of a *payada* at Sardetti's pulpería, from *Juan Moreira*. INET.

Figure 3.4. Moreira confronts Sardetti in a classic knife fight. Though hard to see in this photograph, both are wielding *facones*. INET.

Regules's dramatic adaption with the same title that the Podestá-Scotti Company first performed in June 1890. Though some of the poem's original verses figure in the play, Regules spun out a new narrative tailored for the José Podestá he had seen in *Juan Moreira* and enjoyed so thoroughly.[13] During years of subsequent performances of the play the entire Podestá family had one or more roles. José, of course, was Martín Fierro.[14] As in *Juan Moreira*, an encounter between Fierro and the law triggered his transformation from hardworking, honest gaucho who lived with his family to conniving outlaw. Thus, in scene 2, lawmen arrive at a *pulpería* where ranch hands including Fierro are enjoying song and drink, only to conscript them and send them off to the frontier to fight Indians. After years have passed, Fierro escapes his bleak fate and, upon returning to where his home was, he pledges to avenge the wrongs committed against him. On this revenge tour, Fierro flees to Indian encampments; gets in knife fights for fun; and then decides to straighten himself out and pass along life lessons to his sons. Like *Juan Moreira*, as well as *Juan Cuello* and *Santos Vega* (Creole dramas similarly based on Gutiérrez's narrative renditions of gaucho legends), the dramatic *Martín Fierro* followed the simple life arc of the hero—good-bad-good. At the same time, this simple story line touched on more profound issues such as relations between ranch hands, Afro-Argentines, and indigenous groups; how the state treated rural inhabitants; and the meanings of patriotism and honor.

Patriotism was front and center of a second group of Creole dramas. These had their share of gaucho toughs. But their authors were also concerned with moments in national history and communicating nationalist sentiment in addition to portraying the injustices of the state. Criollos like Julián Giménez and Juan Soldao—both main characters of their namesake plays—were as gaucho as they came; yet they were not at war with the state. Take the Uruguayan Abdón Arózteguy's *Julián Giménez*, for instance, which the Podestá-Scotti group debuted in Rosario, Argentina, in 1892. Set in the mid-1820s, on the eve of the "invasion of the Thirty-Three" Uruguayans who liberated the territory that would become Uruguay from Brazilian occupation, *Julián Giménez* was often billed as an "independence" play. The play opens in a bar, where several gauchos are playing cards and drinking. Soon a conflict erupts between the Uruguayan gauchos and a Brazilian military officer who is tired of the singing and insults directed at his compatriots. What most irritates this officer is the arrival of Julián Giménez and his talk of having taken a shine to Carolina, a lovely *china* (a woman from the countryside) whose father wants to marry her

off to a Brazilian colonel. These threads of lovers facing obstacles to their amorous union and the imminent clash between Uruguayan patriots and the occupying forces orient the play's action.

This action is varied and follows extensive stage directions, a novelty for
Creole dramas. From the initial bar scene, the play moves to an encounter
between Giménez and his sweetheart; a roaring campfire surrounded by
gauchos lamenting their lot as the first to fight for country and the last to be
recognized; and Giménez soliciting support from his pals for the insurrec-
tion the Thirty-Three plan to mount. Act 1 even ends with the Thirty-Three
landing on Uruguayan shores from Argentina, which, according to the stage
directions, should replicate the famous painting by Juan Manuel Blanes.
Act 2 took spectators to a pulpería for payadas, an impromptu humorous
wedding ceremony for Giménez and Carolina, and then the climax:
Carolina's father and the Brazilian she was to marry whisk her away, Giménez
confronts them, and the Brazilian mortally wounds Giménez as he battles
several enemies. Then, in the final scene, a Basque immigrant pulpero kills
the Brazilian officer to avenge Giménez while an angel holding the flag of the
Thirty-Three spreads her wings over the fallen patriots against a backdrop of
light ("from an electric source or fireworks," notes the directions).[15]

Writing a more "patriotic" Creole drama had been Arózteguy's goal. He
sat down to write *Julián Giménez*—his first such play—the day after seeing
the Podestá-Scotti representation of *Juan Moreira* in 1889. "I must confess,"
he told readers in the preface to his collected plays, "*Juan Moreira* had the
rare ability to make me sob, moving me to my very core. However, I also have
to declare that I found the play to be pernicious for the masses. Thus, I
decided to make the centerpiece of my drama the patriotic gaucho. Patriotism
is the most outstanding feeling among our gauchos."[16] Arózteguy clearly had
didactic aims for the play. This is why he stipulated that as long as José
Podestá or a representative of the company were alive, the play must be performed in its entirety, without suppressing any scenes (especially the longer
monologues) without express consent of the author. He also banked on the
play's patriotic character contributing to its popularity. When he gave the
manuscript to his "friend" José Podestá, he remarked that "he'd written a
play as good as *Moreira*."[17]

A similar explicitly patriotic message resounded along with a condemnation of corrupt state officials in Orosmán Moratorio's *Juan Soldao*, which was
first performed in Tucumán, in northwestern Argentina, in May 1893.[18] *Juan
Soldao* dramatizes the trip of Pedro Paz, a newspaper editor from Montevideo,

to the countryside and whose identity as a black man was significant for reasons we will see shortly. Paz sets out to prove that country residents are living like pariahs, a theme that appeared in his paper. Paz's trip to the frontier originates from a dispute with a minister who asked him to retract his paper's columns condemning the state. Thus, the play stages the visitor's journey to the frontier and back.

In the countryside, Paz is humbled, entertained, saddened, and, finally proven right. He first stumbles across Juan Soldao's ranch, where Juan's father-in-law and wife are roasting lamb, literally, in front of the spectators. The conversation revolves around the meal of roasted meat, which comes from Juan's flock since he would never steal. Paz shares with them that people in the city think all is at peace in the countryside, which provokes strong reaction from Juan and his father-in-law. There is talk of a pesky police commissioner who, because he likes Juan's wife, has given the gaucho trouble, followed by a payada between Juan and Paz, where each praises the other's political leanings.[19] There are horse races in the pit and a great pulpería scene with gauchos ordering up drinks called "rat-killer" (*mata-ratones*) and "horse breaker" (*revienta-caballos*), and playing *taba* (a game of chance played with the different sides of animal knuckle bones). Then the police commissioner arrives at the pulpería and demands his bribe. State corruption continues at an election scene, and when Juan protests, all the gauchos are detained for conscription.

This is the beginning of the end for Juan. He escapes his incarceration only to be tracked down and shot by the commissioner and soldiers. At the end of the play Pedro Paz is back in the city, meeting again with the minister. The catch: there are no consequences of Paz's trek, at least in the play itself. With the minister and deputy shrugging off all the editor has shared about his trip, the play left it up to audiences to conclude what to make of Pedro's presentation of the frontier.[20] Spectators seemed to accept the message, though. According to one review, "The saintly love of country that the play communicates took over their spirits."[21]

A final group of Creole dramas were more introspective in nature. These explored internal fights that led to external transformations. Of the half dozen or so plays in this group two in particular are especially illustrative: Víctor Pérez Petit's *¡Cobarde!* (1894), and Martiniano Leguizamón's *Calandria* (1896).

¡Cobarde! is a gripping story that foreshadows new attitudes toward gauchos and rurality at large.[22] While the setting is the countryside and the cast

is full of stock Creole drama regulars, the stage directions are for the theater, *without* a pit for galloping horses. Like previous Creole dramas, this one makes much of an impossible union between a good gaucho (Pedro) and his china (Natividad), with honor on the line. *¡Cobarde!* opens with gaucho small talk on a ranch. The subject of conversation turns to the beautiful young Natividad, whose father wants to marry her to an Italian immigrant named Rampli. Pedro is not happy about this news since he and Natividad have long pledged themselves to one another. When Natividad tells her father she has no interest in Rampli, he emphasizes that the immigrant is a good man and a hard worker, unlike many gauchos he knows.[23] This disagreement sets up the main conflict. At the party on the ranch that evening, Pedro and Natividad dance together in violation of her father's wishes. Sure enough, the father appears and confronts Pedro, who explains his love for Natividad, to no avail. The two men unsheathe their knives. Natividad screams Pedro's name; after all, he made a promise to her that he would not harm her father. Meanwhile, Pedro's father is screaming at him to avenge his wounded honor. Pedro throws his knife to the ground and walks away. All are dumbfounded and silent, until the two fathers fight, ending in the death of Natividad's father.

We see that, in contrast to previous plays, the protagonist Pedro does not resort to violence, the consequences of which—at least within the framework of the rural code of honor—are unsettling. For most of the remainder of the play, Pedro struggles to escape the moniker of *cobarde*—coward—with which everyone, including his father, has branded him. That is, everyone except the city slicker Joaquín, who tells all the ranch hands that they should give Pedro a chance to explain his actions. Only after hearing what he has to say should they decide whether or not he's a coward. The lesson is simple, Joaquín says, "through conversation, men can come to an understanding of each other."[24] Meanwhile, Pedro meets Natividad by chance and they decide to go far away, though first Pedro must save his father from the local police who, thanks to Rampli, are waiting to capture him. When Pedro arrives, though, his father has already turned himself in. Pedro begins to fight the squad and is wounded, only to die in his father's arms. This last scene of the play ends with the father screaming "(in immense desperation): My son, my dear son! (Sobbing frenetically over his son's cadaver) He was not a coward! He was not a coward! Pedro! My Son!"[25]

The generational differences in understanding honor and the internal struggles that reverberated through *¡Cobarde!* reappeared in *Calandria*. Yet in this play another introspective element was central: the protagonist's ethical reflections on (and rejection of) violence, and his related decision to pursue a peaceful life of work.[26] Calandria is not a good-gaucho-gone-bad or die-hard patriotic one; rather, he is a happy-spirited native son who is perpetually on the run from the law for having deserted the army. His arguments for fleeing are simple: he does not want to shed the blood of his compatriots, no matter their political differences. Each time a police squad catches up with Calandria—whose name is a reference to the flighty lark—he manages to escape without a fight, to the point that his pursuers laugh at and even admire his wit and cunning.

Scenes brim with the pageantry of country life: horse races, taba games, payadas at pulperías, and country dances like the *pericón* and the *malambo* (more on these in a minute). But life on the run gets old even for Calandria, who wants to be with his sweetheart, Lucía. She arranges for his friends—former military and police officers—to surround him the night they plan to elope. Rather than take him prisoner, they explain how they've signed on for ranch work with a benevolent local landowner, and they want Calandria to join them. He gladly accepts the offer, which ends his roaming life and makes possible a settled future. Then he removes his long knife from his saddle bag, examines it thoughtfully, and hurls into the ground exclaiming, "I've been defeated." Everyone shouts, "Vivas," and then Calandria offers the last words of the play:

> The lark has died
> In the cage of my dear Lucía's arms
> But, old friends, in his place
> The hard-working criollo has been born.[27]

Calandria's final comment marked an explicit symbolic end to the Creole drama cycle, both in Leguizamón's mind as well as in the way dramas portrayed gaucho heroes. Of course, he runs from the law, there's a love story mixed in with the country humor, and the rural world still dominates the stage. Yet, Calandria is no *Juan Moreira*. To the contrary, he frowns upon violence and is applauded when he buries his knife. In this play, and in subsequent representations of gauchos onstage, audiences experienced a definitively different hero. This shift in the representation of the hero appeared in the author's dedication of the play to the "noble and simple soul of our gauchos."[28] And it was why Leguizamón demanded that the Podestá-Scotti Company perform the play at the theater—and *not* at the circus.

There were other, less frequently performed dramas, too, in these years.[29] Yet these other less enduring plays existed in the shadows of the dozen or so Creole dramas that monopolized circus and theater billboards and kept audiences coming back for more. The appeal of the country in the city certainly drew on the suspense and story lines of plays noted here. But the real vigor of the Creole drama phenomenon stemmed from the ways these plays wrestled with contemporary concerns. How did they do this?

Rural Humor and Creole Drama Politics

What made the appeal of the country in the city so strong was that dramatic tales of the countryside went far beyond their face value, so to say. Their humor, engagement with issues of immigration and race relations, and portrayal of the unequal rights of citizenship are just some of the avenues through which Creole dramas struck chords with spectators and addressed issues of contemporary concern. The countryside onstage proved to be the perfect site for illustrating the classic story in which simplicity becomes the harbinger of complex meaning.

Creole drama humor was particularly effective in this regard, as humor often is. Humor in the plays provided comic relief against backdrops of violence or more serious themes, which led performers and authors to judge it an essential feature, especially throughout the decade of 1890.[30]

Consider the following examples of "clean" humor, which became a regular component of dramas then. There was the "fool" character, often played by a dim-witted gaucho. Such was the case of Marcos, in Elías Regules's *Los Guachitos*, subtitled a *comedia criolla*. Marcos confuses the railroad (*ferrocarril*) with a relative of Martín Fierro. The phonetic likeness of ferrocarril and Fierro as the source of confusion was ridiculously funny for theatergoers. A wiser gaucho goes on to explain that fire makes the railroad move, upon which Marcos says he'll try lighting a fire in his wagon to see if he gets the same results.[31] A similar character appeared in another of Regules's plays, *El Entenao* (The Step-son, 1892). Here the gauchos Camilo and the dull Miguel talk about fortune-telling powers, with Camilo stating that he can see the last thing his *compadre* ate. He digs a small hole in the ground with his knife, asks Miguel to blow on it, and when he does, Camilo flips up the loose dirt into Miguel's mouth. "Dirt was the last thing you ate."[32] We can imagine people in the theater getting a kick out of this nefarious trick. *Martín*

Fierro made audiences laugh repeatedly, as they witnessed a conversation about a city slicker who tried to take a portrait of one of the ranch hands, for instance. The gaucho was scared off by all the photography equipment (he thought a projectile was going to come out of the camera). In the same play the audience was party to a comical scene of a baptism in which the boy to be baptized asks "if it will hurt," while the priest utters phony Latin at the ceremony.[33] Calandria's ability to hoodwink his pursuers no matter the traps they set for him was similarly lighthearted. There was nothing derogatory about this vein of clean humor; it was fit for a family outing.

A variety of humor that was not so innocent featured prominently in plays, too. *El Entenao* combined its family-oriented funniness with sharper jokes involving two unique characters: the "effeminate" Sinforiano Cascales and his English dandy servant. Throughout this comedy rough-and-tumble gauchos tell Cascales not to touch them or stand behind them; one even boasts of having killed twenty-three people ("though he was not a doctor") to encourage Cascales to keep his distance.[34] Such jokes were not lost on the crowd, primarily men, who prided themselves on their public projection of traditional masculinity. *Juan Soldao* also blended masculine humor with its serious overtones. Thus, the guards watching Juan and other prisoners lament the lack of beef and joke about who will eat beans and suffer the intestinal consequences.[35] In all of these instances, improvisation was key and gave each performance novelty. Performers could run with comical lines as long as they kept up the laughs.[36]

Finally, many of the most humorous moments in Creole dramas involved *cocoliche* characters. In fact, when it comes to Creole drama humor, the incidents with cocoliches were the most important. The term "cocoliche" emerged in 1890 during a Podestá-Scotti performance of *Juan Moreira*. As José Podestá explains, during a jovial scene his brother Jerónimo began a conversation with an Italian immigrant by the name of Antonio Cocoliche. Cocoliche spoke a sort of mix of Spanish and Italian that lent freshness to the scene. The real success of the character, though, came when Celestino Petray's imitation of Cocoliche in the same scene shortly thereafter elicited waves of applause, leading the company to permanently incorporate this "new" character.[37] Not surprisingly, Petray went on to form his own Creole Circus troupe.

From 1890 through the end of the Creole drama heyday, cocoliche figures were staple cast members. Occasionally Basque, Brazilian, or French characters played this role, though the model was the Italian immigrant. Their mangled Spanish, along with the purposeful misunderstandings and mis-communications that resulted from their garbled language and the inability of others to follow them, injected a unique hilarity into Creole dramas that outlived their stage presence. Carnival participants disguised themselves as cocoliches; illustrated magazines included comic sketches of these charac-ters; and today in the Río de la Plata the term "cocoliche" is still used, prin-cipally in reference to—you guessed it—not speaking clearly.

There is no better example of the contributions cocoliches made to Creole dramas than an extended babel scene in *Julián Giménez*. In this instance an Italian priest named Nicola marries Giménez and his sweetheart in a rushed ceremony at the pulpería owned by a Basque immigrant (who speaks his own cocoliche). The fun begins with the arrival of the priest who, upon seeing the bride, remarks: "I'll be damned! (fanning himself with his arms) Now that is one fine woman!" Of course, all those present laugh at Nicola, who keeps the humor going. He asks his sidekick sacristan to write down the names of the bride, groom, and the witnesses, which he does, but with all kinds of mis-spellings. The bride's last name, González, is confused with the Spanish *con sal*, meaning "with salt"; the pulpero Basterreche, who serves as one of the witnesses, is transcribed as Bascoleche, a play on the Spanish *leche* (milk), which leads Nicola to scream at the sacristan to "take out the milk!" (*sacale la leche*). The squabbling between the priest and his assistant continues almost nonstop. Though the full effect of the miscommunication here is not translatable into English, each utterance during the ceremony undoubtedly produced its own comic effect.[38]

Cocoliche characters represented the process of Creolization of immi-grants. And while comical, exchange between Nicola and the gauchos underscored perceptions that were not always flattering to immigrants or that flaunted negative stereotypes. Nicola comments repeatedly in asides to the audience as well as during the ceremony about the ignorance and barbarism of gauchos. Prior to the start of the ceremony he asks Giménez if he has already paid the church for the marriage license. Needless to say, the hero has not, so Nicola suggests that the gaucho just pay him directly to make things easier, revealing the widespread idea of immigrant crafti-ness. At the end of this scene, as Nicola and the sacristan prepare to exit on horseback, the priest struggles to mount his horse, ending up with his legs around the animal's neck, though claiming to be as "gaucho" as any there. Meanwhile the sacristan's horse bucks him. This country humor, of course, has all the gauchos at the pulpería rolling on the ground, while at the same time it pokes fun at immigrants attempting to assimilate in the countryside.[39]

Poking fun at immigrants was one way Creole dramas treated the demographic revolution that was reshaping the region's population. Immigrants and the issue of immigration were sources of both dramatic and real-life tension that, at times, escalated into outright violence. In *Juan Moreira* the Italian pulpero Sardetti's reluctance to make good on his debt to Moreira sends the hero down the slippery slope of crime. In *¡Cobarde!* the immigrant figure vies with the noble gaucho for the hand of the young maiden, which serves as the catalyst for the play's action. In other Creole dramas the equation was similar: immigrants aligned with corrupt representatives of the state against hardworking native sons. The meaning of such a message was straightforward.

Yet Creole dramas also presented immigrants in a more positive light. There was the fact that many of the Creole Circus's most celebrated performers were immigrants themselves (like the Italian showman Pablo Raffetto) or children of immigrants (like the Podestás). Immigrants also swelled stands and theater boxes and were among the most passionate Creole drama enthusiasts for reasons we will see in the next chapter, a fact not lost on performers, impresarios, or authors. A handful of these representations of country life went so far as to paint immigrants in a heroic light. A Frenchman in *Julián Giménez* is one good example. This character has a hard time communicating with the rural clientele at a pulpería. The gauchos joke about the misunderstandings: *Je ne comprend pas* (I don't understand) for the local customers is *no quiere comprar pan* (he doesn't want to buy any bread). But as soon as he explains his desire to lend his services to the Uruguayan patriots, the gauchos all accept him as one of their own.[40] The good-natured Basque pulpero Basterreche, from the same play, grew in stature at the end by avenging the hero Giménez's death. In fact, Basterreche utters the final words, in cocoliche, before the curtain.[41] Likewise, the Italian pulpero in *Juan Soldao* is friends with all the ranch hands who frequented his store and, in contrast to similar characters, is quick to criticize the corrupt police commissioner.[42]

Such a mix of roles for immigrants invited playgoers to contemplate one of the underlying forces of attraction Creole dramas wielded: patriotism and a nationalist, nativist, Creole spirit. The good-gaucho-gone-bad stories brimmed with nativism. The Juan Moreiras, Juan Cuellos, Martín Fierros, and the like, illustrated local color in speech, dress, and attitude. Their plight of the honest native son against a malevolent state whose interests lay abroad, or at least were not seemingly attuned to local concerns, reinforced this Creole spirit. Even the most recalcitrant objectors to the pervasive influence of *Juan Moreira* or *Martín Fierro* felt giddy when thinking about these noble representatives of the "gaucho race," which was, after all, becoming the symbol of all things Argentine and Uruguayan. They still spoke ill of the negative moral influence such plays exercised. But who could turn their back on a good underdog story, especially when the underdog was "one of us?" A reviewer of *Julián Giménez* in Salto, Uruguay, summed up this influence: "The Uruguayan hearts that feel the sacred patriotic flame burning in their bosom cannot remain immobile in the face of this spectacle that pulls them along with a current of indescribable enthusiasm." [43]

Some Creole dramas were more explicitly patriotic than others. Yet they all riffed on threads of patriotism, nationalism, and nativism. They often did so in ways that made these ideologies more complex than simple praise for the local or national. Consider how racial frontiers played out in *Juan Soldao*, where, readers will remember, the Afro-Uruguayan journalist Pedro Paz travels to explore the situation of gauchos in the countryside. When the immigrant pulpero calls Paz a "sack of coal," the gaucho hero of the play tells the storekeeper to treat Paz like any other gaucho. Paz, in turn, ends up being the defender of gauchos and questioning their limited access to citizenship. [44] The final words of *Martín Fierro* are spoken by the brother of a black gaucho Fierro killed: "May God have forgiven'em [Fierro]," to be pronounced with "deep feeling and drama." [45] The words did not lead to an immediate resolution of the racial tension, but the play's open-endedness raised the issue in a provocative way for viewers across social sectors. A black gaucho has a central role in *Julián Giménez*, too. Besides being one of the hero's closest friends, this Afro-Uruguayan takes a bullet for the play's hero in the final skirmish between the Brazilians and the Uruguayan patriots. In this fight another Afro-Uruguayan character dies, too. In both instances the author wrote specific stage directions for highlighting these deaths. [46]

In addition to fighting (and dying) for the nation, patriotism in Creole dramas was about didactic potential. An "intellectual of great fame on both sides of the Plata River" commented this aspect of *Julián Giménez*: "Aside from the play's literary qualities that make it an exceptionally original work," wrote this unnamed source, "it has the goodness to represent the gaucho at his finest, that is, drawing attention to his pristine patriotism. In contrast to the *gaucho malo* 'Juan Moreira,' in a continuous war with the law . . . and whose story does a poor job of educating the people, 'Julián Giménez' encourages audiences to fight for one's country. It inspires heroic feelings of citizenship, and thus, as time goes on, this play will be the true national drama for Uruguayans."[47] This anonymous observer's words point to the root of patriotic and nativist feelings: citizenship, and the rights and responsibilities associated with it.

More precisely, we are talking about *unequal* rights of citizenship for the rural population—the very heroes of Creole dramas. This was perhaps the most powerful, central, and threatening theme of the Creole drama phenomenon. Moreira's story revolved around both his unequal status and its abuse by the state representatives who were supposed to guarantee rights of citizenship, cementing this theme for future dramas. In the eyes of the law, Moreira was portrayed first as a lying thief when trying to collect his debt at the office of the justice of the peace and later as murderous bandit. Similarly, the newspaper reports that irritate the minister and spark the action in *Juan Soldao* speak of pariahs in the countryside who no longer enjoy any rights. In the pulpería voting scene in this drama, the message audiences heard was "suffrage is a farce," for vote rigging begins as soon as the police commissioner arrives on the scene.[48] A variation of the tilted justice message was at the heart of the story line of *Los óleos del chico*, in which a wealthy man starts a fight at a humble family dance in the country to celebrate a baptism. The police—no surprise—side with the wealthy man simply because he represents *gente decente*. Even the more jocular Creole drama *El Entenao*, so intent on entertaining its audiences, communicated a more serious missive of unequal citizenship. One of the play's protagonists sings a pair of verses that sums up this idea: "I am the stepson of this land / First to be called on for war / And last to be remembered afterwards."[49] Finally, despite the fact that *Martín Fierro* presents, in the end, a calm, "domesticated" gaucho, willing to accept his subordinate place in the world, and not eager to pick fights with anyone, the play's representation was prohibited in Rosario in 1893, along with *Juan Moreira* and *Juan Cuello*. The problem with *Fierro* was the emphasis on the expectation that rural inhabitants' rights would be protected. This feature led authorities to fear popular demands for such rights and, subsequently, the order for the play not to be performed.[50] In Córdoba, too, efforts were made to limit Creole drama performances, primarily by imposing heavy taxes on companies.[51]

This thrust of unequal citizenship not only constituted one of the most intriguing aspects of Creole dramas for their viewers. It also combined with themes of patriotism and the Creole spirit to invite audiences to contemplate

national frontiers in ways they would not have been able to do without the
aid of these best shows in town.

Rural Pageantry and Creole Drama Popularity

As we saw at the outset of this chapter, the Creole Circus or Creole drama at
the theater was a rich collective experience with an atmosphere of rural pageantry that was a strong source of appeal. The plays themselves were festive.
They routinely included gauchos playing taba, with all the excitement of the
competition and money on the line. Several Creole dramas had entire scenes
oriented around horse races or sortija games, both of which took place for
real in front of the spectators. Just imagine a group of riders kicking up
dust—that would soon settle over the audience—as they raced past spectators cheering them on. In *El Entenao* the sortija scene adds nothing to the
plot but pure fun. Though participants in this case had to ride in a semicircle
of sorts instead of in a straight run in the countryside, this re-creation was
full of energy.[52] Another component that made the atmosphere was the *fiesta
campestre*, a country party scene that first debuted in *Juan Moreira* and then
became incorporated into several subsequent dramas. Onstage these fiestas
included tents representing all sorts of gathering spots in the pit; peasants
discussing cock fights and pig raffles; an occasional play (within the play),
with ranch hands commenting on the action; children playing; and, not to
be missed, music, drink, food, and dance. Spectators were often invited to
join the performers in the pit during the fiesta scenes.

Dance was central to the Creole drama atmosphere, though not just any
dance. Square dance patterns that were rural forms of sociability drew roaring applause when they featured in dramas. One of these dances was the
gato, which was a standard number in *Juan Moreira* from 1886 through 1889.
At the end of this year the Podestá-Scotti Company was in the right place at
the right time, again. They had just set up in Montevideo for a long run of
Juan Moreira. After the first show, Elías Regules, *padre* (father of the Regules
who adapted *Martín Fierro* as a dramatic hit), suggested that the gato be
replaced by the *pericón*, an Uruguayan dance of two. He taught the performers the steps, and the dance was incorporated from then on, with an even
warmer reception than the gato on both sides of the river.[53] Creole dramas
likewise introduced *milongas* onstage. These were early versions of the form
later recognized as the *tango*.[54]

Figure 3.5. The joyful *fiesta campestre* moment in *Juan Moreira*. Audience members participated frequently in these scenes. INET.

Dance scenes always required live music—guitarists and accordion players, along with an occasional percussionist, vocalist, and, specifically for these square dance forms, a caller directing the dancers on the "floor." The preeminent payador Gabino Ezeiza was a regular musician at Podestá-Scotti shows, where he always roused crowds with his improvisational skills, adding extra flair to dance moments. These dance scenes had audiences swaying (and moving when they could) to the music.[55] They also contributed to another aspect of the atmosphere: the ritual character of these best shows in town.

Although many in the audience already knew the outcome of the Creole drama they watched unfold, attending the show was a ritual. Fiestas campestres were part of this, for they helped bring rural ritual to the performance space. In rural life, fiestas campestres were closely linked to agrarian festivals that followed specific activities throughout the year: branding, castration, breaking new mounts, sheep shearing, and so on. When the tasks were finished, workers, often accompanied by ranch owners or managers, threw a big party. This is no exaggeration. These celebrations could last multiple days, with participants "tying one on," roasting abundant quantities of meat, and dancing past daylight. The incorporation of aspects of these festivals into Creole dramas not only staged this quality of frontier life quite literally, it also tied agrarian rituals to the ritual character of the plays.[56] But the ritual character extended far beyond the scenes of these fiestas. The fight for justice and the underdog, the forces of good versus those of evil, and the maintenance of honor all fed into this ritual aura. Spectators experienced collectively the clash of such forces and the emotional charge onstage before them. As can be expected, being part of such a ritual was enticing.

The gravitational pull of these characteristics was felt by more men than women—men simply outnumbered women as spectators. Moreover, gaucho heroes held a certain masculine appeal related to the notion of the frontier as a gendered space. Yet, the Creole drama atmosphere was ultimately a communal space that attracted families, women, and children, besides the single men in search of a laugh or a story to fire up their passions. A case in point was the 1893 performance of *Juan Moreira* by an all-female cast that, like its counterpart shows, attracted a varied audience.[57] We will come back to the relationship of masculinity to Creole dramas and social clubs known as Creole societies in chapter 5.

Additionally, the vividness of the countryside onstage created a visceral encounter with the frontier. *El Entenao* opens with a scene of sheep shearing that, according to the stage directions, is the *only* sound the audience should hear for several minutes. Imagine that! Dramas had extensive casts with dozens of named, staple performers and then often dozens of others who were the "extras"—gauchos and chinas, soldiers and city folk, immigrants and police squads. Different spectators identified with different characters. Yet, whether center stage or cast for just seconds, the various characters transmitted a sense of authenticity. Among the members of the Podestá-Scotti group was the rule that stated: "It is strictly prohibited for gauchos to appear on stage in collared shirts or fancy boots. They all have the obligation to 'remain gauchos' until the dramas are over." [58] The idea was to make the frontier as real as possible, to allow spectators to feel it in every way.

This goal was achieved in one drama after another.[59] After a Podestá-Scotti performance of *Juan Moreira* in La Plata in 1889, the Spaniard José Valero made his way to José Podestá's dressing room, where he expressed his enthusiasm for the play.

Everybody does something on stage . . . Even the dogs appear to be artists, for they know what they have to do! You all make fiction seem real. During the fights it's easy to feel the urge to scream "enough!" In sum, for those who see a spectacle like this one for the first time, with its coarseness, its language, for those who have to tune their ear to the way of speaking and accustom themselves to the naturalness and enthusiasm with which you perform the show, it becomes clear why audiences feel so connected to the play and grow so enthused.[60]

Others shared similar impressions of *Moreira*. The Italian author and actor Ermete Novelli praised the "amazing naturalness" of an 1894 performance and how the actors who, not having studied theater formally, took what they saw in real life from the countryside and put it onstage.[61] Abdón Arózteguy (who wrote *Julián Giménez*) underscored *Moreira*'s capacity for making the country feel real. In reference to a performance of the drama by the Podestá-Scotti group, he wrote, "I found it to be so truthful. Moreira's story moved me profoundly to feel the despondent life of our valiant native sons and the severity of our rural authorities. For anyone with a true Creole heart, that drama inspires these deep feelings, for Moreira's wounds are lesions to our Creole flesh, and the blood that is spilt in the drama is our own."[62] That Arózteguy also considered the play to be somewhat "pernicious," inspiring him to write a more upstanding drama, makes his remarks on identifying with Moreira even more resilient.

A glimpse at the reception of Creole dramas during their zenith likewise attests to the extent of their allure and influence. The main point to remember about audience turnout is that it exceeded anything authors, performers, investors, or spectators could have imagined. Yet as shows sold out day after day, month after month, all involved began to expect commercial success and popularity. In most cases, the point of comparison was with *Juan Moreira*. Thus, Elías Regules expressed to the Podestá-Scotti Company his concern with the initial mild reaction to his *Martín Fierro*. At the end of October 1891, a little over a year after the play's debut, the company's secretary sent a letter to Regules. "*Amigazo* Regules," it began. "One of your earlier letters explained how you thought your *Martín* would soon be gone from the stage given its minimal impact in Buenos Aires. We told you then that we wouldn't be worth our salt if little *Martinito* didn't make it big. Well, after taking the show on the road here and there, *Martín* attracts more people than *Moreira*."[63]

Julián Giménez, which as we have seen was born out of the experience of watching *Juan Moreira*, garnered quite a following, too. It was performed more than one thousand times on both sides of the river between 1892 and 1896. "Even my wife," wrote Arózteguy, "who is not fond of my gauchesque writings or dramatic representations of a certain lower order, even she congratulated me on my first Creole drama. If it has any merits, one is for sure that it excited the popular classes [*las masas populares*] of my land. And that was my main goal with its performance."[64] Press accounts in both Montevideo and Buenos Aires shared this enthusiasm. One Uruguayan paper noted that crowds "applaud feverishly the scene where the Thirty-Three Uruguayans pose, and other culminating moments." A Buenos Aires paper remarked that even after hundreds of performances of *Julián Giménez*, spectators continued filling the venues where it was on the playbill.[65]

The gold standard, though, was *Juan Moreira*; no other Creole drama drew as many spectators to as many performances for as many years as did this one. It was the original spark. Journalist Carlos Olivera summed up colorfully this point in 1887. "Until now with *Juan Moreira*, debuts of other theatrical productions have all been like attending a wake. Neither the support of renowned intellectuals or even official influence and attendance of the President and his ministers have been able to make a night at the performance of play by one of our own playwrights anything other than an unending yawn."[66] For the most part, though, high society folk, from intellectuals to the wealthy to politicians, all eager to preserve their social status, kept their distance from the early performances of *Juan Moreira*. Like Eduardo Gutiérrez's narrative that had given rise to the play, more "proper" minds labeled the story "pernicious" and one that communicated to the "masses" all the wrong messages.[67]

Yet by late 1889 this attitude was changing, and so too was the makeup of audiences at performances of this founding drama. Some of Montevideo's upper crust attended the Podestá-Scotti performance of *Juan Moreira*, which they gave forty-two times in a row throughout November before embarking on an extensive tour of Rioplatense towns the following year.[68] One Buenos Aires newspaper made such changes the centerpiece of an editorial in November 1890. Until "yesterday," noted the piece, only a certain "shabby" sort of spectator appeared at these circus dramas. But now, "perhaps out of want to alter the tiresome daily routine with a sensational spectacle, because of a desire to contemplate the realistic, interesting episodes of that legendary life, or out of simple curiosity, the circus is invaded by the most distinguished denizens of Buenos Aires." Distinguished urban celebrities from surgeons to generals left their peaceful homes to rub shoulders with the immense mass of circus-goers, all eagerly attending the story of *Moreira*. The author of that editorial asked about the meaning of the change in spectatorship and the lasting presence of circus shows. "Juan Moreira is the *plat du Jour* of the Buenos Aires high-life—does this mean patriotism? I hope so! Or perhaps a relaxation of artistic tastes, the plebianization of the spirit, or signs of originality. . . . Whatever it may be, it is clear from the crowds that this dramatic representation commands attraction." The author praised the representation of the "innate valor of an entire race" (gauchos—we'll see more on the whole gaucho-race question in chapter 5), which should be enough to make people want to see the show. If not, the editorial concluded, people probably went just because others were going: "*Juan Moreira* is in style. On the streets, in social clubs, one phrase can be continually heard. 'Che!, have you seen *Juan Moreira*?' And that's enough to lead one to the circus." [69]

Sure enough, throughout the 1890s, spectators flocked to see Creole dramas. In 1891 Argentine President Carlos Pellegrini attended several functions the Podestá-Scotti Company gave, including *Juan Moreira* multiple times. This company alone performed more than two hundred functions this year in places spanning from Montevideo to Rosario. After the company left Paraná in Argentina, an Italian circus troupe set up there and represented *Moreira* in Italian. Other groups, like that of Pablo Raffetto, followed suit and contributed to increasing Creole drama activity for most of the rest of the decade. In 1894, the Podestá-Scotti Company and its competitors added another half dozen or so dramas to their existing repertoires. [70] Two years later José Podestá remarked on the audiences that drove play offerings as well as run times. "Let's not forget that the spectators of the region were our principal supporters. They gave us the courage to continue at every moment." To put this point into perspective, between February and September 1896 (the year of *Calandria*), when the Podestá-Scotti Company headed to southern towns in Buenos Aires province, they had performed at least 289 shows—and this is a conservative estimate that doesn't take into account the functions from September through December! [71] In the early 1900s in La Plata printers regularly produced between three and four thousand small programs per show, a thousand larger ones, and sixty to one hundred posters for display around the city. [72] In short, it should be clear by now that *Juan Moreira* and subsequent Creole dramas breathed a whole new life into the theatergoing experience.

This appeal of Creole dramas should be understood in tandem with the overlap in shows offered. The exploration of contemporary issues via the countryside onstage was almost nonstop for more than a decade. Audiences had access to a variety of plays during a company's stay in a given location or, at the very least, show after show of the same play. Consider the options for Montevideans toward the end of 1889. In September, among the whirl-wind of announcements for public amusements including formal theater, zarzuelas, and puppet shows for children, came news of the imminent arrival of the Podestá-Scotti Company, to be joined by Frank Brown. In early October the company began offering varied performances that quickly became all the rage, building suspense for the introduction of a Creole drama in November. Throughout that month, they staged *Juan Moreira*. In December and January they alternated performances of *Moreira* with several pantomimes and their trademark acrobatic and equestrian stunts as well as verse and song by Pepino el 88 and young María Podestá, all of which drew "numerous crowds."[73] A little more than a year later, the same company added more variety to their repertoire with several new Creole dramas for Uruguayan audiences, which they then took to Buenos Aires in 1892—the year of our view into a show at the Jardín Florida. The Podestá Company pivoted from *Juan Moreira* one evening, to *El Entenao* the next, then back to *Moreira* before staging *Julián Giménez* and other dramas. They kept up this pace throughout all of February and March, including preliminary enter-tainment with payadas, cocoliche solo numbers, Gabino Ezeiza's virtuosity, and other acts from their "warehouse of originalities."[74]

Three years later, this variety and overlap characterized the company's offerings in Paysandú, where they arrived in January.[75] So many people attempted to purchase tickets that the police had to intervene to limit ticket sales to around 1,200 per night, as well as impose order as spectators entered the theater. Police involvement in ticket sales and queuing audiences had become a regular feature of the Creole drama phenomenon. At the end of February, the Podestá-Scotti Company left town for Salto. There they repli-cated in large measure the overlap of dramas seen in Paysandú, with the addition of a couple novel acts, like Pepino el 88's imitation of the swindler Count Das (one of chapter 2's traveling showmen) and benefit shows for local authorities and flood victims. In Salto they were warmly received. The tal-ented young writer Horacio Quiroga presented José Podestá with a medal of honor, while residents accompanied the troupe to the port when they departed for Mercedes, Uruguay. In both Paysandú and Salto, performances regularly attracted numbers that ranged from around 500 to more than 1,200 theatergoers. Creole drama action did not end when this company pulled up the stakes of its portable tent venue. Another troupe took over where the Podestá-Scotti group had left off in Salto, and others continued to offer dramas in Paysandú, other small towns, and larger cities throughout the region.[76] Pablo Raffetto even starred as Pepino el 87, an imitator of the renowned clown.

These views into audiences at Creole dramas point to the flood of shows, with their stories, humor, and heroes taking over the collective imagination. A reporter for the Salto paper *Ecos del Progreso* captured succinctly the idea: "Though it weighs on those who do not support Creole dramas, Salto residents spend hours of their life at these plays night after night. We return to the circus tent again and again with enthusiasm and excitement that the impresarios of any opera or theater company would envy."[77]

The countryside onstage lured audiences on many levels. Creole dramas were rich sensory experiences, full of fast-paced action, sounds that got the adrenaline flowing, humorous and heart-wrenching scenes, and those smells that lingered in the memory (and the clothes) of spectators. One circus family, led by José Podestá, succeeded more than any other in making Creole dramas the best shows in town, for all the reasons we have covered in this chapter.

A final note on what made these dramatic portrayals of the countryside a main attraction of the Rioplatense entertainment world for the last fifteen years of the 1800s, and something that gave them additional firepower as catalysts transforming the region's popular culture comes from their articulation of tradition and modernity. That Creole dramas staked their character on tradition—on rural traditions, to be precise—made them especially relevant at the end of the nineteenth century, the apex of the modernizing push, felt most profoundly in the capital cities of Buenos Aires and Montevideo, though radiating across the region. José Podestá reflected frequently on this historical significance of Creole dramas. As the phenomenon entered its autumn moment on the eve of the twentieth century, he wrote: "I wander with my people, fighting for our daily bread and holding high the banner of our young theater. We present gaucho feats and characters, here in the birthplace of that legendary figure, so that new generations, some already degenerate, can learn from the examples of those heroes who, through great effort, gave us the liberty we enjoy today."[78] Here we have José Podestá expounding on the clash between tradition, which he believed Creole dramas rescued, restored, or preserved, and the degeneration he associated with the turn of the century, manifest in the forces of change wrapped up in the modernization of the region.

The author Elías Regules had tradition and modernity in mind, too. In the preface to *Los Guachitos* he explained that he was "a great admirer of our race [read gauchos], and I like to observe it without the refinements of modern life so I can see all of its grandeur."[79] That is, he wanted to celebrate a more simple life, free of the pressures that were reshaping daily existence in cities and in the country. Regules was not alone, nor was the urge to be modern *and* celebrate tradition limited to the big city. A reporter for *Ecos del Progreso*, in Salto, Uruguay, makes this point wonderfully. "With the exception of this circus-theater of Creole dramas . . . life in Salto does not offer many attractions at which people can enjoy themselves or grow. We all understand that we are experiencing with much anxiety the transformation of our town into a city, a moment that is best characterized by the constant urge to *live*, to be active, to move, to circulate, instead of remaining stagnant, perched on our elbows."[80]

Attending the circus and its dramas with their antimodern heroes was, ironically, a premier form of being modern in Salto, as well as across the rest of the region. Moreover, the Creole drama phenomenon was giving rise to a new, modern strand of popular culture. This strand demanded not only a flourish of dramas but also cadres of performers, impresarios, printers of the programs and posters, scores of entrepreneurs hoping to profit from selling the excitement of the stories, and surging numbers and diversity of people clamoring to see the dramas. These best shows in town led spectators to live and breathe a Creole spirit and engage in the process of going Creole, the subject of our next chapter.

CHAPTER 4

Going Creole

✦ IN JANUARY 1894, AT THE HEIGHT OF THE CREOLE DRAMA PHENOM-
enon we learned about in the last chapter, a writer for the local paper in the
small town of Salto, Uruguay, described a fascination with the best shows in
town that went beyond merely attending the plays. *Santos Vega, Juan Cuello*,
and *Juan Moreira* have been especially hot topics among residents of the
countryside, we read, who "so thoroughly enjoy treatments of the traditional
gaucho type and Creole themes." You must hear people talking about the
dramas, the writer noted, to get a clear sense of their enthusiasm. "They
relate the smallest details of Vega's or Moreira's outfits, their bravery when
under attack. They all speak at once, interrupting and correcting each other.
. . . there is no lack of men who try to imitate gestures and inflections of
Creole drama protagonists. Some even present their considerations of the
plays utilizing exclamations of the artists of the very same dramas." Other
reporters for the same paper highlighted the presence of the city's "most distinguished ladies," who, day in and day out, added "brilliance" to each function with the "perfume of their souls" and "angelic glances." When the
"brave" José Podestá appeared on horseback as Cuello, Moreira, or another
gaucho hero, these excited theatergoers exclaimed, "Ah, criollo!, applauding
frenetically."[1]

Several years later, Podestá wrote in his memoirs: "How many young people changed their behaviors because of Creole dramas? Without these plays,
how many authors and artists would have followed a different path in life? So

many of our playwrights these days carry with them the Creole drama spirit, having acted in those very dramas."[2]

The writers for that small-town paper, Podestá, and the playgoers who brimmed with enthusiasm in Salto point to the increasing strength and expanding reach of the Creole spirit in the region. Creole dramas not only promoted this spirit, for it was the core of their business, they also engaged spectators, performers, entrepreneurs, theater owners, and a long list of other groups connected to the representation of of the plays, in what we can call the process of going Creole.

Part of this process overlapped with a period of economic modernization that transformed the region in the last third of the 1800s. Specifically, an agricultural revolution shifted the focus of the rural economy away from animal exports toward cereal production, streamlined the labor required in raising livestock, and attracted waves of immigrants to plow new fields. These changes had far-reaching ramifications for not just the ways people made their living across the region but also for folkways in the countryside and cultural practices in urban spaces. Rural residents who had previously made their livelihoods in work related to livestock migrated to cities in search of new opportunities. Immigrant laborers were employed in the construction projects that remade Buenos Aires and Montevideo into flourishing capitals full of Italian, English, and French architectural designs. And the Argentine and Uruguayan governments welcomed colonies of immigrants to settle plots in the countryside.

It was in this context of demographic change and social upheaval that accompanied the reorientation of the economy and its opening to world economic flows that the Creole became such a powerful anchor point. This was when stories about native sons became tales of Creole heroes, when run-of-the-mill gauchos from years past became mythic figures of the present. This was when a "Creole discourse" Adolfo Prieto details infused the region's print culture and became a staple of the printing industry for decades to come. And it was when authors of Creole dramas tapped into accounts that allowed rural and urban audiences to see some of the negative bearing economic modernization had on country life. One of the results was that spectators from a variety of backgrounds felt a special connection to the plight of the downtrodden within an unfair system, for unfairness was part of daily life for so many. That Creole dramas and their protagonists challenged this modern system and offered hope for making it just the slightest bit more equitable was appealing across diverse groups.[3]

This newfound value of the Creole spirit as representative of individual and collective struggle and an embodiment of regional nativism was clearly wrapped up in the broad contours of this historical moment. Yet the celebration of the Creole as synonymous with the popular by the end of the century, and the increasing association of broadly accepted (and deployed) understandings of national archetypes with fanciful Creole heroes owed to the resonance of Creole drama stories, the experiences people shared at the functions, and the swirl of related content that infused print media as well as social interactions distantly related to the dramas. These stories and experiences allowed Argentines, Uruguayans, and immigrants both at and beyond the spectacles to be protagonists in their life stories in new and different ways, in large part by adopting the Creole spirit or at least agreeing with the idea of its representative character.[4]

For the region's inhabitants, the significance of going Creole hinged on converting what was mythical, fantastic, fictional, or even downright exaggeration into something very concrete, real and, therefore, true. When Creole drama goers applauded or imitated the heroes onstage, or when consumers of the dramas' by-products such as pulp fiction, slang, or musical influences effectively launched commercial success stories, they were embracing a sense of authenticity based on embellishment or even fantasy. But that very embrace of the Creole, however much it was rooted in nostalgia, hyperbole, or pure fiction, rendered it real and sincere. It was that conversion of the fanciful into reality and the ability of fantasy to convey essential truth that made the spread, generalized acceptance of, and participation in the Creole spirit— or the process of going Creole—so consequential during these years.

But what did this process look like? To begin, the presence of the popular where the elite had reigned was becoming the new norm. By the early 1890s, then, it was common to see Creole dramas at venues where opera and formal theater had until recently been the predominant forces, such as the Politeama Argentino and Teatro Doria in Buenos Aires, the 3 de Febrero theater in Paraná, or the Teatro Solís in Montevideo. Thus, the Podestá-Scotti Company performed its 1894 season in Salto at the Ateneo Salteño, which Salteños called "our first and premier cultural, moral, and intellectual center," where the city's crème de la crème usually gathered.[5] The shows oozed with *sabor criollo*, or Creole flavor, that led crowds to soak up the emotional power of the local and participate in the exchange between "high" and "low" cultures. Experiencing sabor criollo with its emotional vibrations was a central feature of going Creole.

Going Creole was also about sociability. That is, Creole dramas were at heart social events. They provided leisure spaces for children and parents to enjoy entertainment celebrating local themes. These spaces in turn helped shape spectators' understandings of the social connections knitting together various types of communities, from neighborhood to nation, and their roles within each. The forms of association and sociability that Creole dramas facilitated were key in this respect, and they spilled over into other areas of public life, like carnival.

Finally, we can see the process of going Creole at work in the marketing methods traveling companies employed, and in the related phenomenon whereby the Creole spirit and Creole dramas influenced the marketing of other cultural products on the eve of the new century.

This chapter centers on these three core elements of going Creole: experiencing sabor criollo, promoting association and sociability, and marketing. These components were felt intensely across the region, at times too intensely, as the final section on Creole counterpoints will show.

Sabor Criollo

The countryside onstage made for a more personal theater experience with local content that was rarely part of opera or acrobatic performances during previous decades. It was in part through the local that Creole dramas tapped into the emotional power of sabor criollo. This emotional current was behind people getting riled up at performances; it was on display in the local music and folk dances that permeated these; and it fueled their changing audience makeup. Combined, these features and their emotive qualities enabled Argentines, Uruguayans, and immigrants to appreciate tradition at the same time they were living the modern changes unleashed at the end of the 1800s.

Creole drama music offers an illustrative place to begin exploring sabor criollo. Performances invariably included musical numbers to welcome spectators, as part of or between acts, and to accompany people filing out of the venue at the night's end. Companies employed local musicians in the towns they visited or, as with the Podestá-Scotti group, traveled with their own bands. Occasionally military bands supplied the music, suggesting either implicit state support for the shows or the desire to capitalize on their popularity.[6] Though some musical numbers required large numbers of musicians

Figure 4.1. *Sabor criollo* on display, with Dr. Roberto Bouton, dressed in his friend José Podestá's outfit for performing *Juan Moreira*. Montevideo, circa 1890. Bouton spent much of his childhood in the Uruguayan countryside and grew more fascinated with rural traditions and ways of life in his adult years. He practiced medicine in rural Uruguay, amassed an extensive collection of what he considered "Creole heritage," and wrote at length about folkways. MHN Colección Fotográfica, carpeta n° 57, 23.

and complex instrumentation, Creole airs or local folk selections were the most frequently played pieces.[7]

Another musical feature of these shows was the payada, where a local troubadour improvised verses as he strummed chord progressions and traced melodic lines on the guitar. As mentioned in chapter 3, whether solo or in competition with other payadores, these musical tales were woven into the dramatic action. Juan Moreira and Martín Fierro, to name just two protagonists, were consummate payadores, and when they played, audiences hung on the notes. Payadores were very much in line with the Creole Circus spirit, for they, like the itinerant acting groups, traveled from town to town to make a living, trying their luck with different audiences and playing until they wore out their welcome.

The contemporary writer Ernesto Quesada was a vocal critic of payadores. In his 1902 essay that attempts to explain the roots of criollismo, or the ideology associated with the Creole spirit, he grumbled about the attraction payadas commanded at the circus and theater: "Gaucho payadores, 'legitimate' ones, 'improvising' for money at a theater in the city! There is a cruel sarcasm in the idea, which demonstrates the decadence of the gaucho race." He continued criticizing the idea of gauchos at the theater: "A payador at the theater is an enormous contradiction: songs of the pampa turned into dramatic fodder. Yet, people eagerly attend those theaters to hear those 'Circus payadores,' where they acquire a vague idea of our gaucho troubadours whom they have never had the chance to hear, nor will they ever."[8] Quesada's critique aside, the figure of the payador was obviously popular enough to be written into Creole dramas where some of the virtuosos got their own acts. There is no better example of a virtuoso payador than Gabino Ezeiza.[9]

By the time Ezeiza joined the Podestá-Scotti Company in early 1891, launching a fruitful relationship that would last a decade, he had already become the region's preeminent payador.[10] At the same time, he was black—not an uncommon phenomenon throughout the countryside, but not the standard image of the heroic gaucho payador people had been reading about in gauchesque literature for decades or seeing onstage at Creole dramas. Ezeiza wowed audiences and became one of the moment's most sought-after performers. "Attention fellow *criollos*!," began the news of his first appearance with the company. The announcement presented him in the most praising way possible: Ezeiza was "the one and only worthy emulator of the immortal Santos Vega [a mythic gaucho payador who had become the hero of several poems, a Gutiérrez narrative, and a Creole drama]" who, in addition to his song lists, would improvise on "whatever themes the public requests."[11] An iconic representative of the Creole, Ezeiza demonstrates the intersection criollismo had with ethnicity. As Ezequiel Adamovsky relays, the Creole had the ability to reconcile ethnic and racial difference, effectively smoothing over certain tensions.[12] Gabino Ezeiza was also a representative—though not purposefully so—of the Afro-Argentine community. So while his verses and chord progressions vibrated with native appeal, he helped Afro-descendants on both sides of the Plata river feel part of the heroic community story, much like we saw with Pedro Paz in the drama *Juan Soldao*.[13] This theme of belonging that sabor criollo helped promote will come into clearer focus below.

Ezeiza had his challengers, and there were occasions when competitors were swifter with their verses or sang smoother than he. Yet Ezeiza continued riding the wave of popular support for sabor criollo throughout the 1890s. He was the guy others had to "defeat" to capture the mantle of the region's top payador.[14] By playing Creole airs and *estilos nacionales* (national

Figure 4.2. Gabino Ezeiza (seated front left), with one of his *payador* opponents, Maxmiliano Santillán (front right), in 1889. Note the interesting presence of the children between the two musicians among an otherwise all-male group. Ezeiza and Santillán engaged in a days-long payada not far from Bahía Blanca, Argentina, where this picture was taken. Museo de Arte Popular José Hernández, Fondo Documental Carlos G. Daws, Album 4, Foto 528.

jigs), Ezeiza capitalized on a musical vein that had emotional appeal with audiences. Furthermore, variations on these traditional folk tunes were often composed by a handful of composers connected to Creole drama groups. The most notable among these was Antonio Podestá, recognized as a "national composer" in circus programs in both Argentina and Uruguay.[15] Beyond local color that payadas and their practitioners like Ezeiza lent performances, they show important connections between notions of tradition, sabor criollo, and claims to symbolize the nation, even though the payada was ultimately a transnational, Rioplatense cultural phenomenon.

A handful of dance traditions similarly added to the sense of pride for the local felt at Creole dramas. The *pericón* and other regional dances like the *gato*, the *minué*, and the *tango africano*, as it was sometimes called, or at others simply tango, conveyed core notions of tradition.[16] These were, after all, local dances. Attendees knew them well, and when the performance space allowed it, dance scenes invited audience participation. It's no wonder that such dances routinely received rave reviews after they became obligatory features of the dramas. And though the dances carried regional overtones, they often appeared in prominent positions in play announcements and were introduced unashamedly as "bailes nacionales."

The pericón, an Uruguayan dance of two, is a case in point. Toward the end of 1889, during a successful season in Montevideo, the Podestá-Scotti Company began incorporating the pericón into performances of *Juan Moreira*. From that moment on, this folk dance guaranteed crowds. In fact, the pericón kept shows afloat when they fell flat, as in the company's representation of *Santos Vega* in Montevideo at the end of 1894. Reviewers for the paper *El Siglo* criticized the monotony of scenes, the poor stage arrangement, and general inability of the company to capture the audience's attention. But the pericón received warm applause.[17] Similarly, in Paysandú the following January, reviewers for the local paper commented that the "pericón nacional," as the dance was often called, gave the *fiesta campestre* scene in *Juan Moreira* an air of "grace and mastery" and was simply the best part of the show.[18]

The impact of the pericón and similar dances was not just confined to the circus tent or theater. A writer for the Paysandú daily *El Paysandú* noted with enthusiasm the transcendent quality of dance in Creole dramas. "With their corresponding gatos and pericones these plays have produced a renaissance of certain customs that European civilization had forced us to hide. Now, the pericón is going to become the dance of choice in the most aristocratic salons of Buenos Aires and Montevideo." The note goes on to cite "proof" of this prophecy in Buenos Aires. The city's *El Tiempo* had observed that "'the great novelty in our dance halls this winter is the pericón nacional.'"[19] The point is that rural dance traditions were central to sabor criollo. More important, thanks to the rising popularity such dances enjoyed because of their inclusion as prized Creole drama numbers, they appeared in other entertainment areas and spaces of association, such as dance halls, exemplifying the Creole taking hold in different social contexts.

A similar pattern of influence is evident in the ways audiences engaged with the local content they saw during and after shows. Getting riled up was half the fun of attending a Creole drama. The press commonly referred to "boisterous manifestations" audiences made, noting cheers, jeers, sighs, and other expressions of emotion as the plays unfolded.[20] Just imagine the atmosphere at an April 1892 performance of *Juan Moreira* in Carmelo, Uruguay. The director of the company decided to introduce some novelty into the play by having Moreira's throat slit, which really upset the crowd. "Among all the shouts of protest and general uproar," the audience called for Moreira to be spared. Some called the director, Napoletano Barullo, "an ugly scoundrel" for having added this scene. The local paper noted that Barullo escaped a mysterious "nasty gift" the crowd would have given him only because a "distinguished" family was in the audience. As the number of dramatic offerings increased and attracted larger audiences, new regulations were introduced to control spectator behavior during shows and manage ticket sales. When these events moved to more formal performance spaces in Montevideo, for example, spectators were prohibited from standing in hallways or on the edges of bleachers. Remaining in one's assigned space for these action-packed shows was a tall order.[21] After all, this high-energy spectatorship, we can call it, was part of what made attending Creole dramas a memorable experience.

Also memorable was another engagement linked with the representation of violence. There were many instances when playgoers interrupted performances to defend their gaucho heroes from corrupt lawmen and injustice, as they saw it. The most well-known examples come from spectators charging the stage during performances of *Juan Moreira* to either prevent the hero from being stabbed in the back as he attempted to escape the police forces that had him cornered, or to avenge the cowardly act. The excited audience members generally approached with real weapons as opposed to the actors' stage props, resulting in the occasional scare among actors and having to start the scene over.[22] In his memoirs José Podestá tells the story of a guard who, during a performance of *Santos Vega*, jumped onstage toward the end of the show to prevent a fight between soldiers and gauchos. The guard's superior was going to incarcerate the employee but desisted when the actress María Podestá implored him to go easy on the man.[23]

The rough edges of Creole drama stories and their figures also influenced behaviors and actions outside performance venues. The Salto newspaper *Ecos del Progreso* published detailed regulations for horse races that increased in number because of circus shows.[24] In November 1893 Montevideo's *El Siglo* reported an altercation that took place in front of the theater following a *Juan Cuello* show. A spectator by the name of Juan Rossi got into an argument with a police official, and then attacked him with a knife. The officer responded with pistol shots, though all missed their mark. After the ruckus had attracted other police, both men were taken to the station and treated for minor knife wounds. Rossi had left the show itching for a fight, and that is what he got. In contrast to spectators charging the stage during performances, here we have what seems to be a Creole drama–inspired act of violence against a police figure, and right outside the theater.[25] Up in Salto there was both news of some toughs getting into fights at the Podestá-Scotti circus during several nights in January 1894, and a statement from the company assuring authorities and the public that *none* of its members were involved.[26]

Several observers commented on this phenomenon across time. The Argentine intellectual Ernesto Quesada cited police reports of knife fights that broke out at or after performances of Creole dramas, and lamented the trend of delinquents who prided themselves on being like Moreira, to the point of calling themselves Moreiras.[27] His contemporary Vicente Rossi also remarked on the "fashionable" presence of Moreira-like figures in the chronicles of delinquency and how "the *pueblo* was becoming like Moreira."[28] Florencio Sánchez, who was later an outspoken critic of the Creole fashion as well as the region's most celebrated playwright of the early twentieth century, wrote of the gravitational pull toward mimicry of masculine toughness. "For a moment, taking on the police squad was a sort of fantasy close to reality in the popular imagination. Who knows if many of us can claim innocence from having engaged in that youthful game of pretending to dole out, with our wooden knives, as many blows as Moreira did."[29] A couple decades later, José María Obaldía, an author and educator from Treinta y Tres, Uruguay, recalled playing "los matreros" (bandits) with friends in the early 1930s. "After the circuses and their dramas, including *Moreira*, left town, we played 'los matreros' at night in the town square."[30]

Knife fighting had a deep history in both rural and urban spaces, with intimate links to masculine honor and the symbolic uses of violence. What is significant about this practice at the end of the 1800s is its uptick in cities, presence in the media, and connections to the Creole drama movement. Jorge Luis Borges even attributed the attitudes of *compadritos*, or urban tough guys who gained fame in Buenos Aires and Montevideo at the outset of the twentieth century, to Creole drama influences.[31]

Though there are less direct connections between Creole drama influences and knife fights that occurred at masked balls, altercations that were waiting to happen during carnival, or tussles that made the news otherwise, the spirit of *Moreirismo* was in the air. As will become clearer below, Moreirismo meant different things to different people—forms of speech and dress for some of its proponents, "the national cult of bravery" and criminal conduct for many of its detractors, or the rapid production and avid consumption of *Juan Moreira*–like tall tales throughout the decades of 1880 and 1890.[32] Regardless of this variety of meanings, men were the primary advocates of Moreirismo, and they were predominantly associated with the Creole overtones of physical violence. Even so, occasionally news of female Moreiras surfaced.

Soledad Varela was one of these, and by early 1894 she was becoming "quite a celebrity" in the Montevideo press for her clashes with the police. Another such confrontation came at the end of March. This time Soledad caused a scandal of some sort (no details provided) in the Podestás' old neighborhood, which attracted the attention of police. As an officer led her to the station office, she pulled a knife on him. He responded in kind, and both ended up in the hospital. The press asked her later why she did what she did. Her reply: "So the officer remembers me when looking in the mirror, even though he's already very ugly!"[33] There is no mention of Varela attending any Creole drama. But her attitude and action fit right in with the behaviors of those dramatic heroes, as one of Moreirismo's most pronounced characteristics was its celebration of resisting, rejecting, or disparaging authority.

On a more peaceful note, the emotional power of sabor criollo correlated to the changing audience makeup at Creole dramas. The limited commentary on audiences who attended these plays in their first years tends to paint a homogenous portrait—humble workers, residents from the countryside, immigrants. Yet a significant shift in audience makeup happened at the outset of the 1890s. It was then that the Podestá-Scotti Company, Raffetto's group, and smaller Creole Circus outfits started attracting a following among social elites. The La Plata newspaper *El Día* summed up part of this transformation. Previously, noted the author, those who had a "highly developed sensibility" dismissed Creole dramas. But for various reasons these dissenters began attending these spectacles. "Upon leaving the event, everyone uniformly heard the voice of conscience proclaim that 'everything you saw is true,'" suggesting that the prior disdain of some had morphed into awe.[34] Here again was the transmutation of fantasy into reality and truth.

As the last chapter mentioned, in Buenos Aires anybody who was anybody in the city's social world had to see *Juan Moreira* and similar dramas that became the talk of the town. In La Plata the Podestá-Scotti circus became "*the* place to hang out." [35] Reporters for the region's press, especially in smaller towns, were eager to point out new faces at these gatherings. One reviewer celebrated that *Juan Soldao* attracted both the "enlightened denizens of Salto" and the "admiration of our *paisanos.*" In Mercedes, Uruguay, the same play "satisfied even the most demanding spectators and opponents of Creole dramas"—revealing that these opponents were now among audiences. One of Salto's political bosses who attended a Podestá-Scotti show in April 1895, along with "distinguished families and not a few beauties who made male hearts palpitate energetically," ruined one of his fancy gloves from clapping so hard. Simply put, more people were going to Creole dramas, tasting sabor criollo, and, as a result, participating in the process of going Creole.[36]

Different social groups attending Creole dramas constituted one facet of the changing audience makeup. Another aspect stemmed from the appreciation of Creole dramas by the elite theater establishment. For example, in April 1894 during a long stint in Montevideo, the Podestá-Scotti Company took their show from their usual circus tent in which they had been performing for close to a month to the Teatro Solís—the city's premier opera space. Their debut happened on April 19, one of Uruguay's most revered patriotic holidays. There was an Italian opera company in the city during that time, but the Solís's directors chose the Podestá-Scotti Company for this prized performance date. Here, then, we begin to see a new quality attributed to Creole dramas and their performers as powerful representations not just of local color but of patriotism as well.[37] Moreover, the attribution came not from Creole drama regulars but from elite entertainment circles.

The program that evening exemplifies this point. It began with the national anthem, followed by a dazzling pericón. Next José Podestá sang a series of patriotic verses. Then the national anthem was performed again, this time by six guitarists, before viewers saw a skit depicting the arrival of the Thirty-Three Uruguayans, which was in honor of April 19. After some circus music, the show finished with Elías Regules's lighthearted *Los Guachitos.* For the next several days the company went back and forth between the Solís and the circus tent, selling out at both locations.[38] The appeal of the shows that season was so strong that the company remained in Montevideo into June, moving their operation to the Nuevo Politeama Theater where all the action took place onstage. Not to worry, though, advertised the company. "Those who are eager for that true Creole experience, with the thundering hooves of horses and warmth of the campfire, won't miss anything. Horse, kettle, and fire will all be on stage."[39] That is, sabor criollo for everyone.

Appealing to expanded audience expectations led companies to vary not only their repertoires from day to day but also to vary acts within a show. At times this meant novel acrobatic stunts before the Creole drama performance or the participation of a guest artist. At others, companies staged an entire drama and then followed it with a scene or an act from another. The fact that pieces of dramas could be performed suggests that by the early 1890s audiences developed a common local, collective knowledge of story lines. When only the fiesta campestre from *Moreira* was staged or when viewers saw only the first act of *El Entenao*, they filled in the rest of the story thanks to having seen the play previously or the connections they inferred from experiences at other dramas.

That audiences were able to exercise some influence over repertoires, requesting certain dramas to be performed or repeated during a company's stay in town, was significant as well. Even if this influence owed more to making a profit for the company than other considerations, it nonetheless points to the weight audience preferences carried and highlights audience engagement in fomenting a Creole spirit.[40]

Summing up, local music and folk dances, people getting riled up at and because of Creole drama performances, and the changing constitution of audiences who attended these plays exemplify Creole spirit and its expanding regional presence. Local content was compelling, and it generated patterns of influence of the sort this section has examined. But sabor criollo would not have packed this punch were it not for the collective social experience and consumption of these local stories, characters, and concerns.

Social Affairs

Creole drama performances were real social affairs at which various social circles mingled and where spectators crossed class and ethnic divisions daily. Such frequent rubbing of shoulders was significant to the forms of association and socializing, together understood as sociability, that Creole drama venues promoted and that spilled over into other areas of social life, like ballroom dances and carnival. This cross-pollination of sabor criollo reached its height in the late 1880s and 1890s. The ramifications were profound on several levels. To signal some of the most salient, in addition to being critical members of Creole Circus troupes themselves, immigrants attended the shows regularly, in part to experience a sense of belonging; personal memories became collective ones; and spectators developed a more complete understanding of community bonds, evident, for example, in generous attendance at benefit shows for a range of causes. These social affairs allowed spectators to ponder the mixing of social frontiers in which they themselves were protagonists.

Many features of Creole drama events made for attractive family outings, beginning with entertainment for children. One way the Podestá-Scotti Company appealed to children was through performances arranged specifically for them such as the "grand children's pantomime Napoleón 1," with more than one hundred youth actors. This skit remained in the company's repertoire for years.[41] For its first several seasons in Montevideo, this company performed right around the corner from the Teatro de Niños, where families took kids to see puppet shows each night. The fact that the Teatro de Niños was only two blocks from the Creole dramas taking place at the Politeama 25 de Mayo theater generated lots of family foot traffic for the Podestá-Scotti Company.[42] Raffles and other diversions for children following performances also kept families coming back.[43]

A handful of other elements were likewise important for families. Showtimes were significant in this regard, with matinees being the most popular time for family attendance. Children routinely outnumbered adults at matinees, where programs tended to be lighter.[44] Consider an afternoon showing of *Juan Moreira* billed as an "homage to the world of children" in Buenos Aires in March 1892. Children actors, among whom the oldest was nine, performed half of the show. Family-friendly scenes from other dramas also were performed at matinees over the years.[45] Additionally, ticket costs for Creole dramas, even more so than for other entertainment options, were generally free or greatly reduced for children under age eight. Finally, venues constantly advertised their innovations in comfort, primarily for women spectators, who were honored with free entrance and drinks. The effect was evident early on in the boasting companies did of their success with families. To cite just one case, Pablo Raffetto and friends drew close to two thousand people per show in 1890 in the small city of Paysandú. They did so largely by reaching out to families.[46]

In addition to providing motives for family outings, thereby helping youth spectators establish a strong relationship with the theater and the idea of a blossoming Creole enthusiasm from an early age, Creole dramas attracted people for more basic reasons, like "passing time," as one commentator noted. The space where the Petray Company set up in Salto in April 1895 was appropriately named *El Pasatiempo*.[47] In La Plata, where the Podestá-Scotti Company began performing in 1885, the circus tent "rapidly turned into *the* fashionable place to be."[48] More than ever before, these spectacles offered new chances to go out, to socialize, and connect with others enjoying leisure. Conceiving attendance at the functions as a leisure activity is important to understanding their role in fostering more frequent social interaction among disparate sectors of the population. Moreover, what many thought was simply going to be a leisurely night at a show turned into something much more meaningful. Thanks to conversations had, the collective experience of the story and the range of emotions audiences felt together, and sharing that moment of time out of time, these leisure spaces made going Creole an enjoyable, even easy process.

Consider some aspects that facilitated this type of sociability. To begin, leisurely conversation at these dramas was a hallmark of pre- and post-performance activity. There were many occasions on which companies complained of audience members conversing and commenting during performances, too, to the point of being bothersome for the actors.[49] The Creole Circus also provided middle- and upper-class spectators with the chance to see and be seen. With the increasing popularity and changing audiences at the dramas through the 1890s, their venues gained stature as leading places to be recognized in social circles. This was the very reason behind publishing the names of the most "distinguished social figures" who attended the plays, primarily in small-town newspapers.[50] One of these in Salto noted that countless women filled all parts of the theater in January 1894. Some were there because of the stories onstage, while others, noted the paper, were clearly locking eyes with potential courtiers. The following month a reporter wrote that some of these women were sending "sparks from their eyes that penetrated the hearts of some Don Juan in the crowd."[51] Even when unknown plays staged by little-known groups filled an evening's program, locals continued flocking to the dramas, despite the hope among some observers that popular tastes should have become "more refined."[52]

Just how many people were going out to these shows? More than ever before, as the daily numbers posted at Creole dramas evidenced. In Buenos Aires the functions regularly attracted between two thousand and four thousand people, depending on the venue. Once the Podestá-Scotti Company moved from its tent to the Politeama 25 de Mayo in Montevideo at the end of the 1880s, around 2,500 people attended the nightly shows, seated in balconies and standing in different areas throughout the theater. There the company presented *Juan Moreira* more than forty times to full houses in November 1889 alone.[53] In Paysandú companies attracted more than one thousand theatergoers on an ongoing basis. Here, as we have learned, police not only intervened to control ticket sales but also showed up at performance spaces to prevent overcrowding. Even the small town of Mercedes, Uruguay, saw large turnouts. When the Podestá-Scotti Company was there in May 1895 around one thousand people, including most of Mercedes's adult population, jammed into the company's tent.[54]

Affordable ticket prices encouraged these crowds. "The usual prices and showtime" was often the last line on show announcements, pointing to a familiarity with ticket prices and when shows were routinely performed. When the Podestá-Scotti Company reduced prices for shows at its Pabellón in Salto in March 1895, audience members were ecstatic. One young man proclaimed, "What a deal, eh? I won't miss a single show; I'm going to memorize all of Pepino 88's songs." Thanks to the new, even lower rates, the local press applauded that everyone had the chance to "spend a couple entertaining hours admiring the skills of the artists and enjoying the many great dramas. These have something the acclaimed foreign productions lack: they're eminently moral, and they keep alive the vibrant memory of traditions and ways of being among our *paisanos*."[55]

Ticket prices were only part of the equation. The Creole drama social affair was also about belonging and a sense of community. For many spectators the plays offered analogous representations of their own trials and tribulations. Though the dramas had their starry protagonists and heroic bluster, the stories themselves were ultimately about community and community struggle. This collective character was central to their appeal and function as social anchor points that helped audiences see broader themes in the often fantastic, fictional plots. Because these themes paralleled life experiences of spectators, they were ones with which audiences could identify in varying degrees.[56]

Both belonging and community were at the center of benefit shows Creole Circus troupes performed. Benefit shows utilized sabor criollo for specific causes—support for local institutions (such as schools, mutual aid societies, hospitals), clubs, or specific people, like performers or local authorities.

Companies counted on the support of audiences to make such performances worthwhile. For many spectators, attending these benefit shows was simply another opportunity for entertainment. But for others supporting the cause of the day was the point. Moreover, these benefit shows provided a direct link between Creoleness and a more expansive sense of community. So, when a company like the Podestá-Scotti group devoted Creole drama performances to the "Italian community" in different locations around the region, more than good will was exchanged. Those who attended, including many Italians, expressed their support for the community and celebrated a larger bond *through* the Creole experience, in addition to having a good time.

Contemplate a performance of *Juan Moreira* the Podestá-Scotti Company gave in April 1891 in Montevideo to benefit the actor playing Cocoliche. Most important about the benefit show was the widespread public display of support for the immigrant character.[57] Or this example: the same company gave a benefit show for the Escuela Italiana Benevolenza in Salto in April 1895. The local paper encouraged Italian residents in Salto to attend the performance, thanked Salteños for their patronage, and applauded "distinguished" women for distributing tickets. As we saw in chapter 2, benefit shows helped companies develop social and political capital. This was especially true when the leading Creole drama company praised members of immigrant communities. Such gestures did more than ingratiate the company with newcomers, they also contributed to creating a sense of belonging in the new national community.[58] There were many other gestures like these. While members of the region's political elite and the more well-to-do who were invariably present at such shows could have donated to the causes of benefit shows through other channels, they often chose Creole dramas for their philanthropy. This was because they were high-profile ways to show support and sympathy, with all the associated publicity.[59]

Belonging and community were likewise part of the dramas in which immigrants played Creole heroes. There were versions of *Juan Moreira* entirely in Italian—in Paraná in late 1891, in Mendoza in 1892, for example. An Italian showman starred in the mediocre rendition of *Moreira* in Carmelo, Uruguay, in 1892 that, nonetheless, attracted spectators.[60] The Petray Brothers and the Queirolo family, both of which consisted of several generations of immigrants and had worked with the Podestás early on, put on a parody of *Moreira* in Paysandú in early 1895. It was a parody in part because Moreira was performed by a "napolitano," as was the justice of the peace, while the pulpero Sardetti imitated Spanish modes of speaking and a "Galician" look. These characters would have elicited much laughter, which was one of the motives behind the selection. At the same time, and like many of the cocoliche characters mentioned in chapter 3, this parody was an olive branch of sorts to the local immigrant population and aimed to connect with them in ways that suggested assimilation and an embrace of the Creole.[61]

The sense of belonging and community these spectacles fostered was visible in other areas of public life. Balls and carnival offer some of the best illustrations of this cross-pollination and how forms of association spread from the sites of the dramas elsewhere. Masked balls were among the premier social events during the summer months of January and February. These usually began around 10:30 p.m. and lasted well into the night, if not until dawn. Toward the end of the century the main places for these balls were the very same theaters across the region where Creole dramas roused audiences. The Nuevo Politeama in Montevideo, for instance, often hosted dramas through December, then transformed (as in removed) the seating area to accommodate dancers before moving back to theater mode. Simply put, masked balls shared the same space with these dramas, with the participants in the former becoming the spectators in the latter. Balls also offered moments for Creole Circus–inflected music to appear, such as the pericón, or the "happy Habanera" titled *Juan Moreira*.[62]

Even more than balls, carnival activities involving costumes and competitions between parade groups, which were large-scale forms of association in public spaces, reflect the process of going Creole and the extent of this process's impact on community. In the last third of the century, each February carnival offered residents across the Río de la Plata a prime moment for socializing, in part because of the "anything goes" attitude that ruled.[63] In the port capitals of Montevideo and Buenos Aires, carnival brought out most participants. Though the multiclass and multiethnic profile that had characterized the festivities for the previous two decades began to dissipate in the mid-1880s, carnival as a site of civic expression and criollismo turned out to be even more important, evident in the costumed dance groups or *comparsas* that became a staple feature by the late 1870s. Afro-descendant and blackface comparsas were numerous, as were the comparsas immigrant social groups presented to compete in carnival parades.[64] Among the most popular costumes and characters these comparsas took up were varying versions of Cocoliche, Moreira, and other theatrical gaucho heroes.[65] By the turn of the century these characters that had first circulated in print and later made the rounds through dramatic representation had become quite the carnival stars.

Carnival festivities held in *La Prensa's* headquarters in 1900 provide a telling picture. There competitions between choral groups, carnival floats, and Creole societies (the subject of the next chapter), with men, women, and children dressed as gauchos and cocoliches, lasted for days. Upward of ten thousand people participated in the contests alone on any given day, not even counting those who came to watch! [66] One scholar who has studied this phenomenon remarked that carnival allowed participants and spectators a moment to dramatize their relationship with the nation; carnival in Buenos Aires "extended a site for the negotiation and contestation of shifting national boundaries." [67] There was certainly an element of ethnic and racial negotiation at work as immigrants played gauchos during carnival across the region. Through this performance of Creoleness, many sought to escape the disparaging associations of immigrants with biological (racial) inferiority swirling at the turn of the century, and, in the process, draw on the cultural capital of Creole whiteness, or the power of the Creole to bridge difference. [68] At the same time, immigrants and migrants from the countryside often lived in the same neighborhoods in capital cities as well as smaller towns along the Río de la Plata. Many newcomers shared with good criollos resentment for the rich and disdain for obstacles to social mobility; and like lower-class rural migrants, they sought ways to participate in Rioplatense society. [69]

So even while immigrants were the butt of humiliating jokes in some scenes, carnival comparsas and Creole dramas provided a sense of belonging that hinged on associating with others through sabor criollo. This association again was a source of irritation for Ernesto Quesada. He blamed Eduardo Gutiérrez's *Juan Moreira* and "its imitators," all of which were "deplorable dramas," for "inflaming the imaginations" of immigrants at carnival. "That is the explanation for why those whose only link to our *paisano* is a costume, and who have spent their lives next to some machine . . . show up on carnival in spurs and with a *facón* to talk about the police persecuting honorable countrymen and justices of the peace making off with someone else's sweetheart." [70]

Immigrant imaginations were not the only ones being "inflamed." The popular illustrated magazine *Caras y Caretas* reported on a man by the name of Martín Biava who swore he was going to dress up as a gaucho for the 1904 carnival, against his wife's wishes. He spent a portion of his savings on a wig and hat. From one of his wife's throws he improvised a *chiripá* to wrap around his legs. He utilized a long kitchen knife to simulate a tough-guy facón. And he let his beard grow out, believing that all this would help him show up those gringos (i.e., the immigrants) who appear during the carnival season as Moreiras. In the accompanying image of Biava running to catch the street car, he challenged his wife to say that he didn't look like Moreira himself. She sighed and told him that he reminded her more of Jesus Christ.[71]

The Podestá-Scotti members were keenly aware of these representations and how they might impact audience turnout at their shows. The company formed its own carnival comparsa that capitalized on sociability at carnival to fan the flames of the Creole spirit and advertise their upcoming performance seasons.[72] Advertising, after all, was a booming business, and whether in the press, during carnival, or with a pitch at a live show, no company missed the chance to tout its offerings or Creole cred.

In short, the forms of association Creole dramas stimulated in and out of the circus tent and theater helped develop community bonds as well as a more thorough understanding of these. As one observer noted in 1894, there was a direct correlation between the ripple effect the Creole spirit had in public life and "our sociability in formation."[73] By 1900 the public embrace of the Creole was undeniable and seemed to infiltrate more and more corners of daily life. Marketing played a central role here.

Marketing the Creole

The proliferation of marketing methods employed by Creole drama troupes and the makers of products like cigarettes, guitars, and carnival costumes both reflected and advanced the general attraction of all things Creole toward the turn of the century. These methods constituted clear attempts to influence the shape of sabor criollo's appeal, to boost ticket sales, and to secure financial gain. Naturally, then, these strategies were part of the process of going Creole.

Publicity for the Podestá-Scotti Company from the late 1880s through the 1890s illustrates well the development of these marketing methods. Following a strategy that many entertainers had used, in the second half of the 1880s the company invested in publicity before arriving at a locale to drum up interest in upcoming shows. These promotional announcements were highly detailed, elaborating on the equipment, artists, the mode of transportation used by the company, the repertoire of "applauded Creole dramas," novelties that season, and so on.[74] The company distributed tickets to members of the press in hopes of the performances receiving positive reviews. For a debut show at a Montevideo theater they even invited the public to enjoy tables full of "exquisite wines and fine pastas," with the press there to report the pre-show feast and the public's excitement.[75]

Marketing strategies became more focused around everything Creole in the early 1890s. It was then that the Podestá-Scotti Company started branding itself differently. Up until 1891 the group labeled itself—and was referred to by reporters—as a "Grand Equestrian and Acrobatic Company." Yet the Creole vibe resulted in a name change for them as well as other performance groups. For a series of shows at the Jardín Florida in Buenos Aires in 1892, posters announced the Podestá-Scotti Company as the "*Grand Equestrian, Gimnastic, and Acrobatic Company, and the Creators of DRAMAS CRIOLLOS.*"[76] "Creators" was the operative word, for the company sought to harness the claims of originators and authenticators of the movement.

There were practical motives behind the rebranding as well. One was to ward off competition from other, upstart companies. None of these smaller outfits managed to overtake the Podestá-Scotti Company's hold on the Creole drama market. But they could cut into audience turnout and give the plays a bad rap before the Podestá-Scotti Company arrived in each location. This was precisely the complaint waged by the company secretary in 1891 after Luis Anselmi's competing troupe had copied Podestá-Scotti performances of *Martín Fierro* in Buenos Aires. He urged the play's author, Elías Regules, to pursue legal measures requiring Anselmi to remain confined to small towns where the Podestá-Scotti troupe would not perform.[77] Several years later the Podestá-Scotti brothers filed a court complaint against Anselmi charging that he had infringed on their rights by offering unauthorized performances of *Julián Giménez* and *Nobleza Criolla*, plays which the plaintiffs asserted were created expressly for their company. The judge—none other than Ernesto Quesada—sided with the plaintiffs. In the process he railed against Creole dramas and their popularity. By the time the decision was made in 1903, Anselmi had reaped the plays' benefits. His group continued to perform other Creole dramas that the Podestá-Scotti Company had made famous, but by the beginning of the twentieth century was leaving behind for more formal theatrical productions.[78]

Another motive of the rebranding was economic. By promoting themselves as the "creators" of Creole dramas and the "only National company," the Podestás and the Scottis sought to leverage that identity for local tax breaks where they gave performances.[79] On other occasions the company expressed concern about competitors affecting ticket sales by setting prices for much less than the troupe normally charged. Thus, as they prepared for a series of shows in Mar del Plata beginning in late 1892, the secretary suggested to a group of impresarios the placement of posters and newspaper ads announcing the "immediate arrival" of the group in order to secure the marketplace. Such news, wrote the secretary, would be enough to dissuade any competing Creole drama troupes to set foot in Mar del Plata since the public "always prefers us."[80]

In the mid-1890s the company continued tweaking its name. It was "The First Creole Drama Company" in 1894. In March 1895, for instance, the Salto newspaper *Ecos del Progreso* used this title and praised the return of the "creators of Creole theater." The reference to "theater" here was especially important at this moment of the Creole drama phenomenon, with the transition from circus spectacle to one more attuned to the space of the theater. This is exactly the idea summed up by the reporter who commented on improvements to the shows that would "elevate the moral and material qualities of the circus shows to the proportions of the theater." The Podestá-Scotti Company also advertised itself as the "Grand Creole Drama Company," attempting to sell its theatrical qualities more than its prior circus character as the group performed more extensively in theaters.[81]

Rumor was also a powerful marketing tool, such as when speculation of a possible visit from the Podestá-Scotti Company to Mercedes, Uruguay, in April 1895 made front-page news in the local paper. "Word has it," started the column, that the company would soon be in town. "If news of their arrival is true—and we do not have any further information on this point—our neighbors will have the opportunity to judge for themselves one of the most reputable drama companies in all of South America." It is clear here that even the rumor of the company's visit was effective marketing, precisely because of the Creole spirit. When the company actually showed up in Mercedes at the end of April for a month-long stint, it was the talk of the town. Despite many of Mercedes's "distinguished" residents attending a benefit show put on by none other than the mysterious and mischievous Conde de Das (recall him from chapter 2) the same evening as the Podestá-Scotti debut, the drama overflowed with spectators eager to see "those meritorious artists devoted to their work." In addition to the talented acrobats and highly trained animals, we read in the town's paper that what sets this

company apart from others is its specialty: the "drama nacional," performed by "artists who are true criollos."[82]

Soon after other troupes began representing Creole dramas they also
attempted to cash in on labeling themselves as Creole companies devoted to
performances that embodied criollismo. Thus, when the Petray and Queirolo
Brothers, who were newcomers to the entertainment world, set up in
Paysandú's main theater in February 1895, they made scenes from *Juan
Moreira* the center of their shows. Writers for the town paper admitted their
skepticism regarding criollismo at the theater from these performers, but
they were impressed with the new group's skills and the positive reaction
from the audience.[83] A couple months later, when the Petray Brothers followed on the heels of the Podestá-Scotti Company's departure from Salto,
they sold themselves as a Creole drama company, too, and from then on,
played on the symbolic capital of the name.[84] Even in 1900 when they joined
the larger Circo Americano, the entire outfit promoted itself as "a great gymnastic and Creole drama company" whose slogan was "order, culture, and
morality." This Circo Americano sold out shows regularly, benefitting from
the attraction to Creole stories previous companies had cultivated, illustrating the depth of the fascination with Creole as well as its marketing power
even in the Creole Circus's twilight years.[85]

Descriptive comments attached to announcements for dramas likewise
deployed these marketing strategies. *Juan Moreira* was often advertised as
"the national drama of Creole traditions." From 1892 on, *El Entenao, Martín
Fierro, Julián Giménez,* and other plays were also all "national dramas of
Creole traditions." The declaration of "national drama" appeared for shows
in both Argentina and Uruguay, pointing to their regional impact as well as
to the widespread acceptance of the dramas as legitimate representations of
the nation on both sides of the Plata river. In effect, the plays lent to a general
transference of Moreira's, or Fierro's, or Giménez's plight onto the outlines
of Argentine, Uruguayan, and Rioplatense history at the close of the century.
One poster for *Julián Giménez* claimed that the Creole customs the Podestá-
Scotti Company performed had sown the "roots of NATIONAL THEATER."

Authenticity and links to notions of tradition were similarly paramount
in these marketing maneuvers. In this vein, *Juan Moreira* was a drama that
was "genuinely gauchesque" with "PURE CRIOLLISMO IN EVERY SCENE,"
as one play poster from 1892 proclaimed.[86] *El Entenao* was announced in 1893
as a "drama criollo y social" (Creole and social drama), which captured not
just the idea of tradition but also the role of such plays in presenting social

portraits and giving audiences that special time to socialize.[87] Even while "tradition" was a cornerstone of the Creole drama experience, there were several layers of connections tying the marketing of the Creole to modern life at the turn of the century. Modern marketing techniques, which depended in part on new print technologies, allowed for the massive distribution of ads in newspapers, posters, and magazines. And modern transportation companies often plugged the newly constructed streetcar routes to take theatergoers home after shows in the same announcements for the dramas, suggesting how these companies saw an opportunity to make sizeable profits.[88]

There were also a range of products whose makers sought to benefit from the fame of these dramas. The Argentine cigarette manufacturer La Popular, which produced around one hundred thousand packs per day, churned out Juan Moreira–, Martín Fierro–, and Juan Cuello– branded cigarettes, among its other labels, throughout the 1890s. Each of these brands contained collectable cards with scenes from the story and abbreviated captions—the Moreira series had twenty-two cards, Cuello thirty-six, and Fierro thirty.[89] During the Podestá-Scotti Company's 1895 stint in Paysandú, they gave out Los Guachitos cigarettes at a performance of *Los Guachitos*, apparently to great applause. A reporter commented that the smokes were just as good as the show, which drew a full house that hoped for repeat giveaways.[90] Adolfo Prieto highlights some other products that underscore the marketing power of the Creole: sketches of Moreira on matchboxes; guitar sales that rose to the hundreds of thousands per year; and the use of phrases from gauchesque characters and Creole drama figures to promote Argentine wines.[91]

Finally, the press played a significant role in marketing the Creole. First, the stream of advertisements in the public diversions section of papers was constant, making news of the plays a feature of daily life. Then there were the reviews or commentaries of dramas that often spoke of the excitement in a given locale surrounding the arrival of the performers, or encouraged readers to attend shows. Even many of the critical reviews suggested that the dramas were worth seeing. Such secondary publicity for the plays reached a growing readership toward the end of the century as papers augmented print runs to satisfy an increasingly literate public.[92] The allure associated with the press as the preeminent form of modern communication at the end of the century added legitimacy to the ads for and news of the plays, as well as sabor criollo more generally.

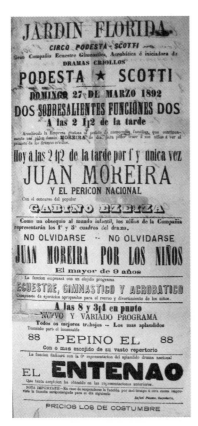

Figure 4.3. Poster for a Podestá-Scotti performance of *Juan Moreira* and *El Entenao* on March 27, 1892. The program is full of the regular variety: folk dancing; Gabino Ezeiza; Pepino 88's clown act; and acrobatic stunts. Standing out, though, is the mention of scenes from *Moreira* "by children, for children" that will take place in the afternoon. "Don't forget!" The company heeded the requests of spectators to offer such a number for kids. INET.

Figure 4.4. Poster for a Podestá-Scotti performance of *Juan Moreira* on March 15, 1892. Note the illustration of Moreira atop his horse, victorious against his persecutors, with his loyal dog below. The program announced that this "genuinely gauchesque drama is full of PURE CRIOLLISMO IN EVERY SCENE." INET.

After all, the region's press helped to both consolidate the ubiquity of sabor criollo and to circulate ideas of the social importance of the Creole. Even our critic Ernesto Quesada reluctantly acknowledged this in his 1902 essay about criollismo, where he bemoaned the "immense popularity" of "lowly Creole theater" and those "gaudy dramas of men gone astray."[93] The plays were his specific target, but his more general lament was about the Creole spirit, the dramas as social affairs, and the marketing phenomenon we have seen.

Counterpoints to Going Creole

The process this chapter has traced was felt intensely across the region. Sabor criollo was magnetic; the sociability experienced at Creole dramas had far-reaching ramifications; and there were profits to be made from the economy of Creole products. Yet the portrait of this Creole fever would not be complete without considering a handful of counterpoints, namely a lawsuit filed against the Podestá-Scotti Company; records of ticket sales to other, competing types of performances; and, last, criminal activity seemingly pointing to the process of going Creole getting out of hand. At first glance these counterpoints suggest obstacles to the spread of the Creole spirit and limits of its impact that would seem to undermine the very story followed thus far. Ultimately, though, this counter-evidence underscores the reach and intensity the process had in the region at the end of the 1800s on into the twentieth century.

It was the very success of sabor criollo that inspired Eduardo Gutiérrez's widow and children to file a lawsuit against José Podestá and Alejandro Scotti in 1893. The plaintiffs' lawyer petitioned for Podestá and Scotti to abstain from further performances of *Juan Moreira* and *Juan Cuello*, and that they pay the Gutiérrez family what his widow estimated to be their rightful share from the shows given up to the date of the suit. The argument was that Gutiérrez was the author of the plays' original content, and therefore his heirs were entitled to royalties from his works. Podestá and Scotti disputed the charges and claimed that Gutiérrez was not in fact the author of the plays themselves. The judge in the case ruled in the first instance in September 1893 that the law only allowed him to order the company to abstain from future performances of *Juan Moreira* and *Juan Cuello*, but that they would not be obligated to pay any portion of their past earnings to

Gutiérrez's family. The defendants of course appealed. Four years later the final ruling confirmed the abstention order and ruled out any kind of payment.

Based on the legal briefs, the judges ruled against Podestá and Scotti more out of eagerness to prohibit or limit future performances of these dramas than because the evidence was all that convincing. Aside from pointing to the language of the plays overlapping with that of the novels and the testimony of spectators who obviously saw similarities in the stories, the ownership of the rights to the works was unclear. In fact, the case was one of the early attempts to define intellectual property rights in Argentina. Add to this the fact that Podestá, and not Gutiérrez, had given the plays their dialogue. While alive, Gutiérrez had never expressed an interest in Creole dramas after his initial adaptation of *Juan Moreira* as a pantomime, which appeared to be the only performance he attended. Rather than a vested interest in the works themselves or legal precedent, the commercial success of the Podestá-Scotti Company motivated Gutiérrez's widow to demand compensation.[94] By the time the final ruling was issued in late 1897, the company was adding other types of plays to its repertoire and moving away from Creole dramas. Moreover, the Podestá-Scotti Company, as well as several other less famous troupes, continued to perform *Juan Moreira* and *Juan Cuello* in subsequent years. So, on the one hand, the lawsuit illustrates an unsuccessful attempt to cash in on the financial success of the phenomenon, and, on the other, the effort of the judges involved to reign in the appeal of blockbuster performances, albeit toward the end of their heyday.

The dramas and their performers faced a more urgent hurdle from competing entertainment options in the 1890s. Annual statistical registers from Buenos Aires and Montevideo reveal some data on ticket sales that pose questions about audience loyalties and turnout at Creole dramas. We can glean, for example, that in Buenos Aires in 1887 close to 210,000 people attended circuses, out of a total 1.5 million spectators for the year. The following year eight circus companies staged 636 performances, attracting 233,000 attendees out of the 1.8 million who attended performances in the city. These figures are important, yet at the same time for several years (1887, 1888, 1890, 1893) neither the Podestá-Scotti Company nor the Carlo Brothers feature in the tally of shows and spectators.[95] The number of Creole drama shows in Buenos Aires dipped slightly in 1894 to around 200, and then rose to 359 in 1896, when the phenomenon began to wane. Statistics for this year did include both the Podestá-Scotti Company and rival Circo Anselmi, but the number of Creole drama spectators only reached around 60,000 out of a total of 1.8 million for all spectacles, which appears low for the number of shows and size of venues.[96] During this same year in Montevideo the annual report noted that the Pabellón Podestá-Scotti held 55 Creole dramas. Combined with the Pabellón Nacional, a site for dramas and acrobatic shows, the locales accounted for a meager 10 percent of the year's public diversions in the city. According to the reports for both cities, there were more *zarzuelas* (a Spanish form of light opera) and comedies than other shows offered, and these carried the largest numbers of spectators.[97]

These figures suggest two conclusions. First, the statistics appear to challenge the extent of the Creole drama phenomenon's popularity, at least in the capitals. At the same time, the reports presented incomplete information, especially on circuses and Creole dramas. This is the more important revelation. Not only are the numbers limited to performance activity in the capital cities—we know that Creole dramas had a rich following in other towns and pueblos across the region—they also leave out from the results some of the most active performers. Why would the municipal reports deliberately not include the ticket sales for the Podestá-Scotti or Carlo shows over several years? And how many smaller Creole Circus groups set up tents in Buenos Aires and Montevideo but went unaccounted in the numbers?

Though no definitive conclusion can be drawn, the speculative answer has to do with shaping the official record of the performance landscape. Erring on the side of lower ticket sales to these dramas or ignoring references to certain circus troupes during these years was one way to influence how entertainment would be remembered. When paired with the debates on the effect Creole dramas had on public morality, which we will take up in chapter 6, the intention of the reports' authors to mitigate the impact of going Creole becomes clearer. Moreover, zarzuelas bore the brunt of criticism in the reports, being called in 1893 "exotic productions of dubious taste, confusing morality, and detestable form."[98] The following year the same municipal publication in Buenos Aires complained about the commercial success of zarzuela and proclaimed, "We must react against the corruption that threatens the artistic taste of our capital's residents."[99] There was still hope for zarzuela, though. After all, it was clad in European garb and performed often by Europeans themselves. And though zarzuela stole some of the fire from opera, it was still wholly distinct from the world of Creole dramas. The critique of zarzuelas *instead* of Creole dramas seems to be an attempt to lessen their impact by ignoring the shows.

Of course, it was hard to ignore this impact, as this chapter has shown, and as the last counterpoint hints. Occasionally the process of going Creole went too far. Nowhere was this more evident than in cases of hypermasculinity on display with Creole tough guys. Some of these engaged in playful knife fights following attendance at Creole dramas, with nicks, scratches, or other light wounds being the extent of the confrontations. In these after-show tussles, we can observe an immediate reaction (and mode of reception) to the Creole spirit. Others, however, employed the knife-wielding tactics dramatized onstage to commit real-life acts of violence—true crime—repeatedly, the marks of which appear in police records or, in a few instances, in the apotheosis of the criminals themselves. Rather than dissuading people from going Creole or attending the dramas, these figures became beloved icons of resistance and protectors of the downtrodden.

Moreira himself was the epitome of the criminal-turned-national icon, though a couple other examples illustrate men with a similar trajectory, beginning with the Uruguayan bandit Martín Aquino. Born in 1889 Aquino was a police office, herder, and contraband smuggler on the Brazil–Uruguay border. Some allege he fought with the Uruguayan caudillo Aparicio Saravia in the country's last civil wars in 1904.[100] Aquino adopted the nickname "Moreira" when serving in the police force, and he had a picture of Moreira above his bed in his childhood room in Canelones.[101] He clearly admired Moreira, and the picture and nickname suggest that Moreira's story was present in Aquino's process of going Creole. There were parallels between their lives, too: both were "noble" country men in real life, though ultimately slid down the slippery slope of crime. Like Moreira, Aquino became an outlaw. And upon dying both grew into legend in the popular imagination.

The Argentine Antonio Gil, better known as "Gauchito Gil," was a similar figure who had the Robin Hood reputation of robbing the rich to give to the poor. The police captured and killed Gil before the Creole drama phenomenon took off. But it was after his death that Gauchito Gil became a folk saint revered at points throughout Argentina. His primary shrine outside of Mercedes, Argentina, still attracts tens of thousands seeking to pay tribute each year.[102]

Last, the Uruguayan Alejandro Rodríguez, better known as "El Clinudo," committed acts of true crime in the early 1880s. In the years after he was captured in 1882, tales of his crimes were fodder for *folletines* (serialized narratives), "causas célebres" crime sections in papers throughout Uruguay, and even the inspiration for a lost play the soon-to-be-star-dramaturg Florencio

Sánchez wrote. Clinudo was the chief protagonist.[103] In life El Clinudo's reputation was one of a criminal, pure and simple, who never became a beloved
outcast in the popular imagination. This did not prevent his lawyer from
attempting to present a man forced into crime due to circumstances in the
countryside, and to portray him as a victim of the state as well as of the folletines that had already rendered public judgement. Sound familiar?

I am not suggesting that the process of going Creole resulted necessarily
in an uptick in banditry or a particular variant of criminal activity, though
this would certainly be a fascinating avenue to follow. Data does show,
though, curious spikes in the number of crimes committed with knives or
"other sharp objects," wounded victims, and attacks against law enforcement
officers during the period from 1889 to 1901.[104] Instead, part of the attention
and posthumous glory certain criminals enjoyed owes to the Creole spirit
that primed the public to celebrate their type as folk heroes, even when the
crimes they committed would have been reason to condemn these men in
other circumstances. In this interpretation the diffusion of the links between
the Creole and notions of authenticity and community was a filter through
which the region's inhabitants understood criminality. Certain criminals
were transformed into ideal social rebels, perfect for the making of tradition
that we will see in the next chapter.

The counter-evidence from such figures who seem to exemplify the process of going Creole getting out of hand, from the lawsuit against the Podestá-
Scotti Company, or the statistical reports of ticket sales to performances
competing with Creole dramas, certainly raises questions about the reach,
intensity, and the forms in which people experienced sabor criollo. But if
anything, the counterpoints here reinforce its influence.

In this chapter we have seen deep emotional vibrations of sabor criollo, social
connections that fanned out from the Creole drama experience, and the
commercialization of the Creole spirit toward the end of the 1800s. Sabor
criollo was felt in music, dance, and the ways in which spectators engaged
with the themes of the plays. It was the force behind the forms of association
that brought together rich and poor, peasants and upscale politicians, immigrants and locals, at the performances and in other areas of public life such
as dances and carnival. These were the core elements that drove the widespread acceptance of the Creole as synonymous with collective values and
representation. The public embrace of the Creole spirit transformed the stuff

of myth, fantasy, and fiction into reality; it made what we might see as exaggerated or invented notions of authenticity sources of essential truth.

Ironically, as the process of going Creole grew more intense across the region, Creole dramas shed some of their initial characteristics and rougher edges. In 1893 the Podestá-Scotti Company announced that audiences would no longer have to put up with the dirt of the circus tent since they were the only company to possess a special rug that cut down on floor dust. The transition of companies from circus tent to theater likewise provided for an improved experience. Yet, their Creoleness and emphasis on tradition remained intact. The link to tradition—that is, the idea that these dramas referenced a heroic past and kept it alive for younger generations—was one of the reasons why sympathizers as well as critics of the plays began speaking of them as the foundation for national theater. According to the Salto newspaper *Ecos del Progreso*, having such a theatrical tradition whose story could be told and retold was a hallmark of "great and noble countries."[105]

Ultimately the process of going Creole reveals the consolidation of a regional identity that was synonymous with national belonging and the making of tradition. Creole dramas were pivotal in this process, but they were not alone. As we are about to see in the next chapter, *sociedades criollas*, or membership clubs devoted to "playing gaucho," which began proliferating in the region in the mid-1890s, made regional identity, national belonging, and tradition the font of their business and enduring presence.

CHAPTER 5

Playing Gaucho and the Making of Tradition

✢ ON A LATE FALL DAY IN MAY 1894, DR. ELÍAS REGULES TURNED HIS
dream of a Creole Society into a reality. At the time Regules was Dean of the
School of Medicine in Montevideo, yet he was growing ever more passionate
about all things Creole and spent as much time as possible at his rural retreat
outside the city. On May 24 Regules and a group of friends held a *fiesta criolla*
at a small ranch on the northern edge of Montevideo. Decked out in gaucho
regalia, the group had paraded on horseback through the city's streets past
newly constructed elegant shops and apartment buildings that gave the city a
touch of Paris. The horsemen pictured against this cityscape, as we see below
in images 5.1 and 5.2, offered a fabulous contrast. Along the way they added
contingents until they numbered close to two hundred (pictured in image 5.3),
before riding back to the ranch where they celebrated in proper rural fashion,
meaning with plenty dance, song, *mate* (a traditional South American tea),
and a barbeque blowout.

The men chose the following day, May 25, for its patriotic overtones to
launch officially the *Sociedad Criolla*. At 3 p.m. Regules and thirty-two
friends gathered in the Podestá-Scotti circus tent downtown for the inaugural ceremony. Among these "founding members"—all men—are some familiar names for us, such as José Podestá, who was close friends with Regules,
and the soon-to-be-famous short story author Horacio Quiroga. Orosmán
Moratorio, who had written the play *Juan Soldao*, was the society's first vice
president. Regules held the reins of the group, which pledged to "welcome
under its traditionalist banner any and all who hold the true concept of the

129

Patria."[1] Then the members paraded out to their ranch for another fiesta.
According to the local paper *El Día* the men on horseback made for a "beautiful spectacle ... of youth who brought back proud memories of the feats of
our gauchos from yore."[2] After the meal a group of aficionados put on a representation of *Juan Moreira*, then they all disbanded and went about their
routines. Several months later, in September, the ritual and party were
repeated, this time with the addition of the Sociedad's newly "sworn-in" flag
that closely resembled one used during the wars of independence.

Scenes from those celebrations in both May and September could have
been from any number of Creole dramas, which was only fitting. After all,
the members of this new Creole Society had baptized their club under the
circus tent of the region's preeminent Creole drama troupe, and they had
included an impromptu version of the most successful Creole drama as part
of their inaugural festivities. Yet for all the merriment characterizing the
parades and barbecues, despite the amusement of playing gaucho, and
though we can picture members joyfully dancing or laughing with the musical improvisation, these were serious events, too.

Figure 5.1. First outing of some of the Sociedad Criolla's founding members in Montevideo in May 1894. There is a sharp contrast between the men on horseback and the
elegant urban architecture behind them.

Figure 5.2. Regules (center) with two other Sociedad Criolla members. All three stand out against the urban backdrop, though the one on the right especially so. Note his riding crop in hand and the *boleadoras* (indigenous hunting weapon consisting of stones tethered together) wrapped around his waist. Sociedad Criolla Elías Regules.

Figure 5.3. The contingent grew along the route to Montevideo. With the goal of creating the society clear in mind, the group posed for a picture along the "paseo criollo." May 1894. Sociedad Criolla Elías Regules.

Seriousness was behind the careful calculation of symbolic numbers (thirty-three friends, like the famed Thirty-Three Uruguayans who had launched the country's final fight for independence; the selection of May 25 for the inauguration, in reference to the patriotic holiday celebrated on both sides of the river commemorating autonomy from the Spanish empire). They were serious as well because this was "real" life. Participants and spectators were involved in an intense moment of theatricality during which there was a concerted effort to invent—or protect, in the eyes of the Society's members—*tradition*. Tradition offered a good excuse to enjoy leisure time and fortify bonds, but it was also serious business.

Elías Regules's Sociedad Criolla was the first among hundreds of similar societies, clubs, and smaller Creole unions (*agrupaciones* or *aparcerías gauchas*) established from 1894 through the 1910s in Uruguay, Argentina, and southern Brazil. It is no coincidence that the remarkable initial growth in the number of Creole societies—the general term we'll use to speak about the variety of groups comprising the phenomenon—followed the arc of mass immigration to the region, which as we saw previously slowed in the 1910s. Part of the appeal of these societies was their nativist, nationalist outlook, cloaked in the call to preserve tradition. Tradition here was inseparable from an often romanticized understanding of rural life, folkways or cultural practices, and modes of work and speech. Tradition was linked to the land, to life on horseback, or around the campfire. The rhetoric of tradition conveyed this earthiness. And the gaucho, which at the end of the 1800s had been refracted through decades of literary interpretations and the Creole drama phenomenon, came to be both the iconic representative of tradition and emblem of freedom, bravery, and national identity, making it possible to invoke with ease "feats" of those "gauchos of yore" who exuded authenticity and local roots. These notions meshed perfectly with an increasingly widespread anti-immigrant sentiment and anticosmopolitan ideology at the turn of the century. Such ideas informed what Regules, his followers, and subsequent Creole society members conceived as the cause of traditionalism or the traditionalist movement.

Traditionalism dealt in historical memory and the ways tradition was invoked, celebrated, and communicated. Traditionalist centers and groups were prime architects of social identities. These, in turn, relied on myths of origin concerning gauchos in the political and ethnic formation of the nation.[3] Traditionalists "remembered" the wars of independence as the wars gauchos won (true to some extent), or the periods of forced recruitment of gauchos to fight along the frontier and their resistance to what they deemed corrupt forces of the modern, cosmopolitan state. Creole societies spearheaded the traditionalist movement that intertwined with the spirit and success of Creole dramas as well as the gauchesque and criollista literary traditions. Their idea of preserving rural tradition, though, was in effect one of creation, which relied both heavily on the popular cultural power of Creole dramas beyond their places of representation as well as on committed members, including plenty of immigrants, to animate their activities.

Why did so many of these societies appear, and what did their members get out of participating in activities? What relationship did these societies have with popular culture and the budding popular culture industry? This chapter addresses these questions by looking first at the proliferation of Creole societies and their activities at the turn of the century, focusing, in particular, on the Sociedad Criolla that Regules founded and stressing the direct line connecting Creole dramas to Creole societies. As predominantly male organizations, these societies yield insight into links between masculinity and political culture taking shape in these years. Then we will turn to how these groups represented ideas of tradition, and how they promoted understandings of ethnicity and race as central to club—and national—identity. Finally, the chapter closes with an emphasis on Creole societies within the framework of civil associations emerging at the turn of the century. In this context they not only facilitated political participation in an evolving public arena, they also constituted very concrete representations of popular culture and contributed to its dissemination.

These clubs illustrate perfectly the movement of Creole drama stories and the Creole spirit from one space and medium to another, the fusion of high and low cultures, and another instance of all things Creole driving the region's popular culture. Their members hailed from the full range of socioeconomic spheres and even ideological backgrounds. What drew them together was a traditionalist interpretation of Uruguayan and Argentine history, the fun that could be had when playing gaucho and invoking tradition, and considering how that vision shaped their imagination of the future.

Invoking Tradition in Gaucho Garb

Let me share an anecdote to help us imagine what it was like getting into gaucho garb. I was fortunate to spend one July pouring through the Sociedad

Criolla's files and records, which have been accumulating since 1894. I was granted access to all the documentation in the club's "museum"—letters from Elías Regules to Creole drama actors; framed programs from the society's events; banners used in parades. In the shedlike building next door I scanned thousands of photographs of members in their gaucho attire dancing, eating, giving speeches, participating in demonstrations. There were pictures of Regules with his family and as the head of the Society throughout the years—referred to then and now as *el patriarca*. All the while the winter wind blew in through the building's wide doors, left open, through which a rooster or two would occasionally come in, examine the red-tile floor, and then return to pecking the ground outside. It was the perfect setting for the Creole spirit to take hold. In the director's office located in the compound's oldest building I came across some of the society's accounting records, Regules's written impressions of *Martín Fierro*, and photographs the Podestá brothers had given Regules, touting their friendship. There was no order to this archive. But there was clearly a wealth of material there that spoke to the joys, pastimes, and relationships members had in gaucho garb over the more than one hundred years of the Sociedad's existence. My time at the Sociedad Criolla made it even more evident that this Creole society, as well as the many others that followed suit on a smaller or larger scale, was a critical social and leisure space, and a complex social institution. When members dressed up and played gaucho, they did so for fun and for just a handful of hours at a time. Yet donning the costume at the society compound or on a stroll through town was a public ritual that could be formative or transformative, too, as the photographs and abundant other records, and material relics of the gatherings communicated.

Given Elías Regules's interest in and desire to celebrate rural life, it was only fitting that he chose the Podestá-Scotti circus venue for the inauguration of his Sociedad Criolla, underscoring the link between Creole dramas and Creole societies. Regules had developed a close friendship with the company and had already written two successful plays for them. Moreover, with the company's role in the dissemination of theater to remote towns in the countryside and their growing fame among cultural elites, the Podestá-Scotti venue provided the perfect place to contemplate the curious mixture of modernity and the longing for tradition.

Regules himself embodied this blend. On the one hand, he was a professor of modern medicine who held prominent teaching positions and served as the Dean of the School of Medicine as well as the head of the entire

Figure 5.4. Postcard of Regules in a *desfile* in Montevideo. 1925. Sociedad Criolla Elías Regules.

Uruguayan university system. Yet, he felt most at home in the countryside and devoted his free time to the Sociedad, writing poetry and cultivating the ideas that would fuel the traditionalist movement in Uruguay. Regules was born in Montevideo but spent his adolescence in the interior near the town of Durazno, several hours from the capital, where he later returned to study. He crafted and read verses and speeches for each anniversary of the Sociedad, which held most activities at a ranch belonging to one of the members until acquiring its own space in the Atahualpa neighborhood. At that time the area was still quite rural though it bordered the Prado, where elegant homes and a luxurious hotel were soon constructed.[4] Photographs of the group's activities present Regules on horseback (his favorite place to pose for pictures), dancing, giving advice to young members eager to get in on the fun and learn about tradition, or leading a march of gauchos and chinas through the modern city in the name of tradition (as in image 5.4). Regules continued as head of the Sociedad through the 1920s until his last days, when his sons took over the administration. Tradition—like the circus—was a family affair.

Like Regules, members of the 1894 cohort as well as subsequent generations who joined were gauchos only at the Sociedad's events, after which they went back to their regular lives. Their participation was far from insignificant, though, as the proliferation of similar organizations in the region over following two decades demonstrates. The development of these civil associations in neighboring Argentina and what they themselves called the traditionalist movement showcases this point.

The first documented Argentine societies date from 1899 and were scattered across the republic. Like their Uruguayan counterparts, they charged a small fee to join. Among these new clubs, some lasted only a few months or a year, while others continued for much longer.[5] In his 1916 study on the ramifications of the Santos Vega legend in Argentina (recall that Vega was the story of a larger-than-life payador), the German anthropologist Robert Lehmann-Nitsche noted that in the city of Buenos Aires alone, where immigrants and their children constituted the majority of the population, there were around fifty societies in existence. Members represented all areas of professional life, from government employees to hair dressers, illustrating the growing middle class also took an interest in what the clubs had to offer. In addition to the societies operating in 1916, close to 220 others had risen and fallen in the city during the first decade and a half of the century.[6] Having spent several decades in Argentina, Lehmann-Nitsche was an eyewitness to this phenomenon.

Names of these centers reflect the Creole spirit and the goal of framing a collective understanding of tradition. Some chose Creole drama titles as their namesake (Nobleza criolla; El Entenao) in hopes of capitalizing on the plays' success to guarantee their own attractiveness to potential members. Others aimed to highlight the general idea of tradition and its incarnation in honorable gauchos, such as La Tradición Argentina (1900), Tradición de Santos Vega (1901–1907), and Los Gauchos Nobles (1901–1906). Still others opted for the simple, rural aura: El Fogón (Campfire, 1899–1901); El Cimarrón (Bitter Mate, 1899–1902); and Amor a una tapera (Love for the Ranch, 1903) are good examples. The Parias de la Pampa (Pampa Pariahs, 1900–1902), Los Despreciados (The Downtrodden, 1900), and Los Matreros (The Outlaws, 1899–1904) clubs riffed off the notion of gauchos as the downtrodden rural residents who were persecuted and became outlaws out of desperation to protect themselves and their honor.[7] Outside the capital, provincial centers and smaller towns had their Creole societies as well, even if, as the musicologist and scholar of Argentine folklore Carlos Vega puts it, "We're only talking about a room to share mate and strum the guitar."[8]

In addition, there were carnival comparsas whose members took on gaucho dress as their costume every February. By 1910, when the centennial celebration of independence in the region gave tradition especially strong resonance, there were more than one hundred of these gaucho comparsas in Argentina.⁹ Their members rehearsed aspects of their performances throughout the year, thereby maintaining social bonds and connections to their acts. Several Creole societies likewise participated in carnival. According to one colorful description, these had their "floats converted into florid ranches, full of affectionate chinas and window sills decorated with jasmines and carnations. Along the parade route they exhibited their hearty lyricism and linked it to the sweetness of *zambas* and *vidalitas* [styles of Creole airs] that suggested images of the pampa and scents of wild flowers." The rising-star tango singer and later actor Carlos Gardel was a member of the Creole society Los Patriotas during 1907. He participated in its activities during carnival and throughout the rest of the year. Gardel was not alone. Numerous well-known actors and singers were members of traditionalist centers or, at least, collaborated with them during carnival for performances of song and show.¹⁰ For both gaucho comparsas and Creole societies that had carnival contingents, participants—and their audiences—took their competitions seriously, not willing to let inclement weather prevent them from performing.¹¹

In Brazil's southern-most state of Rio Grande do Sul, Creole societies formed at the turn of the century, too. The first of these appeared in 1898 in Porto Alegre, where João Cezimbra Jacques founded the Gremio Gaúcho. His goal with the club was "to maintain the character of our great state and consequently of our great traditions by means of regular commemorations of dates and facts that made the Southern Rio Grandian people famous."¹² Six other traditionalist groups formed between 1899 and 1901, and these would later become recognized as pioneers for the emergence of a traditionalist movement in Brazil. Several decades later the 1948 creation of the Center for Gaúcho Traditions in Porto Alegre led to an explosion in the number of Creole societies, making Brazil home to the largest number of these by the end of the twentieth century.¹³

At the outset of the twentieth century, then, the numbers of such associations were clearly on the rise in the Río de la Plata, and they were gaining a foothold in southern Brazil. But what went on at their meetings and who were their members? Here is what we know, given fragmentary documentation surviving from these early clubs.

Creole societies and traditionalist clubs large and small in the Río de la Plata as well as in Brazil held similar activities that had as their general theme the evocation of the "gaucho soul." These usually included an inaugural

ceremony that almost invariably started in the early morning hours, sometimes before 7 a.m. As we saw in the description of this event for the Sociedad
Criolla, there was a parade, most often down main streets and around central
squares, with significant public attention and fanfare, then came a hearty
meal for the new members. Food and drink offered opportunities to bond,
such as when members shared in the drawn-out process of roasting lamb or
entire steers skewered over fire pits, or when they sat for hours conversing
after the meal. Descriptions of these inaugural feasts, and of other moments
when food was a prominent activity on societies' schedules, reference regularly *carne con cuero* as a featured item, for this beef cooked with the hide
still attached hinted at the way it was done in the countryside, or at the way
members imagined heroic, nomadic gauchos doing it in the past. And there
was the omnipresent *amargo*, the colloquial term for bitter mate that members shared from the beginning to the end of their reunions.[14] There were
variants of ceremony, too, that involved gatherings on national holidays or
dates associated with regional feats or figures, often including speeches
tinged with patriotic overtones and stories exemplifying best practices of
gaucho life. Regules was always eager to give these grandiose presentations.

Apart from these characteristics of foundational moments in Creole societies' trajectories or gatherings oriented around national holidays, at most
meetings members and guests played games from the countryside, like taba
and sortija, ran horse races, played the lottery, occasionally staged Creole
dramas or scenes from these, and engaged in a series of "national diversions"
or practices meant to convey a sense of rootedness.[15] Dressing up was one of
these. Donning rural attire, either as a gaucho (or china, as women participants occasionally did), had its ritual quality that transported members out
of their daily routines for a couple hours at a time. Writers for *El Fogón*
picked up on this point when detailing the festivities for Paysandú's new
Creole society in 1900. After the standard program of activities held just outside town, at 5 p.m. everyone went back to Paysandú "full of joy and amid the
greatest happiness."[16] The authenticity of rural attire was taken to heart by
many society members who participated in contests recognizing the "most
Creole" outfits.[17] At times photographers from the local press were present at
society events to gather images for periodical publications, thus giving members opportunities to have their pictures taken (see figs. 5.5–5.8).[18] Some were
thrilled with the chance to record their Creole credentials. Members of the
Gremio Gaúcho in Porto Alegre carried props to invoke the gaucho spirit.[19]
The description of the festivities held for the Calixto El Ñato society included

members playing *fútbol*, which was ironically the very opposite of a rural pastime as it was an immigrant sport, though one that was rapidly undergoing a process of Creolization. Music and song, be it in the form of poetry recited or chanted, popular ditties, improvisational battles unleashed by payadores, or tunes sung by the entire group with guitar accompaniment, were also central elements of the gatherings. Dance was another core component, and it merits a bit more attention since, like the parades, it illustrates links between these clubs and the outside world.

Rural dance forms in the region were widely disseminated through the interaction of Creole societies with the broader public. The *pericón* is the best example. As noted in chapter 4, the pericón made its way from circus dramas to upscale dance parties in the early 1890s. In the following decade certain wealthy families who aligned with the traditionalist movement began hiring dance teachers to help family and friends learn the pericón's moves. Between 1905 and 1914 "charity organizations, aristocratic clubs, and, public schools

Figure 5.5. Some of the Sociedad Criolla's members pose for a photograph in September 1905. Note the range of ages. Regules is in the center of the front row with *mate* in hand. Sociedad Criolla Elías Regules.

Figure 5.6. A member of the Sociedad Criolla poses for a photograph
in his gaucho attire. Note the
painted background. Sociedad Criolla Elías Regules.

Figure 5.7. A member of the Sociedad
Criolla poses for a photograph in his
gaucho attire. Note the painted
background with a bridge leading
into a misty forest, reminiscent of
scenes from London. Sociedad Criolla Elías Regules.

Figure 5.8. A 1913 signed postcard image of the actor Luis Vittone, dedicated to Regules. In the note Vittone wrote he called himself a "falsified gaucho who danced the pericón for Spain's Princess Isabel." Sociedad Criolla Elías Regules.

each developed their own version of the pericón. During festivals, days of remembrance, or as part of the activities celebrating the end of the school year, school children offered their pericón to packed audiences of family members and neighbors, who always gave warm applause."[20] The inaugural events for the Blandengues de la Tradición society in San José, Uruguay, in April 1909 were supposed to be capped off with an evening at the town theater where local children were to dance the pericón. This show had to be canceled, though, due to the overwhelming number of people who clamored to enter, which one report estimated to be around two thousand, twice the venue's capacity.[21] That the dance did not take place is of minor importance when set against the high number of people who came out in recognition of the Creole society, and who were simply eager to see the pericón onstage.

All of these activities—games, food, dress, ceremony, music, dance— featured in the public establishment of centers and were critical to renewing meaning over the course of their existence.[22] These activities were festive ones, and they were collective. Many of these were also literally and figuratively dramatic. That is, being part of a Creole society gave members a chance to play a part and participate in a social drama. Recreational activities allowed participants to escape from daily routines and hardships; they surveyed aspects from a supposedly simpler life, linked to group identity where ideas about nationalism and cosmopolitanism were of chief importance; and their theatricality elicited a type of reflexivity that led members to ponder and perhaps better understand elements of their own lives and collective concerns.[23] Some society activities, like the pronouncements of preserving the heritage of "our great gaucho race," the lofty speeches, or determination to conjure notions of bravery, honor, virility, and authenticity through gaucho dress carried a definitive ideological charge, explored below. Yet this charge fused with the associative character of Creole societies and the leisure opportunities they provided. The clubs were at heart recreational spaces and social clubs, where members expanded social networks.

Sketching the profile of membership at these different societies is more difficult than outlining their activities, primarily because there are few records of who joined, and when, in contrast to the extensive documentation of membership in mutual aid societies during the same period. We do know, however, that these were male-dominant groups and aspects of masculinity coursed through their veins.[24] Kristen McCleary has shown how masculinity in Argentina at the end of the nineteenth century was closely related to rural patriarchy and its influence in family life and national politics.[25] This same notion underpinning the masculine ideal holds true for Uruguay. After all, caudillos had been dominant patriarchal figures in the region throughout the century, and their legacy remained a powerful presence in political life, social circles, and collective understanding of gender roles.

The gaucho heroes of Creole dramas shared much in common with caudillos: they were the perfect portrayals of "real" men who displayed virility, bravery, skill with weapons, and relentless defense of a sense of honor. They symbolized freedom and control of their environment (including livestock). Those who had families were very much patriarchs. Such characters as well as Creole society men also took pride in their ability to shine on the dance floor. Juan Moreira was a talented *malambo* dancer—a country dance consisting of fast leg movements, plenty of stomping, and foot sweeps. Showing off one's dance skills at a Creole society gathering was one way to build up a manly image. Other sources of masculine credibility included finessing language related to rural life, through both vocabulary and accent, and commanding or at least appearing to command knowledge of rural work and pastimes as well as national history.[26] Similar to the goal of showcasing authenticity through gaucho dress, or sitting around with a group of men eating large quantities of meat, there was something deeply virile about deploying specific lingo and knowledge. Writers for *El Fogón* summed up this idea: "The gaucho, my friends, has gotta be hardened to be gaucho." [27] That hardening, went the thought, reflected experience and appropriately Creole wisdom.

If we think more abstractly about Creole societies' engagement with masculinity, there is a link between male social bonds, identity, and nation that is visible in the sources, and that was present to some extent in the imaginations of society members. Vestiges of patriarchy informed how authority was constructed and perceived in the region's political culture. This political culture, in turn, overlapped with the concepts of group identity circulating at Creole society gatherings. Club activities allowed for exhibitions of masculinity (as well as patriarchy) and a mode of political identity rooted in the idealized trappings of rural life, but that was envisioned as national in scope. Members of these societies did not interpret their behavior in these terms. Nevertheless, playing gaucho, with all the masculine overtones, implied acceptance of at least elements of this political identity. [28]

While the clubs were mainly gathering spots for men, women and children participated in activities, too. References to women members and supporters of Creole societies point to them in a handful of roles. The most common among these was dancing. The ubiquitous pericón was a couples dance as were several other popular folk dances that took place at the clubs, so women were crucial to this cultural icon's vitality. Photographs often show women dancing or preparing to dance. At the second anniversary of the Sociedad Criolla in Montevideo. Regules commented that there was "a large group of ladies who, like on other occasions, animated the party." [29] The night after the establishment of a new Creole society in Tacuarembó in 1900 sixty couples from among the members participated in a dance at city hall, including some of the most "select" families. [30] That same year in the Uruguayan town of Fraile Muerto a group of "patriotic" Uruguayan women sewed a flag for the local Creole club "as a gesture of thanks for the important contributions the club makes to sociability." [31] At these societies women also had the chance to dress up for a moment of leisure, though not necessarily in any particular costume, have their photograph taken, and at times feature in the local press. [32] Similar comments appear repeatedly throughout the early twentieth century. While those accounts suggest women took part regularly in the recreation, their roles were not defined clearly aside from dancing and enjoying the food with others. Children occasionally had lead roles in club activities, such as reciting verse, singing, or dancing. Yet for the most part they were present because their parents brought them along for the day.[33]

This outline of club membership helps to explain the contours of recreation and the potential deeper meanings of activities within these societies. Playing gaucho certainly offered its share of fun. Yet beyond or because of the diversion, society members were able to belong to communities and to access social opportunities that did not exist in the same manner outside the clubs. These were all compelling motivations for people to join Creole societies in the first place, and they encouraged continued involvement. The main reason to become a member of a Creole society, though, and what was behind the proliferation of these groups in the late 1800s and early 1900s had to do with tradition. The concept of tradition underlying all things Creole was inseparable from a particular understanding of ethnicity, the glories of staging the frontier, and the gathering momentum of a burgeoning regional popular culture.

Patriotic Traditionalism

In his 1910 history of national theater in regional perspective, Vicente Rossi was convinced about the success of the Creole drama phenomenon in communicating not only the intersection between patriotism and tradition but also the meaning of this combination. "When watching that perfect evocation of the gaucho," he wrote, "if anyone born on Uruguayan or Argentine soil does not feel his heart beat with pride for the gaucho race and ancestry, then be wary of that person's patriotism and nationality."[34] Feeling such pride was not a matter to be taken lightly.

Creole dramas had effectively coupled ideas about tradition with powerful references to race and the nation. As performers took their gaucho characters from one stage to the next, it was hard *not* to associate such figures with a glorification of rural life and ancestry, melodramatic struggles of good versus evil, and broader historical processes related to nation formation. That is, these shows both helped consolidate the heroic image of the gaucho and contributed to the invention of national traditions that converted the gaucho into "the basic icon of Argentine [and Uruguayan] nationality" by the early 1900s.[35] Creole societies took the relationship between tradition, race, and nation much farther, in part because of their mass appeal outside the theater, and in part because of their role in the definition of the traditionalist movement.

Behind club activities, the dramatic interaction of members with the broader public at events such as dances outside a society's gathering area, parades that involved onlookers who had not (yet) joined, and the practice of dressing like rural residents for fellow citizens to admire in public spaces, was the cultivation of a sensibility and "particular sociability" oriented around a traditionalist idea of the past. Societies were central to broadcasting a new vision of Argentine and Uruguayan history in which the ideal gaucho was a protagonist inseparable from the processes of nation formation.[36] There were other groups that contributed to the process of expanding the reach of traditionalism. These included intellectuals and academics, politicians and public figures, and those who were not members of Creole societies but who subscribed to this conception of the gaucho. Yet because of their growing numbers, wide geographic distribution, and the simple fun of activities that interfaced with the more dry messages involving national history, Creole societies enjoyed a unique position when it came to boosting the intersections among patriotism, history, and tradition.

Elías Regules was an early advocate of Creole clubs taking a lead in the dissemination of such ideas. The speech he gave at the Sociedad Criolla's inauguration in May 1894 is an excellent example. For the occasion he covered Uruguayan history in broad strokes, though he was always careful to place the gaucho at the center of the story. After Europeans settled the Americas, he told the members gathered in the Podestá-Scotti tent, the years passed and a new type of "local" inhabitant emerged in the Río de la Plata. This local type wore "the rustic clothing of our gaucho. We have seen his masculinity and resourcefulness in his triumphs over nature's obstacles." With this line we can imagine his audience nodding in approval. "This is the gaucho who, with headband and sleeves rolled up, brandished his knife in the countryside to liberate our patria. That gaucho, that native son who lacks education, is emblematic of the Uruguayan race."[37] Now, with the crowd riled up, Regules goes on to claim that those who are unashamed of their native Uruguay and who do not seek legitimation through foreign ideas or behaviors, can, with head held high, "embrace that model of our race." He ended the address by proclaiming the goal of the Sociedad to "sustain our virile national customs" and pledging allegiance to the "colors of the patria" visible in the flag José Artigas had memorialized during the independence wars.[38]

Here was a deliberate attempt to paint the Sociedad Criolla's activities in direct relation to the actions of past figures, like Artigas, whose image at the end of the century as Uruguay's founding father was just beginning to overtake his previous legacy as revolutionary thorn.[39] Thus, when Alcides de María, who cofounded and served as editor in chief of the illustrated weekly *El Fogón*, gave the inaugural address to the 130 or so members of the Los Criollos society in San José, Uruguay, he ended it with a full-throated shout-out to the memory of Artigas that such clubs help preserve as the "defender of our land."[40]

In Regules's speech, which was published later as a manifesto of the traditionalist movement in the Montevideo paper *La Tribuna Popular*, we see a first well-choreographed move of *patriotic traditionalism*. With the publication and performance of his play *Los Guachitos*, his nativist poem "Mi tapera" (My Humble Ranch), and the creation of his Creole society, in 1894 Regules cemented his position as the leader of the traditionalist movement in Uruguay. As Angel Rama argues, "If he was not the inventor of the gaucho, he was behind the invention of 'tradition.'" Rama notes that others like Orosmán Moratorio, the de María family, and Abdón Arózteguy worked toward the same ends. "But none achieved the efficacy of Regules, which transformed him perhaps not into the poet or dramaturg he had imagined, but at least into the *jefe* of the movement."[41]

The following May Regules gave a speech for the first anniversary of the Sociedad, assessing the impact of the initiative and calling attention again to what was at stake. He summoned the joyful memories of the club's foundation, and the events that had stimulated the "national fiber" of those participating in the Sociedad's first parade. Yet weighing on Regules in 1895 was the perception that Uruguayans were living in a moment of "national indifference," which made even more necessary the plea for cultivating national traditions. That time of apathy also gave the anniversary celebration, as well as the traditionalist movement, heightened symbolic urgency.[42] In fact, one of the chief justifications for the creation of Creole societies and the promotion of tradition year after year was the claim that patriotism, at least as insofar as it was understood to originate in the countryside, was on the decline. Close to fifteen years after Regules's lament, a writer for *El Fogón* told the members of San José's Blandengues de la Tradición society that they were the "last criollos." Just as the national spirit was disintegrating around them and institutions were losing strength, the Creole society was there to help shore things up. This was a lofty goal for a recreational organization, but one that gave members an added sense of purpose to their gatherings as well as one that infused added value into the idea of tradition. The speech closed with a mention of how the landscape facilitated a glorious moment of recreation, as well as the call for "the soul of our great heroes to urge us toward the union and harmony of all criollos."[43] It was clear that the celebration of tradition was as much about political identity and sense of patriotic duty as it was about leisure.

In effect, the traditionalist movement was at its core a political one that aimed to generate political mobilization, despite Regules maintaining that the movement was apolitical. The historic gaucho of independence that Regules and other traditionalists referenced was the people's political advocate, and the early gauchesque had been an example in the literature of political outreach. The criollista phenomenon of the late 1800s no longer operated as political outreach, but it was linked to ideological threads of nativism and nationalism as well as positions regarding immigration, fears surrounding the rise in the number of labor unions, changes to types of labor, and collective identity. It was no coincidence, then, that the proliferation of Creole societies paralleled the growing number of immigrant communities and the real and imagined social changes for which locals perceived immigrants to be responsible.

Recall that immigrants, primarily from Italy and Spain, made up the majority of the population in the city of Buenos Aires and 30 percent of the residents in Buenos Aires province. Slightly lower numbers were seen in surrounding areas: immigrants accounted for 22 percent of Santa Fe province's demographic makeup, and close to 40 percent of Entre Ríos province's and Montevideo's population at the turn of the century.[44] Though Regules and his followers pushed the positive patriotic message, his brand of traditionalism, in the analysis of the musicologist and folklore scholar Lauro Ayestarán, "was born of an anti-immigrant position" and a stern critique of the increasingly cosmopolitan character of the capital.[45] And yet, immigrants constituted key membership blocks of Creole societies, precisely in the global ports of Buenos Aires and Montevideo.

It was this anticosmopolitan and anti-immigrant position that led to the perception of Regules being opposed to "progress" and that, in turn, attracted critics. One of these was the journalist Carlos Blixen, with whom Regules maintained a running debate in the press. Blixen accused Sociedad Criolla members of "preserving in the city, and thanks to the benefits progress has brought," all of the Creole elements they pretended to make part of tradition. He argued that since the "gaucho no longer exists," to revive him through dress, song, dance, and other activities of the sort seen at the Sociedad Criolla was to go against the very nature of progress.[46] And in reference to the first parade the Society organized through Montevideo, Blixen wrote that "some 200 artificial gauchos rode their poor horses into the city center . . . Oh the youth of today! Such extravagance!"[47]

Of course Regules was not opposed entirely to material progress; he was a medical doctor and aware of the benefits modern science and modern trade facilitated. What he did not want was for local (rural) practices to be washed away by the flood of imported goods, ideas, and ways of life. He summed up this position in an essay titled "Us and Them," where he attempted to explain that progress was not a single defined idea, and that proud Uruguayans should honor national practices (that came from the countryside) rather than hoist a flag from across the Atlantic.[48] The sentiment again revealed the conflation of rural life with national tradition and patriotism. He emphasized this patriotic posture in response to his critics, telling them to focus on more serious concerns and respect the "convictions" of the Sociedad Criolla, whose members respect their compatriots.[49] Underlying this dig was Regules's understanding of how Creole society members represented values of citizenship, including respectful interactions with compatriots and defense of patriotic conviction.

Other society leaders echoed this train of thought. One especially rich area where tradition's embrace of patriotism expanded was print media. We know of the explosion in criollista pamphlets, narrative, and verse in the 1880s and 1890s and the connections between these veins of popular print and the gauchesque tradition that was consumed with increasing intensity throughout the century. Beginning in the mid-1890s a new print phenomenon hit the streets: illustrated magazines that took tradition as their mantra and the gaucho as their spokesperson. The first of these magazines to appear was the weekly *El Fogón*, from Montevideo. It was also one of the longest lived, published from 1895 to 1914. Dozens of others quickly followed. These were produced in small towns like Minas and Rocha (Uruguay) or Arrecifes and Lomas de Zamora in the province of Buenos Aires, and larger cities such as Rosario, La Plata, and Buenos Aires. Like Creole societies, the magazines adopted characteristically traditional titles. To name just a few, there was *El Ombú* (Montevideo), which took the name of a large shrub that became a standard feature in landscape paintings from the region in these years, often associated with the lilt of country life; *El Criollo* (Minas); *La Pampa Argentina: revista criolla de costumbres nacionales* (The Argentine Pampa: A Creole Magazine of National Customs, Buenos Aires); *Raza Pampa: revista literaria de actualidades y costumbres nacionales* (The Pampa Race: National News and Customs, Buenos Aires); and *Hormiga Negra: semanario político de costumbres nacionales* (Hormiga Negra: A Weekly Review of Politics and National Customs, San Antonio de Areco), which adopted the title of another of Eduardo Gutiérrez's best-selling narratives.[50]

Most important for this chapter's focus is that these magazines went hand in hand with the emergence of Creole societies. Many shared news of society meetings and activities as well as helped recruit new members. This was the case, for example, with the relationship between the Sociedad Criolla and *El Fogón* in Montevideo (several similar magazines in Argentina had the same title), which had an average print run of around fifteen thousand copies per week. Such publicity for the Criolla—though not exclusive—was to be expected since the club's first vice president Orosmán Moratorio cofounded the magazine with Alcides de María, after which like-minded traditionalists served as editors. *El Fogón* was an outlet for Regules's criollista poetry, too, which had sold poorly in book form despite going through seven editions.[51] As with the resurgence of folk dances in upscale venues, the spread of these

Figure 5.9. The appropriately Creole masthead of *El Fogón*, from January 15, 1899. The lead article treated "Rioplatense Customs," focusing on *mate.* MHN Giró.

Figure 5.10. Cover illustration for *El Fogón*, January 7, 1901. Literate gauchos, blending modern education with traditional figures, featured constantly on the covers. Women readers formed an important part of the magazine's audience, too. MHN Giró.

magazines points to an additional dimension of the vogue of traditionalism around the turn of the century.[52]

The gaucho as regional icon and historical actor was thus one of the chief vectors of the traditionalist movement. Another one grew from understandings of race and ethnicity, specifically the "gaucho race" (*raza gaucha*).[53] While sources deploy this term explicitly, it is more accurate to speak in terms of Creole ethnicity. References to this idea permeate this chapter because it was one of the components underpinning the traditionalist movement and the invention of national traditions. Creole ethnicity allowed for figures like *Martín Fierro* and *Juan Moreira* specifically, or the nostalgic image of the gaucho more generally, to embody the ideal of the Argentine (and Uruguayan) race, and for their stories to provide narratives that could be mapped onto national history. This Creole ethnicity was exclusive, like all attempts to define ethnic groups, although not rigidly so. Regules's Sociedad Criolla, for example, proclaimed that "around the warm gaucho campfire of the Criolla, all Uruguayans are welcome, as are all people who, coming from other lands, identify spiritually with us." [54]

Under the umbrella of Creole ethnicity, then, one could find the mixed-race gaucho who had come to represent cultural purity, virility, and the ability to control his environment by the end of the 1800s; a nativist spirit and the accompanying privileges associated with birthplace; a cultural outlook that favored the local over any association with the foreign; a banner for opposition to immigration and immigrants; a certain desire to expand the numbers of native citizens who identified with the Creole; and room for immigrants and foreigners who chose to become good Creoles. If this sounds contradictory or even confusing, it is because it is.

Such ambiguity was built into the multivalent nature of Creole discourse. The diverse functions of the Creole among different social sectors lent to the malleability of Creole ethnicity as well as the variety of its operations. Adolfo Prieto distinguished three of these. For rural inhabitants forced to migrate to urban spaces, the Creole had a nostalgic allure in the face of all things strange in the city. This was one of the reasons Creole dramas and criollista literature enjoyed such favorable reception among this group. It was also why one of the great appeals of Creole societies for newcomers to cities was their offering of a simpler life for a couple hours at a time.

Immigrants, as we saw in the last chapter, saw the adoption of Creole ethnicity as a way to assimilate. Immigrant families joined Creole societies and participated in the activities as good gauchos, especially when only light horseback riding was required, and they were members of the gaucho carnival comparsas. We can recall from last chapter the prominent intellectual Ernesto Quesada's complaints of immigrant imaginations being inflamed by the story of Moreira and dressing as paisanos during carnival, or the *Caras y Caretas* story of a porteño who prepared his gaucho costume to show up the *gringos* (that is, the immigrants) during carnival. [55] Descendants of immigrants were among the founding members of Regules's Sociedad Criolla. A certain L. Giudi—an Italian surname—served as the first president of Argentina's Sociedad Criolla in 1899. [56] And in 1901 *El Fogón* ran a biographical sketch of the "Gaucho Ledesma," the pseudonym for a contributor to the magazine. He was the son of an Italian father and a "Creole" mother. According to the profile that combination "resulted in the perfection of his ability to express what he feels, at the same time it has refined the cultivation of his passions for all things native." [57] Ledesma was always inclined to dress as a gaucho to demonstrate his awe for country—read Creole—life. Perhaps the sketch had the intention of modeling assimilation? Similar examples of immigrants and their children finding a sense of community in Creole clubs and habits abound.

With the growth of labor unions and the spread of anarchist and socialist philosophies often associated with immigrant workers at the turn of the century, playing gaucho also provided cover for immigrants who sought to escape the tensions swirling around the changing labor landscape. Part of the ideological backlash against immigrants at the end of the 1800s stemmed from the idea that they had brought class conflict to a nation that offered equal opportunity, in itself a romantic idea, but one that facilitated the conversion of immigrant workers into political targets.[58] There was a fear of newcomers joining anarchist movements, a position that was much more about ideology than race or ethnic discrimination, though often manifested via the latter.[59] One of the most severe manifestations of this fear was the so-called 1902 residence law in Argentina, granting the federal government the unfettered ability to detain or deport immigrants.

Finally, for the upper echelons that included landholders, factory owners, and merchant elites, Creole discourse allowed for an expression of self-preservation. As internal migrants latched on to the Creole in the face of the new and the foreign in the city, elites saw an opportunity to harness their support of the Creole spirit to the need to preserve their social (and, in theory, economic) position.[60]

To these three functions Ezequiel Adamovsky has added one more: Creole discourse "made visible the ethnic heterogeneity of the nation, specifically those groups recognized as non-white." This may seem contradictory in late nineteenth-century Argentina and Uruguay, where places like England, France, and Germany were often idealized as sources for everything from philosophy and public education to models of citizenship and racial makeup. After all, it was the idea that European civilization was supposed to tame American barbarism that led in part to the state-backed initiatives to bring immigrants to the region. Out of this process, went the thinking, would emerge a whiter (more civilized and culturally European) citizenry. At the same time, *lo criollo* was gathering strength. Drawing on local, non-European sources, experiences, and groups, invocations of a Creole spirit and ethnicity functioned as "a powerful integrating force that collaborated in bridging actual ethnic differences."[61] The demographics of the region were still in flux and revealed inhabitants of numerous nationalities and ethnic backgrounds. Yet it was through ideas of racial and cultural mixture and their uniquely local outcome in the "gaucho race" that allowed for the Creole to acquire, in Adamovsky's reading, this unifying character and ability to reconcile difference. This deployment of Creole ethnicity went hand in hand with the displacement of civic national identity by ethnic nationalism, which reached its apex around the 1910 centenary celebration of independence.[62]

These four functions help explain why consuming the Creole and claiming Creole ethnicity carried such enormous political weight. This was especially clear as labor movements gained strength during the first half of the twentieth century. Workers aligned their plight for better conditions with the struggles of real and fictional downtrodden gauchos.[63] To cite just one example of this alignment, the mass mobilization that resulted in the birth of Peronism—Argentina's most enduring political movement—in October 1945 included participants who dressed as gauchos and chinas, rode on horseback, and recited gauchesque poetry. This was a scene fit for any Creole society but was staged in support of a leader who spoke of a "Creole political movement" that had gaucho roots. This leader, Juan Perón, had come face to face with Juan Moreira's skull as a child, which his grandfather received and studied as a medical marvel.[64]

Tradition, ethnicity, and theatricality were closely connected. More than any other organizations in the years stretching from the 1890s through the 1910s Creole societies played the key role in disseminating this triumvirate. Ruben Oliven exemplifies this connection with the title of his anthropology of the Gaúcho traditionalist movement in Brazil, *Tradition Matters: Modern Gaúcho Identity in Brazil*. In the Brazilian south it mattered because regional tradition offered privileged access to the national.[65] In Argentina and Uruguay patriotic traditionalism delivered a sense of stability that overlapped with national concerns during a period of rapid economic modernization.

This connection to national identity and symbolism gave patriotic traditionalism purchase on the collective imagination. Creole societies provided members and spectators opportunities to live tradition, if only for brief periods each week. But the significance of that time, of staging and crossing class, ethnic, cultural, and geographic frontiers, and of re-creating a lifestyle and activities far from where they existed, left a lasting impression that was foundational for the sense of community. When we look at these communities in the broader context of civil associations, it becomes clear how they facilitated political participation in the public arena as well as how they fomented the spread of popular culture.

Creole Societies, Political Participation, and Popular Culture

Creole societies formed during the explosion of civil voluntary associations, mainly mutual aid societies, around 1900. Described at the time by the British traveler John Hammerton as "almost innumerable," these associations were dedicated to supporting and protecting their members, as well as promoting their group's identity and interests.[66] Domingo Bórea, who compiled the section on associations and aid societies for the 1914 Argentine census, emphasized that the high number of these was a sign of the people's civility, "moral evolution," and modernity. He went on to comment that the surge in the number of such clubs even pointed to Argentina as a "great and modern" nation.[67] The same points were part of the welcome speech the former Minister of the Economy gave to Theodore Roosevelt when he visited Argentina in November 1913.[68]

The development of mutual aid societies resulted largely from the arrival of immigrant groups. The first associations to form during the 1850s, 1860s, and 1870s were Italian, Spanish, and French mutual aid societies, where membership helped cover medical costs and provided financial protection from illness and work-related accidents. In one of his studies of Italian immigrant communities in Argentina, Samuel Baily argues that ethnic-based mutual aid societies were the most important institutions for immigrants, though they opened their doors to Argentines and Uruguayans, too.[69] In addition to providing health-care benefits, these associations offered vibrant social spaces as well as a sense of "home" where elements of life left behind in Europe could be experienced or re-created in some degree. As the number of these various associations grew and their memberships rose throughout the 1890s and the first decade of the twentieth century, they played an increasingly important role in the development of the region's political culture.[70]

To grasp the scale of participation in these new associations, let's observe their development in Argentina. During the half century from the 1850s through the 1910s, the number of voluntary or membership-based civil associations rose most sharply in the years between 1900 and 1913. In this period some 560 new clubs were established, more than double the number that appeared in the decade of 1890. By 1913 there more than 1,200 societies serving upward of half a million members, most of whom were classified in the census as workers (day laborers, stevedores, street salesmen, artisans, masons, railway employees, and so on). The majority of these societies were located in the city and province of Buenos Aires and catered to Italian and Spanish immigrants. Around a quarter of the capital's population age fifteen and older belonged to a membership-based club or association, not counting those who were Creole society members. Men outnumbered women on average by a factor of ten.[71]

All of these clubs facilitated forms of political participation that engaged with the evolving public sphere, for they were portals for members to stake out places within local social landscapes.[72] These societies marked positions of public opinion in increasingly visible and important ways, which was significant given that public opinion was surfacing as a new source of political legitimacy in the 1800s. As Hilda Sábato has observed, these associations "promoted and organized most of the civic meetings and demonstrations that were frequently staged in the main cities." Moreover, "different groups and sectors of the population voiced their opinion and represented their claims through their organizations and newspapers, and also more directly, by displaying a physical presence in the civic spaces of the cities."[73] Carnival was one such prominent space, which helps to understand the widespread participation of associations in carnival play.

The presence of Creole societies at carnival and in other civic spaces not only gave backing to their symbolic political value, it also allowed them to make material contributions to and be a highly visible manifestation of popular culture, which had become synonymous with the Creole spirit by the end of the 1800s. How so? We know that Creole societies numbered in the hundreds and enjoyed a public existence at a moment in the region's history when there was greater involvement in politics than ever before.[74] We also have seen instances of club members displaying their Creole pride (patriotic traditionalism) to the wider public. Remember the theatrics of the Sociedad Criolla, as its members paraded through city streets adding new adherents along the way? Or the carnival comparsas that converted playing gaucho into the stuff of serious annual competitions? It was precisely that sort of interfacing with civil society that made the spread of popular culture seem almost effortless—members were just having fun—and, as a result, so effective. The public character of Creole societies likewise intersected with the lucrative commercial potential of marketing all things Creole, heightening their ability to be integral to the burgeoning industry of cultural goods.

A perfect example of Creole societies meeting the industries producing cultural goods comes from strains of folk music. At Creole society activities, like at Creole dramas, it was commonplace for one to hear arrangements, variations, or adaptations of rural melodies. Some were printed and later lost, while others existed only so long as the voices sang and instruments played. At the same time, Carlos Vega noted that these song forms, which were central to society gatherings, "inspired more formal composers and musicians who enjoyed a much higher position in the cultural hierarchy" to publish, with great commercial success, their interpretations of *gatos, vidalitas, estilos, milongas, zamacuecas,* and other Creole airs.[75] The effect was ultimately the circulation and distribution of musical traditions linked to the Creole spirit beyond the entertainment spaces and clubs where the tunes were performed and the aura invoked. A case in point was the Uruguayan composer Gerardo Grasso's arrangement of the pericón deemed to be the model "national pericón." The sheet-music arrangement appeared in at least eight editions that sold out across the region, each with its ornately designed cover page evoking the spirit of the music.

This relation between cultural products that were becoming a market of their own and Creole societies accentuates how these institutions managed to bridge modernity and tradition. The societies facilitated public contact with the circulation of Creole cultural goods, even though this was not an explicit goal of these groups nor were members necessarily aware of their role in this process. Moreover, the majority of early Creole societies were located in urban environments, or on the outskirts of cities and smaller towns, making for what Ruben Oliven calls a curious "urban movement . . . to recoup rural values."[76]

In this sense, at the center of Creole societies' mission and their relationship to the wider public was communicating via representation the value of tradition and its making (or preservation in the eyes of traditionalists). It was in those representations, in the staging of frontiers and the re-creation of a lifestyle and activities far from where they existed geographically and, often, temporally that Creole societies gained enduring meaning. These practices allowed members to experience the vitality of tradition and its performance, and to participate in the creation of a sense of historical depth for those traditions that would lend them authority and authenticity.[77] Thus, playing gaucho was powerful and transformative at the same time it was fun.[78]

Some readers may find the absence of any reference to indigenous groups or figures in society activities to be puzzling or quite alarming. With all the fanfare about mythical cowboys, where were the Indians? Their absence should be understood in line with both popular and official conceptions of the region's indigenous past. In Uruguay the indigenous presence had been

Figure 5.11. Cover of the eighth edition of Gerardo Grasso's *Pericón*. Centro de Documentación Musical Lauro Ayestarán.

dramatically eliminated by the 1830s and rarely figured in official history or collective memory through the rest of the century. In Argentina the history of state treatment of indigenous populations was also fraught, most especially during the military campaign to push these groups southward and settle the overtaken land in the 1870s and 1880s. In both instances, indigenous vestiges were removed from the popular imagination, considered elements to be tamed through modern life—that is, filtered through the lens of "scientific racism" prevailing in the Americas at the time—or absorbed into tales of gaucho heroism. So the lack of an indigenous link to club names, activities, or symbolism is representative of the broader collective mindset of the moment.

Oriented initially around patriotic traditionalism Creole societies are literally and figuratively a spectacular example of the proliferation of the Creole beyond the Creole drama. By playing gaucho, members from different social sectors and ethnic groups helped promote a range of meanings rooted in myths of rural honor, participated in the development of a sense of tradition and narratives about national myths of origin, and represented notions of ethnicity and race central to social identities. At the same time, the activities of these clubs, for members only or especially when on display for fellow residents during parades or at carnival, lent to community building and facilitated political participation in an evolving political arena where civil associations had central roles.

There was of course plenty of fun to be had at society gatherings, not to mention the food, drink, and dancing. At the same time, and regardless of the extent to which members were aware, Creole societies were also integral to the promotion of the region's popular culture to reaches that had not been imagined previously. We will see this process firsthand with *Juan Moreira* on tour in the next chapter, and the growing backlash against the Creole drama phenomenon.

PART 3

Consolidating the Popular Culture Marketplace (1890s–2010s)

CHAPTER 6

Debating Cultural Representation

✦ IN 1902 THE ARGENTINE INTELLECTUAL ERNESTO QUESADA HAD plenty of reasons to be upset. In that year he published his long-winded essay about *criollismo*, a term encompassing the multiplying manifestations of the Creole, where he sounded the alarm about many of these. All were tied to the pervasive influence of stories about gaucho heroes and what he saw as their corrosive effect on public morality and negative impact on national, even regional, identity. "Year after year," lamented Quesada, "Eduardo Gutiérrez's works appear in new editions. These swirl around, inflaming imaginations that are predisposed to remember the feats and customs of the characters Gutiérrez gifted with the brilliance of legendary heroes." He goes on to observe that "even today, at the dawn of a new century, those whose only connection to the countryside is by imitating modes of dress, often don spurs, a coin-studded wide leather belt, and a *facón*. They speak of the police persecuting honorable *paisanos* and of justices of the peace stealing away sweethearts from their true loves."[1] This widespread infatuation with nonsense could not be good.

The prevalence of Gutiérrez's narratives, published in the region's press and later appearing as inexpensive books, was one source of Quesada's and like-minded contemporaries' frustrations. There were others. By 1900 Creole drama heroes and the troupes that brought those characters to life had raised serious questions. The fact was that when performers staged frontiers at the premier opera theaters of Buenos Aires, Montevideo, or at the upscale venues in dozens of smaller cities in the region, or when audience makeup at the shows began including politicians, doctors, and high-society women, Quesada and fellow opponents bristled. Was there not a cultural hierarchy that, however implicitly, demanded respect? Who was responsible for policing that hierarchy, and what happened when it was violated? Who had the authority to represent national culture?

Such questions also played out in the growth of the Creole literary industry that seemed to produce an endless stream of poems, pamphlets, and novels that reprised, re-created, and imitated some of the greatest hits. We can only imagine how Quesada might assess the use of Creole drama stars as the names of new cigarette brands, though we do know that he was distraught by the conversion of Juan Moreira's story into an opera in 1897. By 1900 *Juan Moreira* and other Creole dramas had crossed the Atlantic and landed in Spain for the beginning of a European tour that, in theory, included shows at the Paris Universal Exposition. European crowds were wowed with "ethnographic spectacles" of Argentine (and Uruguayan) customs. While such plays and their performers as cultural ambassadors thrilled supporters of the Creole, others, like Quesada, were frightened by the implications. And yet, by the start of the new century, Creole dramas had passed the apex of their popularity. The beginning of the end of their ubiquitous presence was well underway, a fact that was not lost on the phenomenon's detractors.

The interests and tensions surrounding the movement of these Creole infused stories across media, venues, and geographic space are the focus of this chapter. My aim is to reveal quite literally popular culture on the move and to throw into relief debates of increasing intensity about cultural representation. *Juan Moreira* was again at the center of things. Both Gutiérrez's narrative and the theatrical adaptation that had sparked the Creole drama vogue continued attracting readers, inspiring similar tales, and filling performance spaces. The *Juan Moreira* legend was a tour de force. The Creole societies we learned about in the last chapter were indebted to it. Everyday language was another area in which *Juan Moreira* and similar stories were exercising a powerful—and as we know now—lasting influence.

This influence brought backlash. During this same period stretching roughly from the mid-1890s through the first decade of the twentieth century, a group of opponents spoke out and wrote against the various displays of that influence, who and what could shape authoritative expressions of regional culture, and outlined ideas for what "national" theater should look like. These opponents clashed with voices of support in a heated debate that paralleled and at times contributed to the end of the Creole drama phenomenon around the turn of the century. Ultimately, the debate sheds light on the growing significance and reception of popular culture in the region as well as the role of criollismo in fashioning collective values.

The disintegration of the Creole drama cultural phenomenon turns on much more than a simple chronological tipping point. After all, a lot was at stake in this period fraught with tension. There were concerns about revered modes of cultural expression that were being "invaded" by less desirable elements; the role of cultural representation at home and abroad; and what happened when representatives did not align with certain expectations. Similarly, there were fears of national language being contaminated by "improper" forms of speech. At the same time, performers, impresarios, and cultural consumers began to turn their attention away from representations of Creoleness. The last gasp of Creole dramas and the debate surrounding their extended ramifications signaled that the phenomenon no longer attracted the support across social sectors of previous years.

More than just an example of a fad that had run its course, though, this was a point of cultural inflection. The beginning of the end of the Creole drama phenomenon, with the clash between those who made it what it was and those who sought its demise, entailed a broader conversation about modern popular culture and strands of cultural distinction. What were these, what bearing did they have on public life, and how did they relate to conceptions of transnational identity? Those were all serious questions that came to a head during the downfall of Creole dramas. To see how this pivotal moment unfolded, we begin with popular culture on the move.

Popular Culture on the Move

Eduardo Gutiérrez never imagined the extent of *Juan Moreira*'s impact, despite the lucrative returns he garnered from the daily installments of the story he produced for the Argentine newspaper *La Patria Argentina*. Nor did he live to see the legacy of his hero take flight, the story condensed on collector's cards, or the conversion of Moreira into both a cultural icon and lightening rod toward the end of the century. The movement of Moreira's story from the space of serialized narrative to the opera stage illustrated an underlying principle of the Creole drama phenomenon: that heroes of many a gaucho tale that circulated first in print went on to fight another day. They did so first in the dramas that became all the rage with traveling circuses, in the advertising that the circuses put out, and often in the names and activities of clubs that formed around the turn of the century. But those leaps were just the beginning of what we can call popular culture on the move.

This concept underscores both the rapid growth of popular culture as well as the geographical movement of cultural products and practices, like the dramas or the spread of Creole literature. Popular culture on the move depended on the forceful continuity of stories and their heroes over time, the dissemination of these across media types, and large-scale reception. Recall examples of this process previous chapters discussed. There were the cigarette makers that capitalized on the commercial success and appeal of Creole icons, issuing hero-branded lines beginning in the 1890s. Music and dance that enlivened scenes in narrative or poetry, or that added joy and energy to dramatic shows, likewise found new outlets, followers, and practitioners, including payadores. These wandering musicians offered tunes in cafés and on street corners, and some became stars in their own right thanks to their participation in Creole dramas. The trajectory of the pericón was similar: this folk dance made its way onto stages of circus shows and theaters and then was taken up in elegant salons. Meanwhile, composers competed for the claim—and handsome profits—of having authored the authoritative score for the "pericón nacional."

Among the many more illustrations of popular culture on the move, here I want to emphasize opera, *Juan Moreira*'s European tour, and language "contamination." These three pivotal examples showcase cultural flows, interchanges between elite and popular culture, and point to the looming backlash against the Creole drama phenomenon and its impacts.

To begin, the world of opera was probably the last place contemporaries would have expected to see gaucho heroes onstage. After all, European composers and performers dominated the regional opera scene throughout the century. This dominance was felt even more strongly in the second half of the 1800s. Advances in maritime transportation and new opera houses like the Teatro Colón in Buenos Aires and the Teatro Solís in Montevideo led to increased traffic of opera companies, including star singers, who enjoyed extended stays in the region. Because of their European provenance these companies held a certain allure for local audiences. Moreover, given the cultural authority locals vested in opera during the last third of the century, performances became prime places to see and be seen, especially for social climbers.

There had been near misses between Creole drama troupes and opera-goers in previous years. The Podestá-Scotti Company had played at the Teatro Solís, and the Teatro de la Opera in Buenos Aires as well as several theaters in smaller towns—often the only theaters in those locations—had welcomed Creole dramas. Yet there was comfort in the fact that such shows were *not* operas. This distance shrank in late 1891 when an Italian orchestra director staged an opera titled *Juan Moreira* at the Doria Theater in Buenos Aires, though few took notice. A specialized art magazine included some commentary in Italian on the performance, but the city's major papers made no mention of it.[2] So for all intents and purposes, *Juan Moreira* had still yet to make its big splash in the world of opera.

The renowned Argentine composer Arturo Berutti's *Pampa*, from 1897, changed that. Berutti's family had been close to the towering statesman Domingo Sarmiento, and he had already established a reputation in opera circles in Italy as well as in Argentina. Yet when he announced the upcoming performance of *Pampa* there was pushback. Some of the resistance was because the new opera was based on *Moreira*. Of course, the etiquette of the opera scene automatically led some to question the value of *Pampa*. Berutti's explanation of why he chose his subject matter stressed the need to recognize the moral lessons of the countryside, channeled through the "national type" formed there (i.e., the gaucho). For Berutti that focus lent novelty and authenticity, "so much so that in recent years we can observe that the most popular and accepted productions are those that have taken up this rural character in its diverse manifestations."[3]

Comments like these did not exactly inspire confidence in his creation. The tenor who was cast as Moreira—Miguel Mariacher—threatened to back out given the chilly reception the work was receiving in the court of public opinion prior to its debut. Fortunately for the production, Berutti was able to convince the singer to stay on. In addition to reading Gutiérrez in order to better understand the character, Mariacher followed Berutti's advice and attended the Anselmi circus's renditions of *Moreira* to hone his act. Mariacher's study paid off with his acclaimed performance in *Pampa*, which opened on July, 27 1897, and played four times in Buenos Aires before moving to Montevideo.[4]

The opera as a whole, though, was less enthusiastically received. Berutti was praised for composing the first "Argentine opera." A writer for *La Nación* celebrated that "there can be no doubt Berutti has dared to carve a new path-way to experience Argentine sentiment and thought."[5] But it was precisely the conflation of such sentiment and thought with Moreira that riled our critic, Ernesto Quesada. Folletines like those of Gutiérrez, he noted, and the "never-ending list of *Moreira* imitators, have invaded our dramatic scene through plays that represent deplorable tastes, first at circuses, and now reaching our most important stage in the form of a serious opera."[6] Other reviewers did not hesitate to criticize *Pampa*'s lacking dramatic qualities, which they blamed on the librettist, an Italian immigrant who had settled in Mercedes, Argentina.[7] Curiously Mercedes had been one of the real-life Juan Moreira's old haunts, so perhaps the librettist, as Quesada might have feared, had been influenced by criollismo's magnetism.

For his part, the librettist called attention to the broader, collective implications of the story, which overshadowed the negative criticism. "Don't ask if the protagonist is Santos Vega, Moreira, or a similar figure," he wrote. "No, it is the gaucho, the small town, the province, all of the pampa, as well as that little ranch whose inhabitants suffer . . . it is the symbolic refuge of the pains and hopes of a people. . . . Thus, the action . . . emanates not from an individual, but from the community."[8] *La Tribuna*'s social critic echoed the community impact angle, proclaiming, "Never before has a debut at the Opera theater awakened greater public interest than did *Pampa* last night." The writer added that "from the point of view of a social gathering *Pampa* was a brilliant success."[9] The author of this comment notes that spectators showed up on time for the show, which defied convention. Former and soon-to-be president-again Julio Roca was in attendance. And in what a local Italian periodical called a "particular curiosity," the police official who had stabbed the real-life Moreira in the back was working as a stagehand in a show that "apotheosized his old adversary."[10] *La Tribuna*'s social reviewer was almost certainly highlighting the fact also that opera drew varied audiences consisting of a range of socioeconomic groups, including some of the richest inhabitants of the city as well as working-class immigrants. Claudio Benzecry's study of opera fans in these years has shown that seating was highly stratified, but there could still be quite the "social gathering."[11]

Despite all the praise of the local color *Pampa* brought to the opera (here the music and dance scenes stood out), the libretto was in Italian. Thus, Giovanni (instead of Juan) led the charge against the lawmen in the show. Of course, Italian was one of the characteristic languages of the genre, and the librettist felt more comfortable writing in his native language.[12] But given the content of the story, where immigrants clash with native sons, there was some irony in the mix. Irony aside, *Pampa*, which transformed the story of

Moreira yet again, this time for the genre of opera, and with its lines in Italian, is a clear example of multiple levels on which staging frontiers occurred. In this instance, the story line of the opera as well as its title refer to a nostalgic geographic frontier caught in the whirlwind of modernization. The conflicts that develop—between immigrants and locals, and between locals and state officials—speak to other frontiers—demographic, political— being negotiated at the end of the century. Meanwhile, the libretto in Italian points to cultural and linguistic frontiers and how these crossed or disappeared. *Pampa* likewise allowed for popular and elite cultural frontiers to blur in a multidirectional exchange.[13]

This exchange was a defining feature of popular culture on the move. Just five days after the last performance of *Pampa* the comical spinoff *Moreira en ópera* took to the stage in Buenos Aires, parodying Berutti's work. At the beginning of September, Berutti's *Pampa* was across the Río de la Plata at Montevideo's Teatro Solís for another short run with the same company where it was, for the most part, received positively. The local *El Siglo* announced the debut performance with notable enthusiasm: "*Pampa* comes from a *maestro* full of inspiration; it is a work that has the double merit of both American music and an American story. . . . The plot is one that we all know, based on *Juan Moreira*. Who doesn't know *Juan Moreira*? Its attraction lies in its local story line, the naturalness of the plot, and the emotions generated by its tragic ending."[14] Writing for the same paper, the pen name Delta commented in an extensive note that he had low expectations before going to the opera, but was pleasantly surprised. "*Pampa* is the Creole drama *Juan Moreira* reduced to an opera libretto. Like *Moreira* it is a faithful reproduction of those customs we hope soon disappear, and whose display at the theater has lamentable results. But, all said and done, *Pampa* is interesting."[15] Interesting in large measure, Delta claimed, because of the local flare of the musical numbers (including women *payadoras*) and dance scenes, which were reminiscent of some of the liveliest Creole drama moments.

With *Pampa* we see the movement of a Creole drama story across cultural frontiers, gaining fame on the opera scene. *Juan Moreira* had made it to the peak of refined entertainment, and even the most serious operagoers could no longer shrug off that presence. Judging from reports following the shows that year, opera fans were eager to attend this novel performance, even as they feared that the story's arrival at the opera could resonate in similar ways to *Moreira* in the theater, unleashing a landslide of subsequent Creole operas.[16] That landslide never happened.

Our second case of popular culture on the move comes from the very pronounced geographic movement of Creole drama stories that occurred simultaneously with their circulation across cultural platforms. Chapters 2 and 3 covered the regional performance circuit where dramatic heroes introduced many to the theater for the first time, especially in interior provinces and towns. The network of small towns and coastal cities making up this circuit linked theatergoers in a unique transnational, collective experience of the Creole drama phenomenon. Companies occasionally ventured beyond this circuit. The Podestás had traveled to Rio de Janeiro with the Carlo family in 1884, for instance, while others tried their luck in Mendoza or Tucumán, in northwestern Argentina. Yet none had dared to go as far as the company that took *Juan Moreira* on its 1900 transatlantic tour. This tour signified not only the belief (or hope) that the Creole spirit could resonate in Europe but also the idea that Creole dramas could be representative of the Argentine and Uruguayan experience abroad. This representative character made them exciting and threatening at the same time.

The Podestá family received the initial invitation from an Argentine impresario to take *Juan Moreira* to Spain and then to the 1900 Paris Universal Exposition. José Podestá writes that they "were supposed to do *Moreira* and round out the show with a group of 'authentic Indians' who would exhibit their customs. We could dress them in ornate costumes, even if that meant bending the truth, for the sake of theatrical esthetics and spectator demands." But the plan unraveled, and the Podestá family members went about their performances in the region without further mention of crossing the Atlantic. Perhaps most interesting about the whole affair is Podestá's comparison of this group of Indians potentially performing in Europe to the Indians Buffalo Bill took to on his European tours. This was clearly on the mind of the impresario, too, hoping to enjoy similar success.[17]

Though the Podestás and this group of Indians did not make the trip, the show went on, with the first stop in Barcelona. News of "an Argentine Company" debuting there came in early July 1900. They performed *Juan Moreira* to much applause, despite the theater not offering all the conditions for such spectacles. The local paper *La Dinastía* characterized elements of the play as "genuinely Argentine," drawing our attention to the central aspect of *Juan Moreira* on tour: representation and the dramas serving as ambassadors for national culture.[18] News of the company's stay in the city appeared with more buildup in subsequent announcements in *La Dinastía*. On July 10, for example, readers were treated to these details: "Grand Argentine Company.

Creole Dramas, Never Before Seen in Europe . . . Today, Tuesday, the 6th showing of *Juan Moreira* . . . 39 Artists, 12 horses . . . 12 couples dancing the Grand Pericón Nacional . . . Tomorrow *Juan Moreira.*" A week later there was a benefit show for Joaquín Fontanella, called the "company's lead actor," in one of the very few mentions of performers involved, suggesting that it was most likely Fontanella's company touring. His was one of the lesser-known Creole drama outfits.[19]

The other reference to performers came from a profile of the company published in the paper *Iris*, where the author highlighted aspects that would become problematic for some Argentines and Uruguayans back home. First, the company's rendition of *Juan Moreira* was labeled "the perfect portrait of the life and customs of the gauchos." Second, scenes from the play, including most especially the pericón and the folk songs, offered an "ethnographic document that reveals all the passion of the Argentine soul."[20] What the author stressed was the play's ability and *authority* to represent Argentineness (and we should add Uruguayaness, too).

From Barcelona the company took this authority to Madrid, where they performed in July and August at William Parish's circus space. Parish bet on the sensational and novel quality of the show to attract audiences. As in Barcelona, the company promised Madrid spectators "a spectacle of Argentine life, habits, and customs."[21] One reviewer wrote that "every night the popular drama *Juan Moreira* receives more applause than the previous evening."[22] Another emphasized that Parish's bet had paid off: the company sold the most tickets of the season to the venue. According to Madrid's *El Día*, there were some spectators who showed a lack of enthusiasm for the performance. But Aida Reina captivated everyone's attention and received resounding applause as the star musician. Reina was a student of Gabino Ezeiza (see chapter 4) and became one of the most prominent women *payadoras*.[23] *La Epoca* published a review note praising the show's portrayal of a "legendary type from the countryside, an honorable, hardworking man . . . who became a sort of 'generous outlaw.'" This heroic image, freed from the more complicated and darker sides of the story, sold well abroad.[24] It, too, was a source of concern for skeptics back home.

It was the very same paper, *La Epoca*, that published the most substantial write-up of "La Compañía Argentina," which was how every ad billed the performers. The company effectively developed their reputation for being exactly what the generic name implied—presenters of the Argentine. The reviewer explained the use of the generic name: "the billboard did not name the author of the drama, nor even the actors representing it. We do not know the motive behind this omission." This lack of information was unimportant, though. What mattered was the ethnographic value: "*Juan Moreira* is a living portrait, with palpitating, true gaucho traditions. . . . Everything about the drama and its presentation merits interest: language, the accent of the performers, the clothing, the music, the accessories, everything should be observed. . . . In this simple melodrama there is a great deal for all of us to study." [25]

Accounts in the Spanish press consistently commented on the "Argentine Company's" march toward France for performances during the 1900 Universal Exposition. One Barcelona paper noted that the dramas would surely "attract interest not just in Paris, but in Spain, Italy, and other countries," suggesting a plan for an extensive tour.[26] *La Dinastía* spoke of the company's obligations in Paris, while the *Heraldo* announced that the group would travel to Paris as soon as it completed its stay in Madrid. Yet another paper included descriptions of the "novel views" from the Exposition alongside the announcements of *Juan Moreira* for all the theatergoers who could not make the trip to France.[27]

All this talk of an Argentine company heading to France to stage frontiers was not lost on Manuel Ugarte, one of many Argentines (and Latin Americans) living in Paris at the time. Ugarte wrote a chronicle addressing Argentine theater in Europe, specifically Creole dramas in France. Argentina had invested great resources to take part in the 1889 Paris World's fair (double what the United States put into its exhibit, and almost a third more than Mexico) and had benefited from representation there.[28] In theory displaying the nation in 1900 via agricultural products, infrastructure projects, work opportunities for immigrants, and cultural representation would build on that previous success. Yet the Argentine government canceled its participation in 1900, apparently without much anticipation, due to lack of funds. In its reviews of *Juan Moreira*, the Madrid and Barcelona papers did not register the lack of official participation in Paris. Neither did Ugarte.

According to Ugarte's account the state's absence did not affect the swirl of excitement around theatrical gauchos in Paris, and this possibility had him worried. He cited "recent news of an extravagant flavor from a Parisian daily" announcing the imminent arrival of an "unusual troupe" of Creole dramas. The announcement he referenced went on to tell readers that the shows would be like those of Buffalo Bill and his cowboys. What really unnerved Ugarte was the last sentence of the note: such theater "can give us an exact idea of life in those remote countries" (i.e., Argentina and Uruguay). Ugarte himself seemed skeptical of the news. That such a troupe would soon present examples of "our national theater" could be true or not, he noted. But the very fact that such an idea was circulating was bothersome, for he claimed that "we still do not have theater worth exporting" and called attention to the Barcelona paper *La Vanguardia*'s assessment that *Juan Moreira* represented the "roughness and rudimentary character of Argentine theater." He went on to portray, incorrectly, the minor influence of such dramas in Buenos Aires, and then concluded that if such plays were not well received in Spain (they were), then in Paris they would fare even worse. "It would be an anomaly to stage *Juan Moreira* in the capital of France." [29]

So what happened? Ugarte does not tell us if the company ever made it to France. He does concede that in the right, talented hands the rural customs and lonely heroism of the dramas could be made into something beautiful.[30] The French press and the official documentation from the Exposition make no mention of *Moreira*, similar plays, or the "Argentine Company." There were plenty of places for the company to have performed outside the fairgrounds, many of which were not listed in the official program. Three of these venues hosted regularly a variety of popular spectacles, including equestrian and acrobatic stunts. Could our company have been on the playbill at one of these? Paris's *Tour du Monde* was another location for entertainment. An animated panorama had been installed there, and spectators could attend "exotic theater" or an array of shows put on by "foreign performance troupes." [31] Finally, there was also a long list of shows spanning the spectrum from popular entertainment to modern dance and drama at Loie Fuller's Theater.

The juxtaposition in the Spanish press of *Juan Moreira* with news from the Exposition may have been the closest the drama got to Paris. But the atmosphere there would surely have supported the company, much in the same way Buffalo Bill's shows enjoyed streams of spectators at world's fairs.[32] Besides, it was the very idea of this drama representing the nation and what it meant to be Argentine or Uruguayan that elated some and terrified others.

Back across the Atlantic, linguistic influences and figures of popular speech inspired by Creole dramas became increasingly commonplace. This Creole drama talk, as we can call it, was another measure of popular culture on the move. Like the Argentine Company in Europe, this talk jolted anxiety levels because, ultimately, this linguistic contamination touched nerves of regional identity and sociability.[33] A sample of this talk can help bring into focus the brewing backlash against dramas and their supporters.

Readers will remember from chapter 4 the humorous cocoliche characters who became staple figures in the dramas of the 1890s. "Every night," Ernesto Quesada writes, "the delirious masses applaud furiously" the cocoliche figures at the "gaucho-Cocoliche theater."[34] Their curious blend of languages—primarily Italian and Spanish—added comic relief to the plays, often because of the extravagance of the characters and the confusion they created, while at the same time they explored tensions between immigrants and native-born Argentines and Uruguayans. These characters and their language games were not confined to performance spaces. Cocoliche became one of the most popular carnival costumes in these years, while references to cocoliche characters and language creations began infiltrating everyday speech. On the one hand, Italian influences in Spanish, or the creation of neologisms, were normal considering the demographic changes the region experienced between the 1870s and the 1910s. On the other, authors, artists, musicians, publishers, and carnival promoters cultivated a sort of cocoliche genre to take advantage of the new market niche.

This genre did not sit well with Quesada. He described variations of language contamination, in effect pointing out the emergence of *lunfardo* (the Río de la Plata's unique slang that consists primarily of Italian and Spanish language mixtures and that is intimately linked to regional identity still today), and critiqued cocoliche literature and song where he saw this malicious tendency flourishing. Quesada railed against the proliferation of publications that tapped into the cocoliche vogue in the 1890s and first decade of the twentieth century. Many of these texts were anonymously written, while others came from prolific authors and editors like Manuel Cientofante, Silverio Manco, and Santiago Rolleri, who often inverted his last name on his publications. There were song books, collections of poems, and invented love letters or payada transcriptions. Many had covers that portray stereotypical images of cocoliche figures (e.g., see figs. 6.1 and 6.2). And all were in Cocoliche or included cocoliche compositions along with criollista writings.[35]

As with cocoliche in the theater, cocoliche publications were not limited to reading spaces. Their contents were often sung in group gatherings, thereby multiplying their dissemination as well as stimulating further production of similar material.[36] Thus, the genre continued to reproduce itself,

Figure 6.1. Cover from Manuel M. Cientofante, *Amores de Cocoliche.* Buenos Aires: Casa Editora de Salvador Matera, 1909. Note that the figure here is not dressed in traditional gaucho attire, but he is carrying its accoutrements, the blunderbuss tucked in his belt and a *facón.* Verses on the title page give a sense of the book's flavor: "*Che,* listen to these verses that I've made for my girl / She's so pretty / that I get giddy / Every time I see her in the street." Biblioteca Criolla, Ibero-Amerikanisches Institut.

Figure 6.2. Cover from L. Irellor, *Cocoliche en carnaval.* Buenos Aires, Montevideo: Santiago Rolleri, 1902. The title page announces that "Don Franchisco (Cocoliche) is ecstatic because Carnival is around the corner, and Cocoliche always, always entertains the public." ("*Cocolicho sempre, sempre, a lu plubrico antretiene.*") Biblioteca Criolla, Ibero-Amerikanisches Institut.

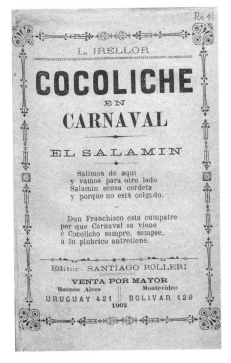

with publishers eager to turn a quick profit. Several criollista and cocoliche authors were self-published and enjoyed transnational circulation of their work, thanks either to the cheapest printings being done in Italy and then shipped back to Argentina and Uruguay, or because of multiple points of distribution. Santiago Rolleri, who edited dozens of pamphlets, is a case in point. His publications, such as *Cocoliche en carnaval* and *Nuevas canciones de Cocoliche*, were for sale simultaneously in Buenos Aires and Montevideo, often with his name doubling as both author and publisher.[37] *Cocoliche en carnaval*, which Quesada wrote "was a book seen in the hands of all those low-lives," matched *Martín Fierro* for the number of official copies sold and in circulation (more than sixty thousand). The spread of Cocoliche language games in the theater, at carnival, and through print provoked heightened concerns when such games became intertwined with daily expression, precisely because they could be observed regularly and as part of public life.[38]

Figures of speech or references that carried Creole drama inflections were on the rise, too, at the turn of the century. The widely read illustrated magazine *Caras y Caretas* yields a good portrait of these. Consider for example the January 20, 1900, issue, which detailed a kerfuffle between two bands of members at the Italia mutual aid society. Writers for *Caras y Caretas* stated that various "Juan Moreiras" were holed up in the society's headquarters. Reference to Moreira here illustrates the use of the symbol in areas of daily life removed from their regular stomping grounds. In March 1901 we can read about a gaucho trying unsuccessfully to light a match that just would not strike: the match "was like Juan Moreira since nobody—not even the police—caught a break with it." Several years later, in 1905, there was news of a "Moreira woman" who gained fame for being a difficult tenant, so difficult that no landlord could tolerate her for any length of time. That September the image of Moreira representing the "people" and standing for popular protest in the debate over the impact of import taxes featured on a cover (see image 6.3). And in July 1910 writers for the magazine invoked a commonly used expression in a story about family members reuniting. According to the tale, a distant son Abraham makes his way home, upon which the mother asks her daughter Olga what she thinks about Abraham's looks. Upon seeing his new style Olga exclaims, "You Moreira, you!" (qui Moreira qu'istás).[39]

References of this sort give a sense of what Creole drama talk felt like, its presence in everyday language, and its ability to transport meaning from drama scenes and moments to interactions and situations that had little or nothing to do with the performances.

Figure 6.3. The September 9, 1905, cover of the widely read magazine *Caras y Caretas*. Here we see Moreira representing the *pueblo* and standing for popular protest in the debate over the impact of import taxes. Neither the real Moreira nor the Creole drama hero had been involved in such a debate, but now it was only natural that the figure was invoked as the representative of the "people."

Our survey of Creole drama influences in the spread of popular culture could also point to the growth in the production of guitars and the establishment of new acting studios, especially for young men who took to learning the instrument or the actor's craft in hopes of becoming the next Podestá. Popular culture on the move showed up in the relationship between police officials and the public (mainly men, as we have noted in previous chapters), as well as in male hairstyles and fashion (longer hair and more boots with heels contributed to the look of the day among certain groups).[40] Catchy tunes from the dramas likewise were disseminated thanks to new recording technologies. In just one example we can read about itinerant puppeteers and entertainers who played wax cylinders with these songs at Pedro Lacaz's café in the Uruguayan border town of Melo, or in other "humble and scattered spots."[41]

In *Pampa, Juan Moreira*'s European tour, and the linguistic influences and figures of speech permeating daily language, as well as in the additional examples listed above, flows and exchanges across cultural frontiers were ever-present. These examples demonstrate the transnational character of the Creole drama phenomenon specifically and, more generally, of popular culture and its emerging industry that were clearly on the move. The movement of popular culture across media and geography produced both great excitement and great anxiety. Such movement also inflamed tensions surrounding what and who had the authority to represent national and regional culture. The clash over authority became visible in a sustained debate about not just the significance of Creole drama influences but also collective identity.

The Backlash against Creole Dramas

Following the departure of the Podestá-Scotti Company's 1893 visit to Tucumán—one of few to the area—a local paper printed an abrasive assessment. The writer asked if "those *dramas*—and let's go ahead and use the term for the sake of argument . . . merit attendance or even public attention. Is their influence beneficial or damaging? . . . The educated residents of Tucumán have given their verdict . . . and seen in the plays the birth of Argentine theater." That meant little to the reviewer, who was quick to rebut the public approval: "With Creole dramas we go back fifty years. Taste has been perverted. They teach nothing. And that which renders no moral or intellectual good has no reason to exist." A similar appraisal was issued in La Plata the following year, where the family and their dramas were generally warmly received. "A single scene from *Juan Moreira*—the only one we could tolerate in this lifetime—was enough to deplore the fact that such a genre has been elevated to the theater, and from there it is destined to do great harm." [42] Comments in this vein clearly went against the grain of public opinion at the time. They also bring into focus an emerging backlash against Creole dramas.

Criticism of the frontier onstage was certainly not new at the end of the century. Early representations of Creole dramas during the second half of the 1880s had drawn out their share of critics. Yet the level of concern rose in proportion to the popularity of the plays, partly as a reaction to their potential and real influences outside the theater. Usually this reaction pitted the "benefits" of such stories onstage against the detrimental effects on public morality, as the reviews above suggest. In the mid-1890s, with the Creole drama phenomenon at its height, critiques of this sort became more frequent and forceful. One recurring feature of this criticism was fear—fear of returning to an age of barbarism; fear of the plays promoting criminal behavior; fear of disintegrating moral values; fear of rising tensions between socioeconomic classes and ethnic groups. In this moment opponents also introduced reflections on "national" art and literature to challenge the place of the dramas as representative of national and regional character. These voices of criticism faced voices of support in what became a debate over collective cultural representation.

Prominent Argentine and Uruguayan intellectuals got into the fray, too. One of these was Rafael Obligado, a prolific poet and essayist, and a friend of Ernesto Quesada. Obligado's fame stemmed ironically from his innocuous take on the legend of the gaucho *Santos Vega*. Obligado was a leading voice of opposition to the influence of not just Creole dramas but criollismo in all its popular manifestations. Perhaps he saw criollismo as a source of competition for his own creative pursuits. In any event, in a June 1894 speech he gave to members of the Buenos Aires Ateneo club his disapproval took on ideological hues. The main argument of the presentation was that art not only has a nationality but can also be associated with specific regional and town identities. Yet "art is not present for us in *Juan Moreira* . . . nor in any other plays of that ilk," Obligado told his audience. "Nor will the new muse of dance be born from the pericón nacional, any more than the new muse of tragedy from the tragic confrontations between gauchos and police squads, or the new muse of comedy from the coarseness of payadores at the theater." [43] This line of argumentation about what constituted appropriate content for "national" theater—and national art more generally—gained steam, with opinions from both sides of the Creole divide.

A contrasting example to Obligado was the Argentine painter Eduardo Schiaffino, who advocated for the Creole spirit as a source of regional identity. Schiaffino had composed landscape paintings of the pampas, which Obligado criticized in his speech. So a month later he addressed the same group at the Ateneo. After hinting that Obligado was just jealous of the sales numbers and reception of *Juan Moreira*, Schiaffino considered the significance of cultural representation. "It seems to me that if *Juan Moreira* has been the most popular theatrical hit we have ever seen, then plausibly it is because the piece is representative, whatever its literary value. . . . Audiences will continue to attend the play until you all replace it with one that is equally human." Delving into the human character was for Schiaffino—and others— one of the play's most salient features. "*Moreira* represents a particular moment of our social evolution as Argentines. It contains that breath of humanity that makes it so attractive and that allows it to embody the people's aesthetic taste."[44]

Representation, humanity, and regional identity peppered the back and forth in the region's press during these years, too. A good example appeared in Montevideo's *El Nacional*, where Javier de Viana and Creole drama author Abdón Arózteguy engaged in another dispute. De Viana adamantly protested the notion that Creole dramas and a national theater tradition could be linked "in defense of art and out of honor for our society that cannot accept such literary affronts." He compared the evolution of the plays to the rapid growth of bacteria, and then told young authors of the dramas they were wasting their time. De Viana concluded that the real problem the plays posed was the cultivation of ignorance of the countryside and its inhabitants through exaggeration and pure fantasy. This ignorance allowed for immorality onstage and falsification of a way of life that was not representative of reality in any way. Arózteguy responded by claiming de Viana confused the heroic fighters for political freedom who appeared at least in his own dramas with electoral caudillos and contemporary urban tough guys. One day, he hoped, the social value of such characters will be clear for all to see. De Viana again countered. Gauchos are one thing, he wrote, but gauchos in Creole dramas something completely different. "The gaucho of Creole dramas is a fake and, like all falsifications, injurious, more so than the real gaucho."[45] De Viana maintained that he was presenting the whole truth about gauchos rather than one littered with invention when it did not suit the story he wanted to tell.

Both men continued to offer their interpretations of the Creole drama phenomenon in subsequent years, though in this spat they defined another general feature of the debate from these years—"good" (real) gauchos versus "bad" (fake) ones. This standoff factored into the connections among theater, nation, and social identity.

Arózteguy elaborated at length on the good-bad gaucho divide in an essay he titled simply "Creole Dramas: The Good and the Bad." For Arózteguy, the main issue with these dramas, which had fueled more conversation than most every other spectacle, was to determine what kind of influence they have on the masses. The genre for the most part was "in diapers," he wrote, with many more poorly written dramas, and even poorer performances, than skillfully composed ones. As a result, the "bad" gauchos—the Moreiras—have triumphed over the more noble patriotic ones such as Julián Giménez, sketched in his very own play *Julián Giménez*. He thus had no problem with the criticism dramas of "bad" gauchos received, or the idea of censuring these plays along with "obscene" sections of other performances such as zarzuelas. At the same time, though, "good" gaucho dramas like his plays should be spared from the blanket condemnation of the phenomenon or criollismo more generally and applauded, for "they represent our customs and ancestors and thus foment patriotism among the people."[46] And where there was patriotism, thought Arózteguy, there must be something "beneficial" for public morality.

Julián Giménez belonged to the group of dramas that aimed to promote the patriotic portrait of gaucho heroes, as seen in chapter 3. Another one of these "good" gauchos was Calandria, who starred in the namesake play in May 1896. The debut of *Calandria* was a turning point in the history of the Creole drama phenomenon. From that moment on there was a definitive model against which previous dramas could be compared and criticized. *Calandria* also gave license to thinking about the frontier onstage in different ways. One of these was the author's demand that the play's first performers—the Podestá-Scotti Company—present the show in a theater and not under a circus tent. Another revolved around the happy-go-lucky protagonist who renounced violence and took up steady work to be with his sweetheart. These new interpretations of the frontier ultimately resulted in different takeaways for audiences.

Just consider a handful of reviews published in Buenos Aires after the initial performances. The popular Argentine journalist Fray Mocho exclaimed in *La Tribuna*, "Finally we have on stage a true national drama that portrays the gaucho with precision." This statement was as much a critique of previous dramas as it was praise for *Calandria*. In contrast to the earlier plays, *Calandria* did not provoke "ill will or awaken passions that civilization has tamed." In *La Nación* Luis Berisso followed a similar tack: "Last night—after so many hideous melodramas we've had to endure—we had the good fortune to see a living portrait . . . composed by a young man who knows frontier life, as well as how to write." This journalist went on to express his disgust with Creole drama talk and to underscore how *Calandria* is far removed from "those bloodthirsty, brutal figures like *Moreira* . . . who have given a very poor idea of what has been called *national drama* and represent a retrograde tendency." Berisso was careful to note that this difference did not take away from the new drama's flavor. *El Tiempo* published commentary likewise disdaining previous representations that pretended to be national dramas and praising "the true gaucho on the national stage" that communicated an alternative understanding of Creole identity.[47]

These and comparable comments surrounding *Calandria* point to the consolidation of this alternative regional identity, in which nobility, honor, hard work, and patriotism, were the defining characteristics. That is, the "good" gaucho gained a clear place as representative of collective values. Absent was the desire for revenge or the use of violence. This did not mean that in the late 1890s older Creole dramas disappeared from venues or failed to attract audiences. But their appeal and the frequency of their performances declined. In Ernesto Quesada's calculation this was due partly to competition from companies that offered Creole-spirited plays without all the crudeness.[48] He was certainly right about competition.

The frontier and the countryside continued serving as backdrops for cultural representation. But no new dramas took up the older tough-guy protagonists. Even the king of the Creole drama phenomenon—the Podestá-Scotti Company—was expanding its repertoire to include performances made mainly for the theater. Thus, Florencio Sánchez—the Uruguayan playwright who would shortly become the region's most famous—chose none other than the Podestá family to debut several of his plays. As we will see in chapter 7, these made use of the formal space of the theater to question rural tradition and hierarchy, examine the margins of urban life, and explore rifts between generations that grew more intense as urbanization transformed cityscapes.[49] The group that had given rise to one type of cultural representation was ushering in another that was on the verge of overtaking the Creole drama phenomenon.

If the backlash against Creole dramas and popular culture on the move had subsided by 1900, the debate over representation, identity, and nation continued throughout the first decade of the new century. However, now that production and performance of these dramas was on the wane, drastically limiting the perceived threat from prior years, the consequences were different.

The prolific Uruguayan writer, avid theatergoer, and public intellectual Samuel Blixen accordingly struck a conciliatory tone in a 1903 speech he gave at the Teatro Solís (remember that this was a top opera destination). "I see in that primitive vein of our dramatic art a guarantee of its future greatness. Its manifestations up until now have been the most powerful and fecund of the immense literary production in this America." Then, aiming to present redeeming qualities of Creole dramas, he told the crowd that "only those dramas touched the popular soul, moved it deeply, and filled it with enthu-siasm. That incipient art . . . has from the beginning had the distinction of sincerity, the frankness of passion. Of course details can be criticized in the name of good taste, but nobody can deny the potency and sureness of its instinct, which came together in *Juan Moreira* in that beautiful rebellious-ness of the gaucho soul." [50] It was precisely that instinct or passion of per-formers and audiences alike that allowed for the Creole drama phenomenon not only to be rescued from outright condemnation but also to occupy a place in national and regional theater history.

Others joined Blixen in this process of reevaluating the significance of the phenomenon. One inadvertent participant was Enrique Rivarola, who pub-lished an extended essay on Argentine theater. Rivarola was no fan of Creole dramas, which he described as plays that "destroy at the same time correctly spoken Spanish and our sense of morality." His comments were rooted in a sense of barbarism he saw invading the world of letters and art. The dramas threatened the ability of theater to represent progress, especially when its characters made their way to the opera, as with *Pampa*. Yet for all the nega-tive qualities of these plays, Rivarola could not ignore them in his survey of national theater.[51] Javier de Viana, who had been one of the fiercest critics tempered his earlier opinions. In a 1909 speech he gave at Montevideo's Apolo club he touted the unpolished actors who helped forge a national and transnational (in the sense of the Río de la Plata region) theater spirit. "Some barely knew how to read; few spoke correctly, and none knew how to wear a suit," he said. But "they opened the doors to a national theatrical tradition. Though their stages were simple corrals and the actors rough around the edges, we must be fair and agree that there is probably more than one theater star who owes his celebrity to the work of those precursors of our dramaturgy." [52]

Finally, there were those who completed the rescue mission. The contem-porary observer Vicente Rossi compared the emergence of the patria to the emergence of national theater: both relied on the "powerful force of gau-chos," providing one of the clearest nationalist interpretations of theater his-tory.[53] Víctor Pérez Petit (author of the Creole drama *Cobarde*) likewise offered a full-throated defense of Creole dramas and their significance to regional identity in an essay titled "Defense of the Creole Drama." For all their rudeness, he wrote, such plays leave the impression of "something great . . . Barbarous dramas! Yes, and that is their greatness! That is the secret of their success. It is the explanation for their popularity and longevity. . . . How could those barbarous dramas not be beautiful and great! They are the drama of our blood and our race!"[54] Here we come full circle, in a sense. Popular culture on the move had its successes, faced strong headwinds, even the most forceful critique. Then, following its decline from the region's entertainment scene, Creole dramas and their far-flung impacts were assured their status as representative of transnational identity.

So what should we make of this debate? On the one hand, we see supporters and opponents of the dramas and their influence struggling to define the parameters of national theater, which depended as much on identifying its "beginning" as it meant selecting "national" dramas and explaining why in fact they were representative of community. Around 1900 it was becoming ever more crucial to claim that there was indeed an "Uruguayan" or "Argentine" theatrical tradition, for that tradition was intimately linked to expressions of cultural nationalism, which was on the rise throughout the Americas.

On the other hand, we have the performers of Creole dramas and linked phenomena like *Pampa* who had other interests at heart. Most were merely trying to make a living and veered from one town to another in search of continued ticket sales. Others, like Mariacher, sought artistic recognition, even fame, on the stage. While some of these performers, such José or Jerónimo Podestá, the Anselmi circus family, or Pablo Raffetto sympathized with the gaucho heroes they played, they were not invested in the debate about Creole dramas. So when audiences began seeking other entertainment offerings, these stars as well as others had no problem switching up their repertoires with new and different performances.

The back and forth we have seen in this section also reveals the shifting meanings of the Creole. There was widespread acceptance of Creole dramas and their influences in the early 1890s, including their stamp on criollismo. However, this acceptance gave way to condemnation and rejection, and a transformation of what the Creole stood for, in line with a more orderly and nostalgic vision. This new rendering gained currency with Creole dramas in their twilight and no longer posing a source of angst for their opponents. This is a simplified periodization of the phenomenon and its decline. Yet what is most important to note is how the evolution of the Creole and its reception point to the evolving topography of modern popular culture in the region. The debate over cultural representation, and the challenges Creole dramas faced as cultural ambassadors abroad, was a debate on the development of popular culture and its growing marketplace.

Popular culture on the move generated serious questions about cultural hierarchy and the authority behind cultural representation. Fears related to the expanded public participation in the world of the Creole as filtered through the Creole drama experience were real. Yet the impact of these dramas and their imprint on public morality was rapidly shrinking around the turn of the century. At issue was the legacy of this phenomenon, how the narrative of that legacy would develop, and its place in the elaboration of a Rioplatense or transnational cultural identity.

The content of the dramas, their commercial success, and their influences that encroached on public and private life, led to the backlash and drove the debate whose arguments we have outlined. Though that debate did not yield a black-and-white outcome, significant strands of cultural distinction emerged.[55] Around 1900 the formal space of the theater began attracting crowds that had previously chosen Creole dramas as their entertainment of choice. Many of the new plays written for theatergoers continued to deal in country themes, but with tame gauchos, younger generations challenging older traditional ways, and stage design that all but eliminated the wild flare of the countryside onstage. No more bonfires or sheep shearing or horse races. There were plenty of other entertainment options, too, that departed from stories of rural life. As we will see in the final chapter, this new entertainment landscape depended on the theatergoing public that Creole dramas had produced, while at the same time it meant the definitive end of the Creole drama phenomenon.

CHAPTER 7

Downfall and Legacy

✢ "IT ALL STARTED AT THE CIRCUS. YES, THE CIRCUS, BUT AT LEAST IT
was *our* beginning. . . . Young artists and authors—there you have the school
of success! Start with the circus!"[1]

Thus wrote an ecstatic—and some would say quasi-prophetic—Carlos
Olivera in his 1885 short article hailing the advent of national theater in
Argentina and a turning point in national culture. The catalyst for his comments was the pantomime version of *Juan Moreira*. Some fifteen years later,
Juan Moreira's movement across media and space, including the Atlantic
Ocean, continued to be a leading edge for the expansion of the region's popular culture. Echoes could still be heard of earlier commentaries linking the
"birth" of a national theatrical tradition in Argentina and Uruguay to the
circus and celebrating the idea of a "humble" company like the Podestás representing regional customs. Playwright, author, and actor Enrique García
Velloso, whose introduction to the world of performance came through
Creole dramas, was one of these voices. In his memoirs he proclaims, "For
thirty years many theater companies have relied on the shadow of *Juan
Moreira*. Our most celebrated actors emerged from these companies.
Whether at the circus or in theaters, *Moreira* always brought success."[2]

The idea of circus shows often leading to more complex theater experiences became a dominant trope in the region's theater history. And as the
1910 centennial celebration of Argentina's path toward independence came
into focus, advocates of cultural nationalism repurposed mythic gauchos as

185

national heroes and attempted to shape their legacy, in part by situating them in patriotic perspective.[3] The nationalist take on theater history was one good example.

At the same time, and despite the dwindling number of Creole drama performances since the late 1890s, the broader currents the phenomenon had unleashed remained a source of unease for critics and opponents. Some of these sought to promote moral or intellectual purity. Gaucho blowouts did not fit into that vision. Others cited public safety concerns or were jealous of the Creole heroes' enduring attraction. In the last chapter we saw this lingering charm in detail through *Juan Moreira* on tour and the reactions popular culture on the move elicited. Yet the seemingly omnipresent references— both positive and negative—to the plays, their actors and authors, and the cultural capital the tales wielded in other areas of public life were not enough to stave off the definitive downfall of Creole dramas. By the turn of the century, performances of such plays grew scant, with just about everyone who had been involved previously in the shows looking for success elsewhere. What was behind this dramatic shift?

This outline certainly suggests a classic rise and fall narrative. The Creole drama modality enjoyed its peak years from the mid-1880s to around 1900, as previous chapters have shown. Then the phenomenon faded into the background of what was an ever more populated sphere of leisure and entertainment options. One possible interpretation of this collapse, though incomplete, is that the dramas had simply run their course, that audiences had their fill and sought something new. However, a fuller account needs to capture the complexity of how new entertainment options built on the success of Creole dramas and their performers, to the point of luring away spectators first, then investors and actors shortly thereafter. The result of that transition was a veritable theater culture and theatergoing public that developed during the first decade of the twentieth century (and continued to expand thereafter), both of which owed much to the enthusiasm audiences cultivated for going out to see frontiers onstage.

While the Creole drama phenomenon's downfall is a centerpiece of this chapter's story, we must also stress that even with the expanded offerings of theatrical entertainment in the early twentieth century, the influence (and occasional return performance) of Creole dramas did not end entirely. Their legacy remained vital to the region's cultural marketplace, with performers making the jump to more formal theatrical venues, and to the new formats of cinema and radio theater throughout the first half of the century. Versions of the popular plays were refashioned in new dramatic formats or for the new medium of the cinema, and melodramas permeated the airwaves, taking the stories and their heroes into peoples' homes in innovative ways. The lasting impact of the plays, therefore, continued influencing ideals of cultural identity throughout the twentieth century. In many ways the rise and fall of the phenomenon paralleled that of so many of its iconic figures. From meager beginnings Creole dramas and their outsized impacts wielded larger than life appeal. Then, the plays saw a fairly hasty end to their time onstage that segued to their rich afterlife.

Sounds so melodramatic, right? That's because it was. And it all started with the disappearing act of the best shows in town.

The Downfall of One Phenomenon and the Rise of Another

By the early 1900s going to the theater was a mainstay of social life across the region. In Buenos Aires and Montevideo as well as in less urban areas, entertainment options had steadily multiplied since the mid-1890s, and during the first decade of the new century there was an explosion of theatrical offerings. Zarzuelas, comical plays that were a sort of light opera, and short dramas in the form of one-act shows called *sainetes* were among the most numerous of these offerings. At the same time public attention to the theater was growing, Creole dramas were losing their foothold in the entertainment marketplace. In smaller towns this paradox played out more slowly given the smaller number of dramatic productions and the continued shows of circus troupes traveling through the countryside. In fact, as Creole drama companies were pushed to operate on the outskirts of larger cities due to rising production costs and shrinking revenues, they found more stable audiences in small-town venues. When the Creole Circus or Creole drama was the only show in town, at times for days or weeks in a row, audiences naturally gravitated toward its performances. But the general outline of the process in small towns is the same: some of the very cultural forces these dramas helped to create, and that had fomented the greater presence of theater in public life, now overshadowed the appeal of the countryside onstage.

These contours frame a story of downfall. Consider some statistics reflecting the expansion of the theater as one of the region's premier leisure sites and places for socializing. From the inauguration of the Politeama Argentino in Buenos Aires in 1879 (this was the venue where *Juan Moreira* and Sarah

Bernhardt almost met) through the end of the century, around twenty new theaters and entertainment venues opened their doors in the city. The number of new spaces almost doubled in the period stretching from 1900 to 1920. These had an average seating capacity of more than seven hundred.[4] Ticket sales increased during these years, too. In Buenos Aires alone, around 2.5 million tickets were sold to theatrical performances in 1889, when the city's population hovered around six hundred thousand; by 1925 almost seven million tickets were distributed among the city's two million residents.[5] On a slightly smaller scale, the same pattern of growth characterized the increasing number of entertainment spaces across Montevideo. These ranged from formal theaters to more informal performance areas offered by cafés, mutual aid clubs, and Creole societies. Venues also opened during this period in smaller cities such as Salto, Colonia, and Paysandú in Uruguay, and Rosario, La Plata, Santa Fe, Paraná, and Córdoba in Argentina. So, across the region numbers of spectators, shows, and places of entertainment were rising.

Yet Creole dramas all but vanished from this dynamic marketplace. In Buenos Aires, where the most complete data on entertainment activity exists for these years, annual yearbooks recorded this trend. Even though their numbers were in decline, in 1900, for example, Creole dramas still feature among the main categories of spectacle. That year's figures noted 348 Creole drama functions among the more than 5,600 total shows across categories, accounting for just over 5 percent of tickets sold. The numbers went up in 1903, with more than 900 Creole dramas. But by 1905 the category no longer appeared; it had merged into the broader "National Dramas and Comedies," which, judging by the elevated numbers of functions, included sainetes and other forms of short plays by local authors. Two years later the additional category "Circuses" complicated the portrait more. This new rubric featured in later yearbooks, leaving the Creole drama category to the past.[6] We can question the completeness of the statistics from these years, but the general picture, especially with the corresponding shift in categories, is one of gaucho heroes no longer on center stage.

While the statistical accounts point to a fairly abrupt departure, signs of the looming end for the phenomenon began appearing in the 1890s. In 1896, for example, the overall number of Creole dramas in Buenos Aires was approximately 350, not out of sync with previous years. However, attendance at these was already lower. In fact, companies were unable to fill seats. The more than 50 representations of *Juan Moreira* in the city that year drew fewer than 10,000 spectators. The Podestá family's performances of *Calandria* attracted fewer than 3,000 people in total to slightly more than a dozen functions. To put this number in perspective, the play's venue—the Victoria Theater—accommodated 1,500 people per show, so we can imagine that crowds were uneven and sparse.[7] Such numbers must be taken with a grain of salt since they represent one stop for companies on the regional performance circuit, and they are likely incomplete. Nevertheless, they point to shifting attitudes in the region's largest entertainment market. Part of the cooler reception of the plays may have corresponded to changing tastes among the middle- and upper-class theatergoers who had become enthusiasts for sabor criollo earlier in the decade, but, because of allayed political fears and increasingly more entertainment choices, joined other circles or sought other modes of social representation.[8]

Creole drama companies, including the most celebrated ones, felt the impact of declining attendance. Though he never shied away from self-promotion, José Podestá writes in his memoirs of the beginning of the Podestá Company's "bad streak." The group had some successes, but overall, he notes, the company struggled to attract crowds in the late 1890s, seemingly, though Podestá does not admit this, because of the selection of shows they offered, whether in Buenos Aires, Montevideo, La Plata, or elsewhere. Finally, at the outset of 1899 the group took an extended break from performing. He laments that "it was the first time, after so many years of success, that we found ourselves obligated to take such a step."[9] The following year the company offered shows in a handful of locations, with mixed results. In the town of San Nicolás, in the heart of Creole drama territory, they had "so little luck" that they stayed a mere ten days. Other stops on the itinerary saw more positive turnouts, with new plays—not Creole dramas—as the source of attraction. The message the company took away was clear: they could no longer count on either gaucho heroics or the well-worn performance circuit if they wished to remain in show business.

Such changes in the entertainment landscape accelerated in the 1900s. The region's premier performance family, for instance, split into several separate companies, with José Podestá going one way, his brother Jerónimo another, and later the younger Pablo setting out on his own, too. All were eager to leave behind the arduous travel schedule of previous decades and establish stable relationships with theater management, financiers, and audiences in a handful of locations.[10] José and the family members who remained with him began performing for diverse audiences at the Teatro Apolo in Buenos Aires. When day laborers showed up in work clothes to one of the early performances, some even without shirts, José became determined to impose a certain dress standard as a way of marking the company's new identity and relationship with audiences. He told the doormen not to admit anyone "without a shirt or who was poorly dressed." If they complained, he added, "tell them it's the municipal code." Jerónimo likewise set up at a local theater. Both groups enjoyed a level of prestige and popular resonance that transferred from their previous successes. José himself drew a straight line from previous experiences to the new phase at theaters, recalling: "Oh the heroic, unsung circus! Its arena was our training ground, where our gauchos made the leap to formal stages. Without the circus we would not have made it to the Apolo."[11]

Both groups' members also benefited from being Argentine and Uruguayan themselves, which gave them an advantage over foreign theater companies (mainly Spanish) that attempted to stage works by local authors. This Creoleness, evident in intonation, song, and understanding of local language codes and gestures, was an asset as well when staging new dramas about regional themes during the first decades of the twentieth century. These new plays dealt with clashes between immigrants and native sons; with living conditions and relationships in *conventillos*, or the tenement houses where immigrants and rural migrants often lived upon arriving in port cities; with lousy working conditions; and, to a smaller degree, with country themes, as we will note shortly. While Creole dramas were interspersed with playlists in the first years of the century, the newer plays, which soon entered a period of virtual mass production, outnumbered and outsold them by far. Just consider the list of shows José Podestá's group staged at the Apolo theater from 1901 to 1903. Of the close to 120 different plays presented, less than 10 percent of these were the old Creole numbers. Even the greatest hits, like *Martín Fierro* and *Santos Vega*, paled in terms of audience turnout and, subsequently, number of functions when compared to plays by the up-and-coming dramaturgs like Nicolás Granada, Martín Coronado, and Florencio Sánchez. Coronado for his part had refused to see Creole dramas and was reluctant for a circus family to perform his work. Yet it was precisely his *La piedra de escándalo* (loosely, Trouble) in the hands of José Podestá at the Apolo that resulted in the greatest recognition he had received so far in his career.[12]

In effect, such dramas opened the next chapter for the Podestás as well as others, and for the course of the region's theater culture.[13] The countryside still made it onto the stage, but from a radically new perspective, often from authors who were highly critical of previous renderings of rural life. Take, for example, Florencio Sánchez, who became an icon of the region's popular culture scene during the first decade of the twentieth century, and who made rural themes central to his plays. Yet he was interested in the growing immigrant presence in the countryside along with accompanying tensions, in children of Creole and immigrant families joining happily in wedlock, and in the generational conflicts of the sort that developed between a traditional Creole father and his city-slicker son in *M'hijo el dotor* (roughly, My Boy, the Lawyer). In this play the son rejects his roots and respect for his rural upbringing, leading to the father's dismay. Sánchez related that *M'hijo* garnered "the greatest applause I had experienced in my artistic career." From that moment on, he said, audiences wanted to see *real* country life (as opposed to the fantasies Creole dramas disseminated), with all its contradictions and challenges. He saw himself as one of the main sources of this type of representation and thus one of the contributors to the region's theater with true artistic capacity.[14]

Entertainment coverage from the early 1900s underscores the transformations at work. Montevideo's *El Siglo* began featuring a "Theaters and Artists" section on its front page in 1904. The newly minted section title had replaced the more casual "diversiones públicas" (public amusements) rubric, hinting at the polished presentation of and general attitude toward formal theater during these years. The variety of entertainment listings, from vaudeville to zarzuelas to sainetes, also pointed to the shifting outlook. These types of spectacles filled the section in subsequent years in *El Siglo*, in Argentine newspapers, and gradually in publications throughout the interior, too. There were Creole dramas from time to time throughout the decade, and with the Podestás gone from that scene, smaller companies tried to capitalize on the chance to make a name for themselves.[15] But the circus-born drama no longer guaranteed widespread appeal.

Even while the frequency of these plays had diminished rapidly in capital cities and would subsequently do so in more remote locations, a notion of Creole pride, referring generally to local, national, or regional connections but without all the heroic overtones, gathered strength. Playwrights composed "dramas of Creole customs" that engaged local stories with local artists, but lacked gaucho toughs. Companies presented themselves as "Creole" or "National" troupes with the same idea of conveying expansive representative character. And journalists who wrote about theater celebrated the Creole as central to the evolution of the region's entertainment. One of these was

Samuel Blixen, the prolific Uruguayan who addressed all things theater-related (he appeared in the last chapter). In a September 1908 article in a Montevideo paper, he pronounced that "our audiences have a distinct predilection for the 'Creole' genre" and that "the theater of national customs, which has been rapidly developing, has almost achieved its peak force."[16] Shortly thereafter another Uruguayan reviewer praised "Creole theater," referring to local theatrical production during the first decade of the twentieth century, as the heart and soul of Uruguay's incipient theater culture. From the "dramas centered on swashbuckling and men in country garb" to contemporary plays, the author noted positive developments in dramatic quality and meaning. Audiences have grown, too, he remarked, and now recognize theater's place in "national cultural life."[17]

That residents in Uruguay and Argentina had come to consider theater a core piece of "national cultural life" during the first decade of the century highlights the rise of the region's theatergoing public and the increasing importance of performance experiences as prime moments for social exchange. This period, in fact, has been termed the "golden age" of Rioplatense theater, partly because of the variety of plays that were staged but also because of the sheer number of shows given and the new social status of drama as a pillar of "national culture."[18] José Podestá's company alone had performed 3,200 shows at the Apolo theater in seven and a half years, from 1901 to 1908. Recall that the Apolo was just one among dozens of theater settings in Buenos Aires at the time.

Particularly important during this golden decade was the *género chico*, which, as the term suggests, consisted of various short dramatic forms. Many authors of these plays were incredibly prolific. Enrique García Velloso (Argentina) debuted more than 140 works; Nemesio Trejo (Argentina) close to 60; Carlos María Pacheco (Uruguay) close to 80 plays; playwright and tango lyricist Alberto Vacarezza (Argentina) some 120 plays, and so on.[19] Género chico authors had often been involved with Creole dramas. This was the case of Nemesio Trejo, who was also a celebrated payador. He showcased his musical talent around the region in cafés, bars, and other gathering spots.[20] Similarly, Enrique García Velloso worked closely with the Podestás back when they did Creole dramas and later expanded his career to encompass writing and directing.

Sainetes were the most numerous and popular among the género chico forms. Between 1890 and 1930 thousands of these were produced, created by the likes of Pacheco, García Velloso, Trejo, Coronado, and others who perfected their relationship with the theater economy. Many sainetes treated working-class struggles or conventillo life in Buenos Aires and Montevideo, featuring characters representing new urban toughs called *compadritos*. Sainetes also surveyed at length labor disputes—which grew in intensity throughout the early 1900s—and the linked backlash toward immigrants that crystalized in a 1902 Argentine law aiming to control immigrant behavior, in particular members of labor unions or anarchist sympathizers.[21] Ethnic communities composed of Italian or Gallician immigrants, or Jewish migrants who spoke Yiddish, for example, and trade groups that had small theaters, also produced sainetes, among other género chico forms, for their members.[22]

With this thematic backdrop in mind it is easy to understand why sainetes took on such significant contemporary meaning.[23] By representing concerns and life stories of popular classes onstage, as one scholar put it, the plays ultimately addressed "the need for political participation by these very groups."[24]

This participation in public or civic life through attendance at the theater was not new at this point. Creole social clubs as well as earlier types of spectacles had offered avenues for such engagement with the public sphere. One of the strengths of Creole dramas was precisely their attempt to relay concerns of popular classes. What was innovative was the augmented range of political issues at stake in plays of the early twentieth century. Additionally, the conventillo as a stage setting turned people's living space into a focal point for social engagement. That, too, lent a new quotidian quality to the theatergoing experience of the golden decade. Because of these factors and the explosion of entertainment options during the first decade of the century, the theatergoing public changed, too.[25] Of course there were more people going out every month—we already noted the jump in these figures. More important, greater numbers of people across class and ethnic frontiers could connect to each other through greater content variety and numbers of performances than ever before.

The ever-present Ernesto Quesada put this expanded social character of theatergoing into perspective. "The inhabitants of Buenos Aires," he writes, "are passionate about theater. The upper echelons, the *high-life*, meet at the Colón Theater; those who are a bit more laid back socialize at the Opera Theater; *decent* people do so at the Alegría Theater, while the rowdy ones take to the Politeama and Variety Theaters." He later concludes that "theater for us is not really theater in the classic sense of the term. It's simply a place to gather and meander."[26]

Though sainete production slowed after 1910, by then there was a thriving theater economy. Alfredo Bianchi was one observer of this economy. He claimed that it took off in the early 1900s, when the "civil era" of dramatic spectacles in the region replaced the "gaucho era"—in itself a telling taxonomy. Bianchi was especially impressed by the amount of revenue the new theater generated. In his collection of essays he titled simply *Teatro nacional*, he also went on to complain about the decline in dramatic quality from the late 1900s through the late 1910s. In an October 1917 essay, he charged that one of the main problems behind the waning quality of plays was the emphasis on making a profit. This industrial model casts aside all concern for art, Bianchi leveled, and theater reviewers were largely to blame given that their measure of success was the potential high number of performances a play could have rather than anything meaningful. He was in effect taking issue with the pervasiveness of popular theater, primarily sainetes, and a theater culture that did not address artistic concerns in the ways he thought imperative.[27] The motives of authors were questioned as well, given the financial relationship many had with dramatic production and the urge to supply what audiences and impresarios demanded.[28]

Bianchi's comments suggest the scale and influence of the theater economy. We can see one good example of this scale and influence in the stricter regulation of theater activity and enforcement of ordinances. Some of these concerned audience comfort—like requiring heating in winter months, electrical lighting instead of kerosene, or respecting advertised start times—while others dealt with building safety and fire prevention. The failure of impresarios or theater owners to follow these regulations, usually out of concern for profit margins, did not end up affecting attendance rates, either, which highlights the economic might of theater.[29]

Evidence of this economic power was also manifest in the boom in theater publications throughout the first third of the century, thanks primarily to the commercial success and cultural appeal of the género chico. During this period more than forty different magazines covering theater in Argentina and Uruguay entered circulation. One of the region's longest lasting and most frequently published was *Bambalinas*, which ran 750 numbers over sixteen years.[30] Newspapers, too, cultivated entertainment beats, with journalists regularly reporting on the latest hits, trends, and performance phenomena. A handful of book publishers rode the enthusiasm surrounding the theater as well. Collections such as the *Library of Uruguayan Theater*, the

Library of Argentine Theater (both produced by the same publisher), and the *New Dramatic and Popular Culture Archive*—a title that sums up how popular culture and theater were thought of together—provided dozens of plays for mass distribution.[31]

What should be coming into clear view is that one of the strengths of the incipient theater economy was its fusion with the popular culture market. A contemporary of Bianchi and Quesada summed up this understanding by noting that the theater business in Argentina is "an important chapter of our national economy," aside from being a "new branch" of Argentine culture.[32] Here we return, in effect, to the concept of national theater, or theater that is central to national cultural life, except with Creole drama notes no longer part of the score. When Vicente Rossi published his *Teatro nacional rioplatense* in 1910—an early treatise on the idea of national and regional theater culture—he attempted to describe this scene. "National theater first appeared on the horizons of the open countryside, with suggestive details of the rural lifestyle. Then it moved closer to the city, spent the night on that frontier between city and countryside, went around the rough city outskirts, and finally landed in the blue salons of bourgeois homes."[33] With the waning of carnival celebrations in Buenos Aires in the mid-1910s, gaucho comparsas and all of the costumed Moreiras and cocoliches similarly faded from the public view.[34] Yet the theater culture we have seen on the rise continued expanding, with literally even greater representation. Between 1919 and 1921 a labor federation of theater workers formed in Argentina. And in the early 1920s, actors, impresarios, stagehands, and other "theater people" created their namesake political party, *Gente de Teatro*. Its candidate was the beloved theater and cinema persona Florencio Parravicini, who won a seat as councilman in the 1926 Buenos Aires municipal elections. Perhaps not surprisingly, Parravicini, like so many others, had gotten his big break two decades earlier with none other than José Podestá's company. We'll come back to Parravicini in a bit.

By the end of the first decade, then, the Creole drama phenomenon was a distant memory, overshadowed by a new entertainment landscape and leisure options. But its participants, from the actors to the audiences, followed these new preferences, and thus continued to feed into the formation of the region's theatergoing public. So, there is some sense of poetic or metaphorical continuity and indebtedness. The Creole drama legacy endured in many concrete forms, too, making the broad appeal of lo criollo one of the hallmarks of twentieth-century Rioplatense popular culture.

An Enduring Legacy

Except for a couple weeks in February, when carnival dances took over Montevideo's theaters, the first two months of 1910 offered plenty of opportunities to see the Creole spirit on display. Throughout January Pablo Podestá, who had begun his career in performance as a youthful acrobat, won over audiences as the lead actor in show after show at the Solís Theater. He (and his company) represented Creole threads in género chico plays by the acclaimed authors of the day. Podestá also staged a sainete rewrite of the Creole drama *Juan Cuello*. This adaptation thrilled theatergoers, in part because of its familiarity, and in part because this new version was *not* a Creole drama. What audiences and reviewers celebrated most, however, was the interpretation of Florencio Sánchez's *Barranca abajo*, or Downhill, which literally portrayed the downfall of older generations of native sons in the countryside. At the nearby Teatro Urquiza Florencio Parravicini—the same one who would later be elected as a Buenos Aires councilman—likewise drew full houses night after night. Some of his performances took up country themes in a subdued light, such as the Javier de Viana piece titled simply *Puro campo* (Pure Country), while others were comical portraits of urban life. And slightly farther away, a horse-taming show promised to be a "social highlight" not to be missed due partly to the presence of "many *good* families."[35]

There were no gaucho dramas of old during those months, but the influences were hard to miss. Just how enduring was the legacy of the Creole drama phenomenon, and where did it show up? During the first third of the century this legacy was visible in a range of prominent cultural practices, most notably theater. There were plenty of plays that took up nativist currents as central themes, so many that some scholars have written of a "nativist theater" system or genre developing during these years.[36] A very few examples of such plays, with telling titles, include *El último gaucho* (The Last Gaucho), *¡Al campo!* (To the Countryside), *Jesús Moreira*, and *San Juan Moreira*. There were also remakes of several Creole dramas in género chico forms, like *Juan Cuello, Martín Fierro*, and *Juan Moreira*, whose story in one form or another just could not be kept off stage.[37] These sorts of adaptations, which continued throughout the century, capitalized on audiences knowing at least the gist of story lines and on the history of prior success. Simultaneously, the promise of variation injected novelty into the mix and helped generate interest.[38]

There were also occasions during which circus groups and even the Creole drama headliners of previous years tried the greatest hits again.[39] José Podestá himself attempted to resurrect the spark of the phenomenon's golden years on several occasions following his transition to the theater. One of these was in 1916, which not only failed to draw spectators but also resulted in financial losses for the group.[40] The other attempt took place in 1925, corresponding to his fiftieth anniversary in show business and his swan song from stage life. Podestá decided to celebrate the moment with a run of Creole dramas in Buenos Aires, Montevideo, and La Plata, and this time the outcome was much more positive. In Buenos Aires he starred in 127 consecutive representations of *Juan Moreira* at the Hippodrome, which he characterized as "the most lucrative arrangement of my artistic career."[41]

Others also considered the farewell tour a success. In Buenos Aires the press seemed unanimous about the full houses and continuous applause *Juan Moreira* drew, and spoke of an "exhumation" of the distant dramas. Some of this enthusiasm shines in the private collection of Carlos Daws, whose library and objects representing all things Creole form the heart of the Museum of Popular Culture in Buenos Aires. Among the collection are albums full of press clippings from these years where we can perceive the amount of attention given to "the exhumation." According to one account, "the work of the Podestá company has been a resounding success, evidenced by the support the public has shown for the resurrection of gaucho dramas. For today's audiences the representation of these plays calls to mind the memories of the first demonstrations of our traditionalist, national theater." Another went on to proclaim, "Years have passed, but the memory of that Creole experience has not been erased." Other reviews were of a similar tenor. Neither the comical portrayals of Moreira at carnival, read one of these, nor the decadence characterizing a new mode of spectacle that took off in the 1920s—the *revista*, a comical act with scantily clad women—have "tarnished the memory of that exemplary man. Juan Moreira, like Christ, is immortal." At the Hippodrome there were so-called *Moreyrólogos* who knew all things Moreira. These specialists could answer questions about the mythical figure or set the record straight for those doubters.[42]

With this tailwind, the company took their shows one last time to Montevideo, and then to La Plata. At the final performance in Uruguay a group of local theater stars and several of the company's supporters presented José Podestá with an album containing letters of praise for his life onstage.[43] An author of one of these letters summed up their focus: "We

Figure 7.1. Carlos Daws (left) and friends going Creole, 1888. Daws was a prominent collector of Creole cultural goods and an advocate for the traditionalist movement (mentioned in chapter 5). Museo de Arte Popular José Hernández, Fondo Documental Carlos G. Daws, Album 4, 78.

cannot speak of the patria without mentioning Artigas, or national authors without summoning the bohemian genius of Florencio Sánchez; nor can we talk about national art without pronouncing, with deep admiration, the name of José Podestá."[44] Another stated, "Podestá has transcended the category of actor to represent a period in history."[45] Enrique García Velloso went even farther, writing in his memoirs that Podestá's work through the decades made possible the development of a cross-class theatergoing public for local companies. "No one," he wrote, "has lived a life in theater more intense, more novelesque, and more full of unexpected twists and turns than Pepe Podestá."[46] The actress Blanca Podestá likewise commented on the extended impact of her uncle José's contributions to the region's cultural life: "If *Juan Moreira* is the symbol of an era, so too is my uncle Pepe Podestá a symbol of a line of artists and an entire theatrical tradition."[47] By all accounts, Podestá embodied the spirit of crossing frontiers and encouraged those who attended his shows to do the same.

It seemed only fitting that José Podestá bid farewell to his life in performance with a final season of gaucho shows—his ticket into the business in the first place. Beyond the celebration of this personality, the number and success of the shows that year (1925) highlight the enduring ability of the Creole to bring people together.

Other cultural objects circulating in the first third of the century illustrate the growing intensity of the legacy as well. Recall from chapter 4 the scenes from Creole dramas, with short captions, that were distributed as collector's cards with a handful of tobacco products named after the iconic gauchos. Those who smoked Juan Cuello, Martín Fierro, or Juan Moreira cigarettes could acquire the entire set of images depicting the complete story. One can imagine the products for sale outside the Hippodrome as crowds arrived for the Podestá Company's last hoorah. Other cigarette brands deployed the Creole spirit in their names—Criollos, El Paisano (The Countryman), El Pingo (Trusty Steed)—and marketing material.[48] Reprints of Eduardo Gutiérrez's narratives continued to be hot commodities, too. In an interview with the book dealer Amadeo Tomassi, son of the sole official book publisher of Gutiérrez's work, Natalio Tomassi, he stated that more than a million copies of the narratives had been printed, and they continued selling.[49] A few years later, in 1928, a newspaper in Rosario proposed renaming a street to Juan Moreira. Like other "mythic caudillos," noted the paper, Moreira had defended principles of Argentine sovereignty.[50] The renaming initiative was ultimately rejected, but similar efforts to name streets after Moreira were later approved in cities such as Concordia and Comodoro Rivadavia in Argentina.

The enduring legacy of the Creole drama phenomenon also figured in new forms of communication and cultural exchange, for example film, which first appeared in the region at the turn of the century (1898 in Uruguay and 1900 in Argentina). Most of the early motion pictures lasted just a few minutes and had no entertainment value. They were newsreels that captured moments of daily life. This meant that, while novel, they did not attract sizeable crowds or become revenue generators until a new kind of narrative silent cinema developed in the 1910s. The first Argentine film of this sort was *The May Revolution*, which played at the Ateneo Theater in Buenos Aires in May 1909 (the Ateneo bookstore on Santa Fe Avenue now resides in the space of the old cinema). This film lasted less than four minutes, though it did follow a story.[51] The following year saw much more experimentation with film as entertainment. In that year the Italian immigrant and one of the pioneers of early Argentine cinema Mario Gallo adapted none other than *Juan Moreira* for film. A handful of similarly Creole-inflected films debuted around the same

Cuello roba á Manuela en el
Pico Blanco

JUAN MOREIRA

RIVADAVIA 1122

A   B

Figure 7.2. Scenes from the collectible card series appearing with the Juan Cuello and Juan Moreira cigarette brands. (A) Juan Cuello rescues his beloved Manuela and races away on his trusty horse, Pico Blanco; (B) The first card in a new *Juan Moreira* series. Key elements from the tale are pictured: Moreira's long knife, his loyal dog Cacique, a guitar, and stocks; (C) Moreira (right) and Sardetti convene with the justice of the peace over the debt issue; and (D) Moreira fleeing the law, looking back as he outpaces his pursuers. Note Cacique seated in front of him. Museo de Arte Popular José Hernández, Fondo Documental Carlos G. Daws, Album 20, 77–81.

C   D

moment, some taking Creole drama titles and following the same plots, such as *Nobleza Gaucha* and *Martín Fierro*. While there were close financial and artistic ties linking film production in Argentina to that of Uruguay, it was not until 1918 that an "Uruguayan" narrative film was produced.[52]

Most notable among these early silent films was *Nobleza Gaucha*, from 1915, which became Argentina's (and the region's) first box office hit. In a matter of months following the film's debut it earned back hundreds of times the production cost.[53] Screenplay writers and production companies saw a valuable business opportunity in the revival of the melodrama and Creole spirit of popular theater. Potential viewers were familiar with themes, titles, or characters of the films. These, in turn, drew on the collective repository of Creole patrimony as way of entertaining audiences eager to enjoy the new medium of cinema. The novelty of the medium likewise added a fresh reason to see a well-worn story. Quite simply, the coupling of mythical tales with modern technology was alluring. Moreover, the timing was simply "right." New marketing strategies were available to impresarios and production companies, and these strategies were deployed to call favorable attention to a variety of connected products. This was the case with *Nobleza Gaucha*. A catchy tango was written for the film, which helped spread the word, as did the production team's decision to sell the naming rights to a yerba mate distributor. Nobleza Gaucha remains one of the dozens of Creole-inspired yerba brands for sale in the region, and around the world.[54]

Nobleza Gaucha was just the beginning of the Creole drama's persistent presence on the silver screen.[55] In 1924 a new cinematic version of *Juan Moreira* was released with a slightly modified titled: *The Saga of the Gaucho Juan Moreira, or The Last Centaur*. This new film played the following year during the Podestá Company's run at the Hippodrome. Advertisements from that moment proclaimed it to be "the greatest, most magnificent National film." The saga was described as an "emotive film" that allowed moviegoers to "experience every aspect of a bygone epoch. Emotion, art, and grandiosity!"[56] Feelings were the heart of marketing nostalgia.

One final aspect of film in these years helps us to understand the complexity and depth of Creole drama influence, namely the casts of actors themselves. Perhaps not surprisingly, cinema enticed former circus and Creole drama luminaries. Some of these were also among the region's first movie stars or promoters of early cinema. Thus, the early silent movie, *El fusilamiento de Dorrego*, from 1910, was screened at both the Ateneo movie house and at the Anselmi circus. Blanca Podestá, daughter of Jerónimo, acted in the 1910 film *Camila O'Gorman*. Enrique Muiño, who got his start with José Podestá's company in 1906, became one of Argentina's iconic silent film personalities, making his first splash in the first cinematic adaptation of *Juan Moreira*, also in 1910. Mario Gallo produced, directed, or taped these films.[57] Celestino Petray, who had toured with the Podestá-Scotti Company and made cocoliche characters a sensation, was another Creole drama regular who made the jump to the new scene. He starred in the 1917 hit *Flor de Durazno*, along with the musical flame Carlos Gardel. Enrique García Velloso also got involved in film, writing screenplays that won praise in the press. José Podestá himself made his mark in Argentine cinema as well, playing the leading role in the 1917 adaptation of *Santos Vega*.[58] Other Podestá family members like Antonio and Pablo took to film, too. Finally, the songwriter and payador Alfredo Gobbi, who often toured with the Podestá-Scotti Company, likewise dabbled in cine.[59]

The number of cinemas or venues that doubled as such grew in both Argentina and Uruguay in the 1920s, pointing to a promising future for film. Toward the end of this decade the cost of movie tickets dropped, eventually becoming less expensive than theater tickets. One of the results of the changing economics of cinema was that movies not only improved their position among entertainment options but also began rivaling the theater for spectators.[60] In short, by 1930, film developed into a major form of entertainment in the region with several of its earliest successes based on the Creole.[61]

In-home audio recordings were another new form of cultural exchange where the legacy made waves. By the turn of the century, it was common to see advertisements for gramophones and phonographs in the local press. These often were promoted as providing "the theater in the home . . . For those who purchase a gramophone boredom is impossible. Be it at home, in the countryside, or at the beach, you can listen to the best operas, songs, military bands, orchestras, monologues, and so on, as often as you like, FREE."[62] Free, that is, once listeners purchased the audio discs. Tens of thousands of these, too, appeared for sale at more and more places throughout the 1900s. Some were imports, with recordings of concerts and musicians from Europe and the United States, though there was a burgeoning local recording industry, developed by some of the same innovators and investors who were involved in the world of cinema.[63] Consider the following publicity for one merchant's store. He offered a collection of "Discos Criollos": Creole airs by Juan de Nava and his son Arturo, both of whom had played with the Podestás; "national" zarzuela tunes; and recordings of the San Martín Theater

Figure 7.3. An advertisement for "Discos Criollos" to play at home. *Caras y Caretas,*
August 23, 1902, no. 203.

orchestra and local police bands, among other discs.[64] Just as critical as the
production of local recordings was the fact that consumers could, in theory,
enjoy these performances on their own time, in their own home. Over the
course of the first two decades of the twentieth century this theoretical possibility was transformed into a reality thanks to gradually declining prices of
new technology and the fact that by the mid-1910s the middle class in the
region was among the largest in Latin America. For them cultural consumption was central to class identity.[65]

What we see at this point with the enduring legacy of the Creole drama
phenomenon is an image of varying forms of popular culture and their
respective markets feeding off one another. Cinema found both inspiration
and acting talent in the theater scene. Popular music, which had also been a
staple at theatrical performances, became available to new audiences as the
sound accompaniment to film screenings and through gramophones. These
concentric circles of association allowed for continuous promotion of the

Creole legacy via different forms of popular culture. They had been a source of inspiration for new commercial opportunities such as the production of sheet music for mass distribution, which we glimpsed in chapter 6, and for tangos, which were being portrayed as "national" music in both Uruguay and Argentina toward the end of the 1910s. That connection of tango to nation passed largely through notions of rural roots and associations with folk music and dance at Creole dramas. It was no coincidence, then, that the tango singer Carlos Gardel, who would also have a film presence, gained momentum when some of his music featured in a 1915 performance of *Juan Moreira*.[66] Beginning in the 1920s, such overlaps in spheres of influence and consumers helped radio take to the air, which would transform yet again the ways in which people could interact with a range of popular modes of entertainment.

Like the initial years of cinema, radio of the 1920s was limited to a handful of outlets, with scarce programming and small audiences.[67] In Buenos Aires—the region's largest entertainment market—there were only eighteen channels by the end of the decade. Outside the capital ten channels were scattered around the country. Music (primarily tango) and some news coverage dominated the airwaves during this moment. Yet in the 1930s the scope for radio underwent a sweeping expansion. In Argentina the number of people listening to radio as part of live audiences and in the home increased exponentially, as did the number of radios in households, evidencing a clear "radiomanía." In fact, in the mid-1930s Argentina had the highest quantity of radios in Latin America (six hundred thousand), while more than one hundred thousand in Uruguay placed it third in the region. These quantities kept their upward climb, taking radio shows to the farthest corners of national life.[68]

It was during the decade of 1930, too, that the radio became a center of domestic life. Expanded programming brought live spectacles into the home. While the gramophone had allowed listeners to hear their favorite tunes "on demand" in the comfort of their homes, live shows on the radio linked people together in new and important ways. A case in point was the Montevideo station Radio Femenina that began broadcasting in 1935 and whose programs were created by women, for women. Its success inspired other stations on both sides of the river to produce content for women listeners.[69] Moreover, with a ratio of nearly one radio for every household in the capital cities of the Río de la Plata by the late 1930s, radio shows had incredible potential audience reach, and their entertaining programs got listeners talking. Most significant among this new mode of experiencing entertainment was radio theater, whose glory years lasted from the mid-1930s through roughly 1950.

Like the narratives of Eduardo Gutiérrez and so many others who took advantage of serialized publication in the late 1800s to create suspense or to keep revenues flowing, and similar to the more modern variant that most readers know as the *telenovela*, radio theater was based on episodes broadcast with regularity over the span of weeks or months. And like these other formats, radio theater employed melodrama to keep audiences tuning in episode after episode, huddled around their receiver. An early example of radio theater, *Chispazos de Tradición* (Sparks of Tradition), which ran on Radio Belgrano in Buenos Aires, was also one of the most widely followed in the region. The program dealt in Creole stories: unrequited love, gaucho heroes and their sweethearts, and questions of honor and revenge. Sound familiar? The *Chispazos* cast was not just a radio phenomenon. They took the show on tour, literally, performing in theaters and neighborhoods around the city and in the Argentine countryside.[70] While radio theater followed other types of stories unrelated to the Creole, *Chispazos* led to further productions that focused similarly on country themes, utilized gauchesque language, or attempted to incorporate sabor criollo as a pillar of their own success on the air. Thus, *Brochazos Camperos* (roughly Country strokes) in Uruguay followed on the heels of *Chispazos*. These radio theater shows utilized the Creole formula for a new medium.[71]

As with early silent film, there was significant overlap between those involved with the Creole theater world or touring circus groups and this new vibe of radio theater. Consider the trajectory of the Argentine Adolfo Marzorati, born in 1910. From his adolescence through his thirties he traveled around Argentina with different circus companies. One of these maintained a repertoire of some fifty plays, among which the Creole dramas were "the most well-received shows." At the age of forty he left the circus behind and joined a radio theater production in Rosario. Other men and women who made their living working with traveling circuses followed similar paths. Their repertoires were expansive, including many of the gaucho plays and sainetes mentioned above. And those who were active in the 1930s through the 1950s often ended their professional careers in radio theater.[72] Then there were "famous" figures whose stories became dramatic fodder in these circles in the same period. The gaucho Cubillos, for instance, entered the imagination of Mendoza's residents via a theatrical rendering of his life by a little-known circus company and a lesser-known author. Cubillos's story bounced from the circus theater to print and back before becoming a radio theater hit in the 1940s.[73] Similarly, the story of Martín Aquino (seen in chapter 4 as a case study for Creole getting out of hand) made the transition from print to theater to radio theater in Uruguay.

In addition to film, gramophones, and the radio, other modes of cultural exchange allowed lo criollo to loom large in the Rioplatense imagination. Folk festivals were critical in this regard. These grew in number and size as the interest in folklore surged in the 1920s and 1930s. Among the first of these festivals was the annual Semana Criolla (Creole Week) in Montevideo, held in Montevideo's Prado park in 1925 to coincide with centennial celebrations of Uruguayan independence. In Argentina popular and official support for folklore combined in the 1921 Encuesta Nacional de Folklore (National Survey of Folklore), a massive undertaking enlisting school teachers in the compilation of oral history, popular poetry, narratives, dance traditions, superstitions, music, and other folkways. In the subsequent two decades the folklore movement took off. For Oscar Chamosa, who studied closely the emergence of this movement in Argentina, the Creole spirit of the late 1800s and early 1900s was a precursor that constructed "archetypes of nationhood" that continued to flourish through folk festivals.[74] These festivals blended regional folkways with local arts and artisans, and competitions of the sort that characterized the Semana Criolla (horse taming, payadas, sortija, and so on). And like Semana Criolla, they and other festivals have continued to grow in duration and attract greater numbers of attendees, as a final glance in our epilogue shows.

This enduring legacy certainly puts a finer point on the story of the Creole drama phenomenon's downfall. There was no doubting the transformation of the entertainment market at the outset of the twentieth century. Spectators, investors, and performers all shifted their interests toward new arenas. These included formal theater options like sainetes and similar género chico formats, the new world of cinema, and, in subsequent decades, radio theater that offered cultural consumers chances to follow live shows from the comfort of home. Creole dramas and their heroes faded from this landscape, making only occasional return appearances in urban centers as time went on. Though smaller groups touring the countryside kept the plays in their repertoires into the 1930s and 1940s, they eventually lost steam among small-town audiences, too. The "best shows" in town had been overshadowed by the new shows in town. Still, their imprint seems indelible, most notably in the rise of a theatergoing culture that benefited so much from the rough-and-tumble plays, and in the persistent ubiquity of the Creole spirit. Downfall led to legacy, and that legacy was vibrant.

The meanings of that Creole drama legacy across time and geography come into sharper focus when set against the backdrop of comparative phenomena in hemispheric perspective. Let's turn to that setting now in our last act, which reveals how frontiers onstage set in motion the development of the region's modern popular culture. But first, we have to make a stop at the world's fair in Chicago.

Curtain

The now-famous Columbian Exposition of 1893 in Chicago—one of several eye-opening world's fairs of the time—revolved around the highly symbolic four hundredth anniversary of Columbus's arrival to the Americas. Almost thirty million ticket holders were introduced to a bustling Chicago, where industry was flourishing, architectural trends were born, and, among other novelties, attendees saw and even rode the new Ferris wheel for the first time.

Among the many monuments to conquest, discovery, and national destiny on display was the address "The Significance of the Frontier in American History" Frederick Jackson Turner delivered to the gathering of the American Historical Association. Turner linked the Columbian voyages of yesteryear to US westward expansion and highlighted the frontier as the defining force and metaphor of the nation's history. So defining and mythic did Turner's idea of the frontier become that he has remained a dominant figure in the story of US history's development as a discipline. His ideas have inspired generations of supporters and critics within the academy and permeated public life.[1]

Turner spoke of the frontier as "the meeting point between savagery and civilization." That was the perfect description for Buffalo Bill's Wild West show, which drew avid crowds just outside the fair grounds.[2] Bill's publicist ran with Turner's idea, utilizing the very words in show advertisements. These proclaimed Bill as the "ORIGINAL–LIVING HERO–LINK BETWEEN SAVAGERY AND CIVILIZAITON." Echoing the exposition's theme, the Wild West company stationery that season portrayed Columbus as the "first pioneer," while Bill was the "last," introducing spectators to the Western frontier, with bravery to match Columbus's treks across the Atlantic.[3]

The idea of the frontier embodying that clash between barbarism and civilization, and the frontiersman as the leading edge of a civilizing force, would remain at the center of the Wild West phenomenon in the following decades. In performances that year its most celebrated and successful star, the frontier man-turned-entrepreneur-and-actor Buffalo Bill, drew some six million spectators day in and day out to dazzling displays of brave native sons—that is, Bill and friends—triumphing over evil and standing taller than the "rough riders" he had assembled from around the world. Every moment of the encounter was geared to bring out the nativism embedded in the frontier motif of the show. Following a rendition of the "Star Spangled Banner," spectators watched Bill and company repulse a group of "marauding Indians" who attacked an emigrant train as it crossed the prairie, rescue a mail coach caught in a similar situation, and so on.[4] It was the frontier and the myth of national progress for show. And fairgoers ate it up.

The Creole Drama Phenomenon in Hemispheric Perspective

Nativist, nationalist, and regionalist inventions can be observed around the world. These ideological currents combine frequently with popular culture to great emotional appeal and, at times, commercial success. Though there are plenty of illustrations of this fact in the Americas and beyond, two of the best points of comparison with the Creole drama phenomenon we have followed throughout the book also combine threads of nationalism and show business, especially the circus, with popular culture and connections to cattle frontiers.[5] A brief look at these two nativist manifestations shows us why the Creole drama moment stands out not just for Argentines and Uruguayans but also within a broader, hemispheric perspective.

The first one of these examples developed in the late nineteenth-century United States, where there was also a parallel frontier onstage. Its most celebrated star was none other than William Cody, better known as Buffalo Bill, who had become the heart and soul of the Wild West Show around a decade before his breakout performances in Chicago. In contrast to many of his Creole drama counterparts, Cody was a man of the frontier whose life as a showman developed as a second career. He spent considerable time as a scout, guide, buffalo hunter, and soldier in the US Army before conquering his stage fright to become one of the most powerful and popular showmen well into the 1910s.

Cody was a master of connecting personal experience to collective imagination. In Joy Kasson's assessment, the awe of westward expansion was filtered through this one man's tales.[6] Early versions of these stories were frontier melodramas in which Cody starred with varying members of his theatrical combinations, as the bands were called, during the 1870s and early 1880s. Critics panned the performances, yet Cody's troupes gave one sold-out show after another. These were full of improvisation, but the main attraction was action: to see frontier men displaying some of their skill in what amounted to "animated dime novels."[7] Cody's big break came in 1883 with the invention of his model Wild West show, promoted as "America's National Entertainment." This new format capitalized on elements from the circus, the theater, and frontier sportsmanship to present a national story.[8]

For the next three and a half decades Cody captivated audiences nationally and internationally. Spectators ranged from those who saved for months to purchase tickets, to European royalty who enjoyed private performances.[9] According to Kasson, the show set audiences on the edge of their seats at the same time that it "reassured them that the rapidly modernizing world was a safe and stable place. . . . Its reliance on a superstar performer whose personal presence became identified with the show itself, made it the harbinger of the modern entertainment spectacle."[10] As Wild West shows marketed their authentic character, they also invented and performed tradition, transformed the past into a sort of future destiny, and bound the personal exploits of heroes to collective identity and interpretations of national history.[11]

If these features of Wild West shows sound familiar, it is because they resemble many characteristics of the Creole drama phenomenon. Both spectacles staged the frontier (or frontiers). Likewise, both Creole dramas and Wild West shows aimed to depict collective history through glorified stories of individuals, dramatizations of pivotal moments in nation formation, or portraits illustrating the climate of the times. This connection to local and national history was vital to these shows' ability to channel notions of tradition. Both entertainment movements derived from stories that followed a similar trajectory: oral history put into print either in popular verse or serialized narratives, which was transformed into dramatic representation before jumping to other media. Moreover, Creole drama authors and performers were vaguely aware of Buffalo Bill's activities and success. José Podestá mentioned Cody in his memoirs, while the hemispheric flows of US circus families to South America likely facilitated more familiarity with the Wild West phenomenon.[12] Movement of families and entertainment news seemed to flow almost exclusively from North to South during this period, though there were occasional exceptions. Rioplatense entertainers, for instance, joined US groups like the Barnum and Bailey Circus to tour throughout the United States and Europe.[13] And Cody himself incorporated gauchos into his shows from time to time under the rubric of "rough riders of the world," though they were disconnected from their Creole drama contexts.

For all the similarities, there were also marked differences between these phenomena. Buffalo Bill's Wild West shows brought the frontier to life in part through the extraction of its inhabitants who ended up onstage. These characters crept into the collective imagination as representative of the countryside they had left behind. Thus, in contrast to the development of Creole dramas, Indians reluctantly participated in melodramas and Wild West shows, usually in violent battles against the "more civilized" white men, who invariably vanquished their adversaries. While the first Creole dramas had their share of clashes between outsiders (often immigrants) and locals, they did not engage in Wild West–style racially charged contests between demographic groups that always ended with Progress on top.

Another significant distinction was the fact that despite the Wild West's tremendous success across the United States and in Europe, the movement did not inspire the creation of membership clubs, like the Creole societies that formed, to allow people to experience the West beyond performance venues. Millions from San Francisco to New York flocked to see the Wild West. But they returned to their lives once the curtain fell, at most with some romantic notions of the West as the space where the natural beauty of the United States was preserved, where modes of life were more pure than those in the cities out East.[14] Others participated in groups or activities that allowed them to "play Indian."[15] Richard Slatta, who has studied cowboys across the Americas, suggests that most immigrants to the United States in the late 1800s remained in the northeast or occasionally ventured farther West to pursue agricultural opportunities in the mid-West, where they were far removed both ideologically and geographically from the frontier. Immigrants did not identify with the West or life on the frontier as they did in Argentina and Uruguay.[16]

Just south of the US border, another cowboy-like figure has long dominated the popular imagination, embodying aspects of Mexican identity and often serving as the national archetype: the *charro*. Like the gaucho, the charro has roots in rural realities and work patterns of the Mexican countryside, most notably those related to cattle ranching. In contrast to Mexico's more rustic *vaqueros*, who, like gauchos, were primarily ranch hands, charros were often associated with the mannerisms and appearance of land-owning elites, though they were not necessarily from the upper classes themselves.[17] The typical depiction of the charro shows him decked out in spurs, fancy clothing, and hat, and gifted with song (think of mariachi groups). The charro symbolized varieties of Mexican masculinity connected to rurality: dominance over animals as well as other men; celebration of amorous exploits; dexterity on horseback. Christopher Conway writes that the charro "is arguably the most universally recognized emblem of Mexican identity around the world"; he's colorful and screams macho.[18] The charro's ascent to national icon was underway in the late 1800s, throttled by protagonists in novels and mimicked by real-life bandits and police forces alike, with the biggest boost coming in the twentieth century after the end to the military confrontations of the Mexican Revolution around 1920. Thanks to film, music, and comics, as well as official state and federal support for organizations that promoted activities related to horse taming, bull riding, and similar rural pastimes, the nostalgic version of the charro as the antimodern folk hero took flight.[19]

As with the Wild West shows, we can see points in common between Creole drama heroes and their Mexican counterparts. The antimodern sentiment that contributed to the rise of the charro resembled that in the Río de la Plata, as did his embodiment of virility. Likewise, both the gaucho and charro myths benefited from twentieth-century mass media dissemination, prolonging and strengthening their relationship to popular culture as well as ideological currents along the political spectrum.

There are differences, nonetheless. Despite the circulation of charro-like men and their characters in nineteenth-century Mexican literature, the charro's position as a cherished figure was a post–Mexican Revolution development. Charros did not attract attention at the theater or circus either, though there was a lively circus and theater scene throughout Mexico.[20] Charro culture faced much competition, moreover, from other prominent cultural icons, such as the above-mentioned vaqueros (more specific to northern Mexico) or the cult of the Virgin of Guadalupe. While Creole dramas and their legacy shared the stage with other modes of popular culture like sainetes, tango, and carnival, competition among these was less intense. And as we have seen in several chapters, influence and inspiration crossed freely among these different expressions of popular culture in the Río de la Plata.

While all of these nativist inventions pose the nostalgic cool of country— and just as often, the romantic myth of wilderness—against the experiences of urbanization and modernization, the Creole drama phenomenon is singular when seen against this hemispheric backdrop. This singularity owes to its ramifications beginning in the late 1800s, the more than century-long market of cultural goods it gave rise to, and the profound and widespread impact that stories of gaucho toughs have had across media, time, class, and race. Quite simply, the countryside onstage throughout the Río de la Plata catalyzed a new vein of regional popular culture whose scale and intensity we can't observe elsewhere.

Creole Roots of Modern Popular Culture

Prior to the zenith of Creole dramas in the 1880s and 1890s, there were, as we have seen, existing strands of popular culture. These included the social world of entertainment and the performance circuit hemispheric travelers forged, as well as partisan poetry written in voices of the countryside and read collectively in the 1830s and 1840s, folk dances, and civic festivities. But performances of frontier life fueled a series of definitive turning points. The first of these transformations was visible in what motivated the region's inhabitants to go out and the relationships they had with entertainment options. Another became clear in the ways in which people associated and socialized. The types and quantities of cultural goods available at the turn of the century characterized a third inflection point.

These changes together led to a decidedly modern strain of popular culture and influenced the rhythms of the region's incipient cultural marketplace, along with the industries that participated in its growth. One of the outcomes was the spread of lo criollo as a hallmark of regional cultural identity. The Creole drama phenomenon's rise and fall had extensive ramifications across the entertainment industry and sparked the creation of Creole-infused products. The plays themselves offered new spaces for socializing, while a sense of Creole heritage was central to others. These places where the Creole was a centerpiece of social interaction included the hundreds of Creole societies that formed, the fancy dance halls where country dance steps became fashionable (owing to their reception onstage), and celebrations like carnival, where costumes, music, and language seemed to flow straight from the staging of frontiers. There was no getting around it: Creole dramas inspired people to go out with greater frequency. Even with the end of this historical phenomenon around 1900, a theatergoing public continued to expand along with the enduring legacy of sabor criollo. That lingering power of Creole identity in nations whose outward projection and self-image throughout the twentieth century were predominantly European (more so, arguably, than anywhere else in Latin America) was yet another testament to the Creole drama's contributions long after the campfire smoke, clash of knife fights, melodramatic stories of gaucho legends, and thunder of horse hooves had faded from the region's entertainment experience.

Around the turn of the twentieth century, frontiers onstage had competitors among the other forms of popular culture that were beginning to attract crowds and consumers. Zarzuelas and other theatrical formats outnumbered Creole dramas and drew larger audiences. Yet the protagonists of those more numerous shows were unremarkable. They did not make it into the collective memory of the region like Juan Moreira or Martín Fierro, Santos Vega or Juan Cuello. Nor did zarzuela plots or characters appear on collectible cards or as cigarette brand names, or stir flurries of adaptations over decades. Readers will remember sainetes that enjoyed long marquee runs, with high numbers of productions through the 1930s. Some of these returned to the spotlight from time to time afterward, too.[21] But like zarzuelas, the high numbers of sainetes did not translate into the large-scale movement of stories or protagonists from one medium to another. Crowds across class lines were also drawn in increasing numbers to another form of entertainment that had deep, informal roots in the region and that, beginning in the 1920s, enjoyed a much more formal status: horse racing.[22]

Other turn-of-the-century indices of popular culture on the rise included print media and carnival, where gaucho heroes, cocoliches, and urban figures were the life of the party. Throughout the twentieth century, carnival expanded its claim as a national festival in Uruguay.[23] Carnival in Argentina faced the opposite fate: the presence of festivities and their ability to attract participants lost ground quickly throughout the 1910s, and in subsequent decades carnival no longer occupied any significant place in the Argentine collective imaginary. But even considering the widespread appeal carnival activities had in the region around 1900, and though performers rehearsed throughout the year, the festival brought people together only for a short span each February. The region's rapidly growing diversity of print media during the 1910s and 1920s, meanwhile, connected rapidly mounting numbers of readers in more private ways. Illustrated magazines like *Caras y Caretas*, *PBT*, *Rojo y Blanco*, and *La Semana*, all of which dealt in humor, current events, and cultural and political commentary, even entered the realm of mass production and networks of mass distribution. Large-scale circulation was similar for pamphlets with gauchesque verses or narratives, and inexpensive book series published by major newspaper presses.[24]

Likewise, tango melodies and musicians made their mark on the region's cultural imagination in this period. Tango imbued the theater- and movie-going experience of the 1910s and 1920s, with live bands playing prior to the start of shows or along with the action onstage or on the screen. The music also became a staple of café life in bustling cities. A new generation of popular singers, including payadores and up-and-coming tango greats like Carlos Gardel, emerged on the scene at that moment and blended rural and urban themes in song. In the 1920s there was a veritable tango mania that gathered strength following the successful journeys of the music to Paris and New York during the previous decade. *Milongas*, where eager tango dancers gathered to dance the night away, formed across the region as important places for people to socialize. But even with the rise in tango's popularity, and although the modern city would be the source of the region's future popular culture icons, the countryside remained a dominant prism through which to express varieties of urban life, at least through the first decades of the new century.[25] Perhaps this could only be expected, as rapid urbanization spawned wistful evocations of rural tranquility.

In this setting of modern popular culture in the Río de la Plata, the Creole drama phenomenon not only preceded but also generated subsequent activities and products. Recall that dramas were early sites of tango performances; that Creole characters inspired celebrated carnival costumes and figures as well as outlines for the short plays that would become staple performances in the 1910s and beyond; that the cinema industry took up gaucho greats; and that the dramatic stories were refashioned, adapted, and modified for radio theater in the 1930s and 1940s. The development of the theatergoing public, with roots in the Creole drama heyday, exhibited the centrality of entertainment (especially theatrical spectacle and theatricality) to the region's modern popular culture.

The main audiences for Creole dramas (and the theatergoing public that grew from them) were inhabitants of urban areas up and down the Río de la Plata estuary, where the majority of people lived. Shows did make it farther inland, but the performance circuit was closely linked to population distribution and river transportation. It was not that urban performers faced a lack of interest when they put on their gaucho hits for people in the countryside; there were plenty of instances where "real" gauchos went to see the staged ones in the interior and left the shows riveted. But the economic incentives for performers and impresarios were simply greater where potential audiences were larger and where companies could stage longer show runs. The result was both curious and complex: country themes and concerns galvanized the attention of spectators as well as the movers and shakers of the entertainment marketplace predominantly in cities that were eager to set themselves apart from the mainly rural interior.

Some of the most significant tensions of the region's emergent popular culture, which have consequently been at the core of themes running throughout this book, present similar ironies. Consider the following examples: antimodern currents gaining prominence in places that aspired to be synonymous with modern progress; fiction, exaggeration, or pure invention standing in for something truly authentic; and immigrants and their descendants creating reference points of Argentine and Uruguayan identity, rooted in Creoleness. We can also contrast the relatively small geographic area where production and consumption of Creole activities and objects were most intense—again, the littoral, or areas close to the Río de la Plata—with the claims these made to national and transnational representation and reach.

While the very concept of the frontier as something that separates distinct moments, communities, or phenomena is built into these tensions, the frequent combination of polar opposites in the making of popular culture suggests that frontiers were often bridged, or that they might (against expectations) cease to be such stark lines of division. How else did circus families of Italian descent gain a monopoly on gaucho dramas? Wasn't the very presence of these plays in the finest opera houses an illustration that the frontier had settled in the city without too much opposition, for a time a least? Didn't the movement of entertainers and cultural goods throughout the region exemplify a constant crossing of geographic frontiers, where the age-old city/countryside divide seemed less of a barrier?

There were obviously multiple frontiers throughout the years we've covered. One corresponded to the geographical dividing line that separated more densely populated areas and settlements from rural life and the country. That metaphor of the countryside as frontier is the one that made such a splash onstage and off. There was the frontier space, too, that was wrapped up in the process of urbanization, where the outskirts of the region's core cities were both spatially and symbolically frontierlike. They were not rural, but they were not orderly like new city centers, either. They had rough edges and rough characters. Economic frontiers were of a different register and perhaps more difficult to overcome. There were the rags-to-riches successes of Creole drama stars, but measuring similar upward mobility for theater-goers and those who consumed products conveying the Creole spirit is more difficult. What was clear beyond a doubt was that when rural migrants, immigrant dockworkers, or day laborers mingled with lawyers, doctors, or white-collar employees at Creole dramas, often cheering, jeering, and laughing in unison, lines of economic difference were breached. Another frontier was temporal and cultural. This one corresponded to the historical moment in the late 1800s and early twentieth century when the market for cultural goods and their enjoyment underwent a profound transformation that resulted in the emergence of modern popular culture in the region. The historical phenomenon of Creole dramas and their ramifications were at the center of that transformative moment.

Among all the frontiers that have come into focus throughout this book, that we have seen onstage, or that we have crossed, this frontier of modern popular culture has been simultaneously perhaps the most intangible, yet the most concrete and omnipresent. How so? Prior to the 1880s and 1890s there were many activities that we have identified as forms of popular culture. Yet it was precisely the Creole drama phenomenon that established a dividing line after which everything changed. This frontier was intangible in a couple respects. One, it advanced over an extended period in the 1880s and 1890s, with greater or lesser manifestations of intensity, rather than at a precise moment during these years. Two, while we can map the general geography of this cultural frontier in the region, it was diffuse, drawn in big cities and small towns alike, and extended its reaches far beyond its primary area of concentration along the Río de la Plata estuary. Last, we might point to how the very experience of the Creole drama phenomenon enveloped its participants in a wave of excitement that they could have understood as innovative, but without being able to necessarily pinpoint why. Our hindsight affords us a much sharper perspective in this regard. At the same time, the very ubiquity of this cultural experience, the proliferation of gaucho dramas, the movement of these stories to spheres beyond the circus and the theater, and the countryside onstage as a source for new cultural icons throughout the twentieth century, also gave this frontier an unmistakable concreteness in daily life.

We have devoted most of our attention throughout the book to the Creole drama phenomenon's rise and fall at the center of this emerging popular culture. Yet the scale of the phenomenon's bearing on activities up to the present day is also significant and worth noting.

Creole societies across Argentina, Brazil, and Uruguay still conjure mythical powers of tradition more than a century after their creation. In Brazil the state government of Rio Grande do Sul began to provide official support for the gaúcho traditionalist movement (GTM) in 1974. As a result, the GTM saw substantial growth in the numbers of clubs and members during the last third of the century. By the early 2000s there were more than 1,500 centers in Rio Grande do Sul alone, and more than 1,000 throughout other Brazilian states, claiming to have some two million regular participants.[26] The movement in Argentina grew similarly, with the number of Creole societies surging in the 1980s after the foundation of the Argentine Gaucho Confederation.[27] Like their predecessors, these took meaningful names, such as the Centro Martín Fierro and the Centro Gauchito Gil.[28] And in Uruguay Creole societies expanded their memberships and intersection with public life. *Semana Criolla*, which became an annual festival soon after its 1925 debut and remains a well-attended event, was an early example of this public celebration of the Creole, with participation of Creole club members.[29] It was in the mid-1920s, too, that Elías Regules lent his support to a monument to the gaucho in downtown Montevideo, where it still presides over a major intersection next to the town hall. Inaugurated in 1927, its base features scenes of rural work and country life as well as a tribute to tradition, depicting an elderly gaucho sharing his wisdom with a younger one. More recently, hundreds of the seven hundred or so Uruguayan Creole societies have participated in the *Fiesta de la Patria Gaucha* in the city of Tacuarembó.[30] This fiesta shares much in common with Semana Criolla, including its week-long duration. Members young and old take part in a parade showing off their gaucho finery and the fancy footsteps of their horses, and in music, cooking, and crafts competitions.[31] The significance of the fiesta's name is not lost on any participant. On each day, speakers celebrate the gaucho history of the nation (the patria gaucha) with taglines similar to those Regules uttered at the outset of the twentieth century in the annual addresses to his Creole society.

For its part, the Sociedad Criolla has continued to adapt. In 1944 the club, newly minted the Sociedad Criolla Elías Regules, moved to a more expansive location on the eastern edge of Montevideo.[32] In 1994 the Sociedad completed work on the re-creation of a nineteenth-century Uruguayan pueblo with a replica of a *pulpería*, a school house, and a "Creole Chapel," where *misas criollas,* or masses, conducted with traditional instrumentation that became immensely popular thanks to the Argentine Ariel Ramírez's folk music group of the 1960s and 1970s, have enthralled listeners. Since the inauguration of this pueblo the club has been a regular destination for school field trips, and a venue for weddings, parties, and corporate events, still blending rural tradition with modern life.[33]

The Creole spirit has also persisted at a range of festivals across the region and appeared in theatrical productions over the past three decades.[34] Consider the Teatro de la Libertad, an experimental theater group in Argentina that started performing in the 1980s. Its first show was *Juan Moreira.* They staged the show some four hundred times in 1984 and 1985, just as Argentines were emerging from nearly a decade of authoritarian rule. Remember that one of the main threads of the play revolved around rights of citizenship and their abuse by corrupt representatives of the state. The choice of *Juan Moreira* as their debut play at that specific moment, then, was especially significant. The publicity for the first performance of Teatro de la Libertad at a 1984 theater festival described the group as "following in the steps of our cherished itinerant actors." The ad went on to remark that in nonconventional performance spaces (squares, street corners, galleries of shops) the company "tried to resuscitate the spirit and language of the classic Creole Circus, the style of those memorable radio theater casts from the 1940s, and pretty much every element related to our theatrical roots." Reviewers praised the shows for "rescuing Moreira and the circus," deemed inseparable from collective memory. In September 1984 the Argentine president attended one of the performances of *Juan Moreira* in Neuquén, reminiscent of the days in the late 1800s when politicians felt it necessary to attend Creole dramas.[35] Modified versions of these dramas have continued to return on occasion to theaters, festivals, and puppet theater productions throughout the region.[36]

Finally, film has fed off of and promoted these narratives, too. Following the 1924 release of the cinematic hit *The Saga of the Gaucho Juan Moreira,* subsequent *Moreira* films were produced throughout the twentieth century, with the last one opening in 1973. Like *Juan Moreira, Martín Fierro* was remade for the movies at least five times. The most recent iteration was a cartoon animation in 2007 based on the drawings of the legendary comic illustrator Roberto Fontanarrosa. Both *Fierro* and *Moreira* also circulated as telenovelas, where viewers, like the serialized fiction readers a hundred years earlier, were kept in suspense from episode to episode.[37]

The sample of activities evidencing the running legacy of the Creole drama phenomenon could go on, but let's end it by pointing to one last example: the use of the term "Creole Circus" to describe the variety show *Showmatch* (a sort of combination of *Dancing with the Stars* and the Univisión classic *Sábado Gigante*), which has had one of the largest television viewerships in Argentina and Uruguay since the early 2000s.[38] While *Showmatch* rarely has anything to do with rural life, it is centered around dance, jokes, the occasional extravagant act, and plot lines oozing melodrama. Moreover, it prides itself on representing Rioplatense—or we could say Creole—humor and sensibility, to the point that the show continually supplies regional cultural reference points. This representative character gives even the most recent invocations of the Creole Circus a hint of its past cross-class pull.

A Last Word

The Creole drama phenomenon staged the frontier between old and new strains of the region's popular culture and catalyzed elements that would dominate its future. Among these elements we can highlight a series of thematic threads and story lines that would return over and over again, in different media; the ways and frequencies with which people interacted with popular culture; the variety of and expanded access to cultural marketplaces; and the evolution of industries that produced (and ideally profited from) cultural goods. The objects themselves would vary over time. Yet the relationships between people and cultural goods, and the social and cultural capital these wielded, gained in strength and constancy thanks to the countryside onstage.

Not surprisingly, this modern popular culture was linked to notions of modern life that set in around 1900, precisely as antimodern heroes reached their highpoint. Argentines and Uruguayans witnessed the transformation of their world through the global integration of their local economies, the establishment of modern public educational systems, and the urge to benefit from the latest trends from abroad in fashion, urban design, ways of thought, medicine, and so on. Throughout such transformations Creole drama heroes saw their stars rise. The novelty of modern life implied crossing boundaries and leaving behind customs and habits that were, at the very least, known behaviors. Antimodern heroes provided anchor points to the past or those behaviors. References were romantic, idealized, or simply disconnected from reality. But they were effective during a moment of crossing the frontier into the modern world.

The emotive and commercial power of the region's antimodern heroes certainly changed over the twentieth century. Yet these heroes, like the idea of the frontier separating urban metropolises from the lilt of country life beyond, retain their presence among the landscape of regional cultural icons. That understanding of the frontier, like in the United States, was padded with perceptions of authenticity, nostalgia, and community, and it is one that continues to roam the minds of Argentines and Uruguayans. This much is evident from just about any copy of *Juan Moreira* or *Martín Fierro*, the latter of which is available in a variety of collector's editions, some with a cow-hide cover (hair still attached) enhancing its Creole credentials. Those Creole roots and their link to the countryside as frontier are part of the backstory to schoolchildren in small towns and big cities who rehearse the pericón for their annual talent shows; they were omnipresent in the payadas of the 1890s and the 1990s; and they inform the Creole festivals that attract hundreds of thousands annually.

These school children, contemporary payadores, and festival attendees are more recent illustrations of what Samuel Blixen wrote about the region's theatergoing public in the early 1900s. They had a "predilection for the 'Creole genre,'" readers may recall, in part because of the patriotic overtones associated with staging frontiers, and in part because of the "genre's" connections to the meanings of collective experience. Audience preferences and the commercial success of the phenomenon led to another of Blixen's observations that is relevant to understanding the force staging frontiers had—and *still* has—on the region's modern popular culture. He spoke of such dramas and the theatrical currents they influenced as having achieved a "life of their own." [39] They fed off each other and their box office success. If Blixen had lived to see the film and radio industries that likewise staged frontiers, or other arenas of the enduring Creole legacy, he would have likely written excitedly about these circles of influence. Perhaps he would have shared Carlos Olivera's enthusiasm, who proclaimed, "It all started at the circus." [40] And then in proper dramatic fashion he would have ended the point with one last word: "Curtain."

Notes

Introduction

1. Poster for the March 7, 1892, performance of *Juan Moreira*, INET.
2. Levine, "The Folklore of Industrial Society: Popular Culture and Its Audiences," 1369–99.
3. Rossi, *Teatro nacional rioplatense*, 51.
4. Levine, *Highbrow/Lowbrow*, 9.
5. Levine, "The Folklore of Industrial Society," 1392.
6. Pérez Petit, "Defensa del drama criollo," 251–53.

Chapter 1

1. Sánchez de Thompson, *Intimidad y política: diario, cartas y recuerdos*, 125; Anonymous, *A Five Years' Residence in Buenos Ayres*, 22–24; Klein, *El actor en el Río de la Plata*, 1:11–33.
2. Caldcleugh, *Travels in South America during the Years 1819–20–21*, 1:122–23.
3. De María, "Cantando y riendo corrijo las costumbres," 1:218; Hidalgo, *Obra completa*, 141–53.
4. De Martínez, *El teatro en el Uruguay en el siglo XIX*, 10, 31–34. As Victor Turner would have it, this escape via performance helped render meaning from daily experience; forms of popular spectacle provided "an explanation of life itself." See Turner, *From Ritual to Theater*, 13.
5. The decision to make Buenos Aires the viceregal center hinged in part on the hope of legitimizing—and thus profiting from—the contraband trade in hides and jerked beef that was on the rise, and in exercising greater oversight over the flow of goods and capital to and from the mining zones of Upper Peru. Making a strong push to claim this peripheral area of the empire for Spain, long disputed

with Portugal in wars over the town of Colonia del Sacramento and the dividing line of the empires, was also at play.

6. Johnson, *Workshop of Revolution*, 28–30, 19.

7. See Johnson, *Workshop of Revolution*, 28–50, on the demographic makeup of the city during the years 1780–1810. For a more detailed exploration of the black population in the city, see Andrews, *The Afro-Argentines of Buenos Aires, 1800–1900*.

8. See Anonymous, *A Five Years' Residence*, 16–17; Johnson, *Workshop of Revolution*, 21, 17–28, for a more detailed portrait of the cityscape in the late 1700s.

9. See Brackenridge, *Voyage to Buenos Ayres Performed in the Years 1817 and 1818*, 58–61.

10. Caldcleugh, *Travels in South America*, 139.

11. Brackenridge, *Voyage to Buenos Ayres*, 57.

12. Taullard, *Historia de nuestros viejos teatros*, 15–16.

13. Pollero, "Historia demográfica de Montevideo y su campaña (1757–1860)."

14. Andrews, *Blackness in the White Nation*, 23–24.

15. The English traveler Thomas Falkner commented on the benefits of the port in his early *Description of Patagonia, and the Adjoining Parts of South America*, 64–65.

16. Davie, *Letters from Paraguay*, 31.

17. Brackenridge, *Voyage to Buenos Ayres*, 44–48.

18. López Cantos, *Juegos, fiestas y diversiones en la América española*, 19–78.

19. I base this description in part on López Cantos, *Juegos, fiestas y diversiones en la América española*; Torre Revello, *Del Montevideo del siglo XVIII: fiestas y costumbres*, 38; and Garavaglia, "El *teatro del poder*: ceremonias, tensiones y conflictos en el estado colonial," 7–30.

20. Irigoyen, "La ciudad como escenario: poder y representación hasta 1830," 98–103; López Cantos, *Juegos*, 26–28.

21. Documentary appendices in Torre Revello, *Del Montevideo del siglo XVIII*, 72.

22. Irigoyen, "La ciudad como escenario," 99; see especially Sansone de Martínez, *El teatro en el Uruguay en el siglo XIX*, 407–25.

23. De María, *Montevideo antiguo*, 2:113–14.

24. Sansone, *El teatro en el Uruguay*, 37–39; Mirza, "Para una revisión de la historia del teatro uruguayo: desde los orígenes hasta 1900," 180–81.

25. On bullfights in the Banda Oriental, see De María, *Montevideo Antiguo*, 1:41–44.

26. Viqueira Albán, *Propriety and Permissiveness in Bourbon Mexico*, 11–26; see also Garavaglia, "El *teatro del poder*," 8.

27. Sánchez de Thompson, "Madame Mendeville Recalls Viceregal Buenos Aires," 23.

28. Sánchez de Thompson, "Madame Mendeville," 23.

29. Sánchez de Thompson, "Madame Mendeville," 25–26.

30. Torre Revello, *Del Montevideo del siglo XVIII*, 42.

31. Documentary appendices in Torre Revello, *Del Montevideo del siglo XVIII*, 73–74.

32. Davie, *Letters from Paraguay*, vi.

33. Davie, *Letters from Paraguay*, 74–80.

34. Davie, *Letters from Paraguay*, 81.

35. Davie, *Letters from Paraguay*, 83.

36. Viqueira Albán, *Propriety and Permissiveness*, 83.

37. Wilde, *Buenos Aires desde setenta años atrás*, 192, 252, 272.

38. Torre Revello, *Del Montevideo del siglo XVIII*, 15, 46–48; De María, *Montevideo antiguo*, 2:113–14.

39. Anonymous, *A Five Years' Residence*, 79–80.

40. There are several excellent recent studies on black nations in colonial and early independent Buenos Aires and Montevideo. See Borucki, *From Shipmates to Soldiers*, in particular chapters 1, 5, and 6; Andrews, *Blackness in the White Nation*; Andrews, *The Afro-Argentines of Buenos Aires, 1800–1900*; Chamosa, "'To Honor the Ashes of Their Forebears'"; and Chasteen, "Black Kings, Blackface Carnival, and Nineteenth-Century Origins of the Tango."

41. De María, *Montevideo antiguo*, 1:277, 280–81; Andrews, *Blackness in the White Nation*, 24–28.

42. Qtd. in Wilde, *Buenos Aires desde setenta años atrás*, 43.

43. Planos del Teatro San Felipe, carpeta 5, cubierta C, Q.6, Bandeja 3; planos 1, 2, 3, 4, 5, 7, 8, MHN Casa Lavalleja. Maps of both cities from this period reveal clues about how inhabitants interacted with the evolving physical geography of city centers.

44. De María, *Montevideo antiguo*, 2:114.

45. See Acree Jr., *Everyday Reading*, 32–42; Burucúa and Campagne, "Mitos y simbologías nacionales en los países del cono sur," 433–74.

46. Beruti, *Memorias curiosas*, 213; Garavaglia, *Construir el estado e inventar la nación*, 33–36.

47. Torre Revello, *Del Montevideo del siglo XVIII*, 56–59.

48. De María, *Montevideo antiguo*, 1:220–22.

49. Anonymous, *A Five Years' Residence*, 102; Brackenridge, *Voyage to Buenos Ayres*, 88, makes a similar observation.

50. See Trigo, "Ideología y política en el teatro gauchesco (primitivo)," 45–56, on the notion of a popular theater cycle comprising "teatro gauchesco primitivo."

51. Ghiano, *Teatro gauchesco primitivo*, 29–30.

52. See Ghiano, *Teatro gauchesco primitivo*, for the text of *Las bodas*; Anonymous, "El valiente fanfarrón y criollo socarrón o El gaucho," 201–62.

53. Seibel, "Prólogo" to *Antología de obras de teatro argentino*, 15–16; Klein, *El actor en el Río de la Plata*, 1:67; Mirza, "Para una revisión"; Mirza, "Los orígenes coloniales de la escena oriental," 307–18; Castagnino, *Esquema de la literatura dramática argentina (1717-1949)*, 34–35.

54. Ghiano, *Teatro gauchesco primitivo*, 71.

55. Ghiano, *Teatro gauchesco primitivo*, 72–73.

56. See Mirza, "Para una revisión"; Anonymous, *Descripción de las fiestas cívicas*.

57. Beruti, *Memorias curiosas*, 168–69.

58. Anonymous, *Relación de las fiestas mayas de Buenos Aires en el presente año de 1813*, 1.

59. Anonymous, *Relación de las fiestas mayas*, 1–2.

60. Beruti, *Memorias curiosas*, 233–34.

61. De María, *Montevideo antiguo*, 1:120–21; Anonymous, *Descripción de las fiestas cívicas*; Acree, *Everyday Reading*, 27–32.

62. Brackenridge, *Voyage to Buenos Ayres*, 88–89.

63. Beruti, *Memorias curiosas*, 368–69.

64. De María, *Montevideo antiguo*, 2:341–56, 360–62; Acree, *Everyday Reading*, 38–42.

65. Brackenridge, *Voyage to Buenos Ayres*, 69.

66. Beruti, *Memorias curiosas*, 435–39.

67. Beruti, *Memorias curiosas*, 540–41; Johnson, "Why Dead Bodies Talk: An Introduction," 1–26.

68. Garavaglia, *Construir el estado*, 12–13.

69. See Myers, "Una revolución en las costumbres: las nuevas formas de sociabilidad de la elite porteña, 1800–1860," 111–45; Barrán, Caetano, and Porzecanski, eds., *Historia de la vida privada en el Uruguay*, vol. 1; Caldcleugh, *Travels in South America*, writes that tertulias are central to social happiness in Buenos Aires, especially among the more well-to-do denizens (170).

70. Hidalgo, *Obra completa*, 145–49.

71. Anonymous, *A Five Years' Residence*, 135.

72. Anonymous, *Fiestas mayas celebradas por el ejército republicano en el Cerro Largo*, 2–7.

73. Hinchliff, *South American Sketches, or A Visit to Rio Janeiro, The Organ Mountains, La Plata, and the Paraná*, 85–87.

74. Klein, *El actor en el Río de la Plata*, 1:73; Bosch, "Viejos circos porteños," 157–61.

75. Klein, *El actor en el Río de la Plata*, 1:73–77; Castagnino, *El circo criollo*, 16; Monzón, "El teatro porteño en el histórico año de la Revolución de Mayo," 3–12.

76. Klein, *El actor en el Río de la Plata*, 1:32–33.

77. Klein, *El actor en el Río de la Plata*, 1:74. See also Beezley, "Introduction," 307–14; and Silva and Beezley, "The Rosete Aranda Puppets," 331–54.

78. Castagnino, *El circo criollo*, 18; Klein, *El actor en el Río de la Plata*, 1:81–117.

79. Beruti, *Memorias curiosas*.

80. Barrán, *Historia de la sensibilidad en el Uruguay*, 1:44–90.

81. Castagnino, *El circo criollo*, 22.

82. Klein, *El actor en el Río de la Plata*, 2:40–41; Chasteen, *National Rhythms, African Roots*, 142–46, 162; Ayestarán, *La música en el Uruguay*, 1:51–71.

83. Klein, *El actor en el Río de la Plata*, 2:43.

84. Anonymous, *A Five Years' Residence*, 23, 32–33; Wilde, *Buenos Aires desde setenta años atrás*, 52; Klein, *El actor en el Río de la Plata*, 2:45; Seibel, *Historia del circo*, 18.

85. Turner, *From Ritual to Theater*, 20–60, 121.

86. Viqueira Albán, *Propriety and Permissiveness*, 29.

87. Taullard, *Historia de nuestros viejos teatros*, 18.

Chapter 2

1. Gottlieb, *Sarah*, 16–17.

2. Gottlieb, *Sarah*, 103–4.

3. Gottlieb, *Sarah*, 98. Gottlieb delves into all these aspects of Sarah's life in his wonderful narrative.

4. Marks, *Sarah Bernhardt's First American Theatrical Tour, 1880–1881*, 87.

5. For more on Bernhardt in Brazil, São Paulo in particular, see Levy, "Sarah Bernhardt en São Paulo," 11–22.

6. Groussac, "La temporada teatral: Fedora Bernhardt," 37–43; *El Mosquito* (Buenos Aires), June 20, 1886, 3; July 4, 1886, 3.

7. *El Orden* (Buenos Aires), July 16, 1886, 1.

8. *El Fígaro* (Buenos Aires), May 24, 1886, 2.

9. See, for example, *El Orden*, July 16, 1886, 1; *El Nacional* (Buenos Aires), July 16, 1886, 1; *El Argentino* (Paraná), July 21, 1886, 1.

10. *El Orden*, July 19, 1886, 1; *El Mosquito*, July 25, 1886, 3.

11. Estrada, *Teatro*, 461–63; see also 474–79.

12. *El Orden*, July 19, 1886, 1.

13. *El Orden*, July 26, 1886, 2; *El Orden*, July 22, 1886, 3.

14. On Bernhardt's travels in Argentina, see *El Orden* and *El Nacional* for late July and especially August. On the Sarmiento-Bernhardt encounter, see *El Nacional*, August 31, 1886.

15. For Pierre Bourdieu "cultural intermediaries" emerged in the mid-twentieth century and formed a distinct occupational group (the "new petite bourgeoisie"). An appreciation of historical cultural intermediaries of the sort that run through this chapter can shed light on sustained cultural circulation long before twentieth-century economic forces transformed cultural production. See Bourdieu, *Distinction: A Social Critique of the Judgement of Taste*, chapters 1 and 6; Negus, "The Work of Cultural Intermediaries and the Enduring Distance Between Production and Consumption," 501–15; Nixon and Du Gay, "Who Needs Cultural Intermediaries?," 495–500.

16. For more on Atlantic theater and performance studies, see Roach, *Cities of the Dead*; and Dillon, *New World Drama*.

17. *El Siglo*, May 24, 1878.

18. Myers, "Una revolución en las costumbres," 124; qtd. in Teodoro Klein, *El actor en el Río de la Plata*, 2:27.

19. Rojas, "El público asistente a los circos, hasta la aparición de 'Juan Moreira,'" 50–58.

20. Rosselli, "The Opera Business and the Italian Immigrant Community in Latin America 1820–1930," 155–82.

21. Rosselli, "The Opera Business." Rosselli makes an excellent general point about separate opera circuits in the Americas in the 1800s.

22. Klein, *El actor en el Río de la Plata*, 2:37.

23. Bilbao, *Buenos Aires desde su fundación hasta nuestros días*, 205–6.

24. De María, *Montevideo Antiguo*, 1:225–31.

25. Castagnino, *El teatro en Buenos Aires durante la época de Rosas*, 1:77–117, 145–68; Borucki, "Tensiones raciales en el juego de la representación," 33–56.

26. Theater invitations printed on silk mention dances to precede and follow an evening's dramas, Hojas sueltas, MHN Lavalleja; Klein, *El actor*, 2:40–41; Bilbao, *Buenos Aires desde su fundación hasta nuestros días*, 205; Ayestarán, *La música en el Uruguay*, 1:274–88.

27. Castagnino, *Literatura dramática argentina, 1717–1967*, 45–62.

28. Haigh, *Sketches of Buenos Ayres and Chile*, 27–28.

29. Robertson and Robertson, *Letters on South America*, 3:123–24.

30. Ayestarán, *La música*, 1:202–12.

31. Vicuña Mackenna, *La Argentina en el año 1855*, 41–43.

32. Salgado, *The Teatro Solís*; De María, *El Teatro Solís*; Llanes, *Teatros de Buenos Aires*, 29–30; Ayestarán, *La música*, 1:208–26.

33. See the articles of the Accionistas de la empresa del nuevo teatro Solís in De María, *El Teatro Solís*, 5–35; Sarmiento, "El teatro como elemento de cultura," 3–5.

34. *La República* (Montevideo), October 7-8, November 13, 1861. Gottschalk toured extensively in Latin America. See Chasteen, *National Rhythms, African Roots*, 1–6. On *Uncle Tom's Cabin* in Latin America see Castilho, "Recrear *La cabaña de Tom* en la Ciudad de México y América Latina," forthcoming.

35. Gottschalk, *Notes of a Pianist*, 71.

36. Ristori, *Studies and Memoirs*, 103–4, 109.

37. Estrada, *Teatro*, 359–60.

38. Bilbao, *Buenos Aires desde su fundación hasta nuestros días*, 210.

39. Pereira, *Recuerdos de mi tiempo*, 222–37, provides an extensive list of performers from the 1880s through the early 1900s.

40. Estrada, *Teatro*, 232.

41. Silva et al., "Estadísticas sobre la inmigración a la Argentina," 13–68; Arteaga et al., "Inmigración y estadística en el Uruguay, 1830–1940," 261–372.

42. Mirza, "Para una revisión de la historia del teatro uruguayo," 179–99.

43. Fernández, *Historia de la magia y el ilusionismo en la Argentina*, 15.

44. Klein, *El actor*, 2:200.

45. *El Nacional*, November 6, 1841; qtd. in Klein, *El actor*, 2:200.

46. AGN, Ar, Fondo y Colección José Juan Biedma 1126; see also Lusnich and Llahí, "El circo," 363; and Aisemberg, "Espectáculos y público," 540; Castagnino, *El teatro en Buenos Aires*, 1:287–90. Playing with knives continued to awe. Consider a woman swallowing seven swords and a bayonet as part of the spectacle offered by the Compañía Amazona, Ecuestre, Gimnástica, Acróbata y Zoólogica (*El Siglo*, March 22, 1884, 2).

47. See Castagnino, *El teatro en Buenos Aires*, 2:418.

48. Castagnino, *El teatro en Buenos Aires*, 1:134–36, 290–91.

49. *El Siglo*, March 10–April 5, 1863.

50. *El Nacional*, June 28, 1864; November 3, 1865; *El Porvenir* (Monte Caseros), February 28–March 10, 1886.

51. Bilbao, *Buenos Aires desde*, 217; *El Mosquito*, December 2, 1883; *El Negro Timoteo* (Montevideo), December 23, 1883; *Ecos del Progreso* (Salto), March 29, 1884.

52. Selgas, *Hojas sueltas y más ojas sueltas*, 307–17.

53. "El hombre mosca" in *La República*, April 24, 1861.

54. *Ecos del Progreso*, February 19–May 18, 1889.

55. *El Siglo*, March 15–April 9, 1863. The zampillaerostation featured in later circus and acrobatic acts throughout the region. See, for example, *La Nación Argentina*, September 28, 1869, 2.

56. *El Siglo*, July 23, 1886–August 1, 1886.

57. *El Paysandú*, June 16, 1890.

58. For a good sample of such groups, see *El Nacional*, October 1868–September 1876.

59. *El Paysandú*, June 30, July 9, 1890.

60. *El Paysandú*, January 19–26, 1892.

61. *La Prensa* (Buenos Aires), March 20, 1894; *El Comercio* (Lima), July 25, 1894, 2–3.

62. *El Paysandú*, March 28, 1895, 2.

63. Centro Gallego (Montevideo), pamphlet March 19, 1895; *Ecos del Progreso*, March 23, 24, & 27, 1895; *El Paysandú*, February 21; March 28; April 1, 6, & 8, 1895.

64. *El Departamento* (Mercedes), April 17 & 22, 1895.

65. Finch, "All about 'Rama,'" 426–34.

66. *Caras y Caretas* (Buenos Aires), December 22, 1900.

67. Klein, *El actor*, 2:45–48; Seibel, *Historia del circo*, 20.

68. Klein, *El actor*, 2:49.

69. Bosch, "Viejos circos porteños," 158–59.

70. MHN Lavalleja, Impresos Col PBA, Programa Jura de la Constitución.

71. Seibel, *Historia del circo*, 20–22; Klein, *El actor*, 2:123–27.

72. Klein, *El actor*, 2:127–32; Bosch, "Viejos circos porteños," 159–61; Seibel, *Historia del circo*, 22; Castagnino, *El circo criollo*, 28.

73. Castagnino, *El teatro en Buenos Aires*, 1:62, 267–86; Castagnino, *El teatro en Buenos Aires*, 2:404–77.

74. *The Standard* (Buenos Aires), November 25, 1862, 3.

75. *The Standard*, December 14, 1862, 3; *El Siglo*, February 4, 1863.
76. *The Standard*, January 6, 1863, 3.
77. *The Standard*, January 18, 1863, 3.
78. *The Standard*, April 2, 1870, 2.
79. *El Siglo*, February 5, 8, & 10, 1863.
80. *El Siglo*, March 21, 24, 1863.
81. *El Siglo*, February 24, 27; March 4, 7, 12, 13, 1863.
82. *The Standard*, December 25, 1862, 3; January 21, 22, 1863; *El Siglo*, February 5, 7; March 17, 25, 1863.
83. See, for example, *The Standard*, December 4, 1862, 3; *El Siglo*, February 6, 1863.
84. *El Siglo*, February 13, 1863. On the water-throwing game, see Chasteen, "Anything Goes," 133–49.
85. *El Nacional*, April 30, 1873, 2; on the Nelsons with the Circo Casali, see December 10, 1873.
86. *Daily Alta California* (San Francisco), November 18, 1864; May 25, 1868; September 5, November 27, 1872; Klein, *El actor*, 2:205–06.
87. *El Nacional*, August 5–October 23, 1869.
88. See *El Nacional*, August 19, 28, 1869; September 8, 20, 1869.
89. See *El Paysandú*, June, 1895.
90. Castagnino, *El circo criollo*, 106; on Brown's reception, see *El Mosquito*, April 6, 1884; Cúneo, *Frank Brown*.
91. Castagnino, *El circo criollo*, 40–49; on the bear, see, for example, *La Patria Argentina* (Buenos Aires), March 6, 1884.
92. Castagnino, *El circo criollo*, 40–49; Aisemberg, "Compañías," 513.
93. *El Siglo*, February 6–March 2, 1884.
94. *La Patria Argentina*, April 17, 1884.
95. *El Mosquito*, April 27, 1884; *La Patria Argentina*, May 16, 1884.
96. *La Patria Argentina*, March 4–July 13, 1884.
97. Castagnino, *El circo criollo*, 65–66; Blanco Amores, "Pablo Podestá," 6.
98. Gottschalk, *Notes of a Pianist*, 440.
99. David Nasaw illustrates wonderfully how going out in the late nineteenth-century United States became socially acceptable. See especially chapter 3 in Nasaw, *Going Out: The Rise and Fall of Public Amusements*.
100. Turner, *From Ritual to Theater*; Huizinga, *Homo Ludens*, 1–46.

Chapter 3

1. Poster for the February 25, 1892, performance of *Martín Fierro*, INET.
2. González Urtiaga, *José J. Podestá y "Pepino el 88,"* 7–8.
3. González Urtiaga, *José J. Podestá*, 8–10; Podestá, *Medio siglo de farándula*, 28–32.
4. González Urtiaga, *José J. Podestá*, 11–25.

5. Klein, "Los Podestá-Scotti," 8; Rossi, *Cosas de negros*, 115–31.

6. Seibel, *El teatro "bárbaro" del interior*, 17; Podestá, *Medio siglo de farándula*, 46–47; González Urtiaga, *José J. Podestá*, 20–25.

7. Podestá, *Medio siglo de farándula*, 51–53.

8. Podestá, *Medio siglo de farándula*, 52; *El Mosquito*, July 6, 1884, 3.

9. Podestá, *Medio siglo de farándula*, 55–58; Seibel, *El teatro "bárbaro" del interior*, 21.

10. Qtd. In Seibel, "Buenos Aires 1890," 23.

11. Seibel, *Los artistas trashumantes*, 309–11.

12. Gutiérrez and Podestá, *Juan Moreira*.

13. Sansone de Martínez, "A manera de prólogo," 27–30.

14. Dubatti, "'Martín Fierro' de Elías Regules," 31–34; poster for the February 22, 1892, performance of *Martín Fierro*, INET.

15. Arózteguy, *Julián Giménez*, 1–94.

16. Arózteguy, *Ensayos dramáticos*, xiv.

17. Arózteguy, *Ensayos dramáticos*, 93, xiv–xv; on *Julián Giménez* as a pivotal representation of nativism see Mogliani, "*Julián Giménez* de Abdón Arózteguy," 195–207; and Pellettieri, "Cambios en el sistema teatral de la gauchesca rioplatense," 115–24.

18. Like his compatriots Arózteguy and Regules, Moratorio enjoyed a close relationship with the Podestá family. He dedicated the drama to José, who played the lead role, and granted the Podestá-Scotti Company exclusive performance rights. This contract guaranteed the play an immediate audience and a head start on a successful run. See Moratorio, *Juan Soldao*, 5.

19. Moratorio, *Juan Soldao*, 21–23.

20. Moratorio, *Juan Soldao*.

21. *Ecos del Progreso* (Salto), January 6, 1894.

22. The author dedicated the play to Jerónimo and José Podestá, whom he called the "true precursors of National Theater, whose creations on the Creole stage still have yet to be surpassed." Pérez Petit, *Teatro*, 1:9.

23. He remarks that "the native sons of this land, well, you can see for yourself: they don't know how to do anything except play the guitar, ride a horse, pretend to be tough, get involved in rebellions, sleep all day, or gamble away their little earnings at pulperías." Pérez Petit, 1:36.

24. Pérez Petit, *Teatro*, 1:128–29.

25. Pérez Petit, *Teatro*, 1:143. The play received a highly negative review in *Ecos del Progreso*, March 8, 1895, in which the reviewer complained of the play's lack of vitality that stemmed from an argument that was far "too simple."

26. Leguizamón, *Calandria*. Like other Creole drama authors, Leguizamón knew the countryside well, having grown up on a ranch in the Argentine province of Entre Ríos. And it was the Entre Ríos countryside that provided the setting for the play that the Podestá-Scotti group first performed at Teatro Victoria in Buenos Aires in May 1896.

27. Leguizamón, *Calandria*, 110
28. Leguizamón, *Calandria*, 56.
29. These included *Los Guachitos*; *Un Otelo en Chiripá*; *Nobleza Criolla*; *Patria y Honor*; *El Desgraciado*; and *Heroismo*, among others.
30. Elías Regules to José Podestá, November 24, 1891, qtd. in Rama, *Los gauchipolíticos rioplatenses*, 2:143.
31. Regules, *Los Guachitos*. Regules granted the company all the rights to the play as well as financial benefits from its performance.
32. Regules, *El Entenao*, 30.
33. Regules, *Martín Fierro*, 41, 53: "In nomine del bautizorum mochachorum qui penete di nombrem Goyitus." Goyito was the boy's name.
34. Regules, *El Entenao*, 95.
35. Moratorio, *Juan Soldao*, 50.
36. Podestá, *Medio siglo de farándula*, 50; Pellettieri, "'Juan Cuello', Novela y obra teatral de la gauchesca al nativismo."
37. Podestá, *Medio siglo de farándula*, 66. Petray called himself Franchisque Cocoliche, and claimed that he was "cregollo gasta lo güese de la taba e la canilla de lo caracuse, amique." Loosely, and playing on the mix of Spanish and Italian, that was "Creole to the bone, my friend." See also García Velloso, *Memorias de un hombre de teatro*, 160–61.
38. Arózteguy, *Julián Giménez*, 67–72.
39. Arózteguy, *Julián Giménez*, 68, 87–88.
40. Arózteguy, *Julián Giménez*, 32–33. The Frenchman says he is there to join the *patriotas* "oguientales," a play on his French pronunciation of the Spanish "r" in *Orientales* (Uruguayans).
41. Arózteguy, *Julián Giménez*, 93.
42. Moratorio, *Juan Soldao*, 31–35.
43. *Ecos del Progreso*, January 20, 1894; see also January 24 & 25, 1894.
44. Moratorio, *Juan Soldao*, 26–27.
45. Regules, *Martín Fierro*, 75.
46. Arózteguy, *Julián Giménez*, 91–92.
47. Arózteguy, *Ensayos dramáticos*, collection of press accounts, 344–45.
48. Moratorio, *Juan Soldao*, 39, 67.
49. Regules, *El Entenao*, 116.
50. Dubatti, "'Martín Fierro' de Elías Regules," 34.
51. Marial, "Los enemigos de Juan Moreira," 64.
52. Sansone, "A manera de prólogo."
53. Podestá, *Medio siglo de farándula*, 61–64, 71–72; Klein, "Los Podestá-Scotti," 11.
54. Chasteen, *National Rhythms, African Roots*, chapters 2 and 4.
55. All dramas mentioned in this chapter, from *Juan Moreira* through *Calandria*, include dance scenes, which were also ripe moments for improvisation.
56. Seibel, *Los artistas trashumantes*, 309.

57. Seibel, *Historia del circo*, 74–76.

58. Qtd. in Klein, "Los Podestá-Scotti," 15.

59. An excellent commentary on this realism appears in *Ecos del Progreso*, March 16, 1895.

60. Qtd. in Podestá, *Medio siglo de farándula*, 61.

61. Podestá, *Medio siglo de farándula*, 85.

62. Arózteguy, *Ensayos dramáticos*, xiv.

63. Klein, "El manuscrito de *Martín Fierro*," 36; Rafael Picasso to Elías Regules, October 31, 1891, f. 85, Colección José de Diego, INET.

64. Arózteguy, *Ensayos dramáticos*, xv.

65. Arózteguy, *Ensayos dramáticos*, collection of press accounts, 342–44.

66. Olivera, *En la brecha*, 317.

67. See Podestá, *Medio siglo de farándula*, 64.

68. *Sud América* (Buenos Aires), November 11, 1890; qtd. in Podestá, *Medio siglo de farándula*, 68–71.

69. *Sud América* (Buenos Aires), November 11, 1890; qtd. in Podestá, *Medio siglo de farándula*, 68–71.

70. Podestá, *Medio siglo de farándula*, 71–72, 84–86.

71. Podestá, *Medio siglo de farándula*, 93.

72. MHN Lavalleja, Hojas sueltas, 2.604.

73. *La Opinión Pública* (Montevideo) and *El Siglo* (Montevideo), October 1889–January 1890. Pantomimes included *Una noche en Pekín*; *Juan Portela*; *José María, o Los bandoleros de Sierra Morena*; one for children titled *Napoleón I*; and *Ferruccio il Siciliano*.

74. Program poster for *El Entenao*, March 10, 1892 (INET); *La Prensa* and *La Nación*, February and March 1892.

75. They performed *Nobleza Criolla* as their debut show, followed two days later by *Julián Jiménez* and then *Los Guachitos*. The big-city success in the port capitals, Rosario, and La Plata of these shows features in the publicity to heighten their appeal in the smaller Paysandú. The company added *Moreira* to their program at the end of the month, concluding their opening week on a very strong note. In February crowds flocked to see *Juan Soldao, Cobarde, Santos Vega, El Entenao*, and *Un Otelo en Chiripá*, among other dramatic tales of the countryside.

76. See *El Paysandú*, January 24–May 31, 1895; *La Prensa (diario de la tarde)* (Salto), April 4–24, 1895; *Ecos del Progreso*, February–May 1895.

77. *Ecos del Progreso*, March 17, 1895.

78. Qtd. in Klein, "Los Podestá-Scotti," 12, letter dated December 12, 1897; see Carmeli, "Text, Traces, and the Reification of Totality," 175–205, for a comparative take on British circus literature and modernity.

79. Regules, *Martín Fierro*, 5.

80. *Ecos del Progreso*, March 17, 1895.

Chapter 4

1. *Ecos del Progreso* (Salto), January 3, 6, 12, & 25, 1894.
2. Podestá, *Medio siglo de farándula*, 78–79.
3. See Marial, "Los enemigos de Juan Moreira," 60–65.
4. Adamovsky, "La cuarta función del criollismo y las luchas por la definición del origen y el color del *ethnos* argentino (desde las primeras novelas gauchescas hasta c. 1940)," 50–92.
5. *Ecos del Progreso*, January 21, 1894, 1.
6. See, for example, *Ecos del Progreso*, March 21, 1894.
7. Vega, *Apuntes para la historia del movimiento tradicionalista argentino*, 43–51.
8. Quesada, "El 'criollismo' en la literatura argentina," 203.
9. Moya, "El circo y el payador," 19–28.
10. José Podestá led the effort to contract Ezeiza for performances. See José Podestá to Gabino Ezeiza, March 10, 1891, f. 43, Colección José de Diego, INET; *El Siglo*, April 14–19, 1891.
11. *El Siglo*, April 15, 1891, 2.
12. Adamovsky, "El criollismo en las luchas por la definición del origen y el color del *ethnos* argentino, 1945–1955," 31–63.
13. On Afro-descendant payadores, see Andrews, *The Afro-Argentines of Buenos Aires, 1800–1900*, 173.
14. Pablo Vázquez claimed to have "defeated" the legendary payador. *El Paysandú* (Paysandú), May 23, 1892, 2.
15. *El Siglo*, December 19, 1894, 3.
16. On milongas and tangos at the plays see Chasteen, *National Rhythms, African Roots*, 55–70; *Julián Giménez* poster, March 30, 1892, INET; see also Vega, *Apuntes para la historia del movimiento tradicionalista argentino*, 50–51.
17. *El Siglo*, November 24, 1894, 2.
18. *El Paysandú*, January 31, 1895, 2. For more on the pericón's origins and moves, see Ayestarán, *La música*, 1:488–90.
19. *El Paysandú*, February 7, 1895, 2.
20. Rossi, *Teatro nacional rioplatense*, 75, presents a summary of these manifestations.
21. *El Siglo*, November 21, 1893, 3.
22. See, for example, Quesada, "El 'criollismo' en la literature argentina," 136; Yunque, "Estudio preliminar," 36.
23. Podestá, *Medio siglo de farándula*, 78; see also Benítez, *Una histórica función de circo*, 50–51.
24. *Ecos del Progreso*, May 10–13, 1892.
25. *El Siglo*, November 24, 1893, 1.
26. *Ecos del Progreso*, January 23, 1894, 2.
27. Quesada, "El 'criollismo,'" 135–37.

28. Rossi, *Teatro nacional*, 75. Rossi writes, "El pueblo se *enmoreiraba.*"

29. Sánchez, "Cartas de un flojo"; "El caudillaje criminal en Sud América"; "El teatro nacional," 44.

30. Interview with José María Obaldía, *El País* (Montevideo), April 26, 2003.

31. Chasteen, "Violence for Show," 47–64; Lanuza and Burri, *El gaucho.*

32. Prieto, *El discruso criollista en la formación de la Argentina moderna*, 148.

33. *El Siglo*, March 30, 1894, 1.

34. *El Día* (La Plata), July 22, 1894, qtd. in Colombo, "Los primeros años del Juan Moreira en La Plata (1886–1894)," 37.

35. Qtd. in Colombo, "Los primeros años," 32.

36. *Ecos del Progreso*, January 25, 1894; February 3, 1894; March 16, 1895; *El Departamento* (Mercedes, Uruguay), May 1, 1895; *La Prensa (Diario de la Tarde)* (Salto), April 15, 1895, 2.

37. *El Siglo*, April 19, 1894, 3.

38. *El Siglo*, May 1894.

39. *El Siglo*, June 2, 1894, 3.

40. Good examples of audiences exercising influence over repertoires appear in *El Paysandú*, February 1895, and *El Tribuno* (La Plata), June 21, 1896.

41. *El Siglo*, November 1, 1889, 1; *El siglo*, November 19, 1892, 2.

42. *El Siglo*, September 29, 1889, 1.

43. For example, *El Siglo*, November 19, 1893, 2; December 10, 1893.

44. *El Siglo*, February 22, 1891, 2; *El Departamento*, May 13, 1895; *El Tribuno*, June 21, 1896.

45. *Juan Moreira* poster, March 27, 1892, Colección Jacobo de Diego, INET; *El Siglo*, April 29, 1894, 3.

46. *El Paysandú*, June 2–8, 1890.

47. *El Paysandú*, April 8, 1892, 2; *Ecos del Progreso*, April 23, 1895, 2.

48. Castagnino, "Juan Moreira: Entre Paradigmas Gauchescos," 36.

49. A good example of this can be found in *Ecos del Progreso*, March 14, 1895.

50. See, for example, *El Departamento*, May 6, 1895.

51. *Ecos del Progreso*, January 6, 1894, 2; February 3, 1894, 1.

52. This specific language appeared in *El Paysandú*, April 4, 1895, 2; an example of a little-known play was *Pajarito*, performed in May of that year in Paysandú with "complete success" (*El Paysandú*, May 24, 1895).

53. *La Opinión Pública* (Montevideo), November–December 1889.

54. *El Siglo*, October 16, 1889, 2; *El Paysandú*, February 18, 1895; *El Departamento* (Mercedes), May 15, 1895.

55. *Ecos del Progreso*, March 12, 1895.

56. On community at the circus, see Benítez, *Una histórica función de circo*, 14–15; Seibel, "Códigos de teatro popular en el Juan Moreira," 54–59; Rama, *Los gauchi-políticos rioplatenses*, 2:132–33.

57. *El Siglo*, April 2, 1891; Seibel, *Historia del circo*, 61.

58. *Ecos del Progreso*, April 7–11, 1895.

59. See commentary, for example, on Salto's high society supporting dramas to benefit flood victims, *Ecos del Progreso*, April 18, 1895, 2.

60. *El Progresista: Publicación Independiente y Liberal* (Carmelo, Uruguay), April 1892; Podestá, *Medio siglo de farándula*, 73.

61. *El Paysandú*, February 13, 1895.

62. On this Habanera variation see *El Siglo*, January–February 1891.

63. Chasteen, "Anything Goes," 133–49.

64. Chamosa, "Lúbolos, Tenorios y Moreiras," 115.

65. Darío, "Psicologías carnavelescas," 77–82.

66. Seigel, "Cocoliche's Romp: Fun with Nationalism at Argentina's Carnival," 56.

67. Seigel, "Cocoliche's Romp," 58.

68. Seigel, "Cocoliche's Romp," 66; Adamovsky, "La cuarta función del criollismo," 52, 84–85.

69. Rama, *Los gauchipolíticos*, 2:144–46.

70. Quesada, "El 'criollismo,'" 151–53.

71. *Caras y Caretas* (Buenos Aires), no. 281, February 20, 1904.

72. See, for example, *Ecos del Progreso*, January 17, 1894, 1.

73. *El Siglo*, May 30, 1894, 2.

74. See *El Siglo*, September 1889, and February 1891, for good examples of this media hype.

75. *El Siglo*, February 21, 1891, 1.

76. See posters from February to March 1892 in the Colección INET.

77. Rafael Picasso to Elías Regules, October 31, 1891, f. 85, Colección Jacobo de Diego, INET.

78. Quesada, *La propiedad intelectual en el derecho argentino*, 3–9, 65–68.

79. Rafael Picasso to Bernardo L. Peyret, September 21, 1892, f. 96, Colección Jacobo de Diego, INET; *El Siglo*, November 8, 1893, 2.

80. Rafael Picasso to E. Rayo y Cía, November 4, 1892, ff. 106–8, Colección Jacobo de Diego, INET.

81. *El Siglo*, October 20, 1894, 3; *Ecos del Progreso*, March 5, 1895; *El Tribuno*, June 18, 1896.

82. *El Departamento*, April 10 & 29, 1895.

83. *El Paysandú*, April 4, 1895, 2.

84. *Ecos del Progreso*, April 1895.

85. *Ecos del Progreso*, December 18, 1900, 2; January 3, 1901, 2.

86. Posters for *Juan Moreira*, February 18, 1892; *Juan Moreira*, March 15, 1892; *Martín Fierro*, March 22, 1892; *Julián Giménez*, March 30, 1892; *El Entenao*, March 10, 1892; all at the INET.

87. *El Siglo*, November 8, 1892, 2; November 17, 1893, 2; December 17, 1893; March 28, 1894, 3.

88. See, for example, *El Siglo*, November–December 1893.

89. *La Nación* (Buenos Aires), June 7, 1892.

90. *El Paysandú*, February 7, 1895, 2.

91. Prieto, *El discurso criollista*, 162–63; *Caras y Caretas*, July 5, 1902, no. 196.

92. Acree, *Everyday Reading*.

93. Quesada, "El 'criollismo,'" 136–37.

94. Quesada, *La propiedad intelectual*, 325–40.

95. Dirección General de Estadística Municipal, *Anuario estadístico de la ciudad de Buenos Aires, año 3, 1893*, 309.

96. Dirección General de Estadística Municipal, *Anuario estadístico de la ciudad de Buenos Aires, año 4, 1894*, xlii; Dirección General de Estadística Municipal, *Anuario Estadístico de la Ciudad de Buenos Aires, año 6, 1896*, 543–54.

97. McCleary, "Popular, Elite, *and* Mass Culture?," 1–27.

98. Dirección General de Estadística Municipal, *Anuario estadístico de la ciudad de Buenos Aires, año 3, 1893*, xxix.

99. Dirección General de Estadística Municipal, *Anuario estadístico de la ciudad de Buenos Aires, año 4, 1894*, xli.

100. On these wars and the towering figure of Saravia, see Chasteen, *Heroes on Horseback*.

101. Abella and Vaz, *Martín Aquino*, 35, 49–50.

102. Graziano, *Cultures of Devotion*, 113–40.

103. Duffau, *Armar al bandido*, 13–14, chapters 3, 4, and 5.

104. Dirección General de Estadística Municipal, *Anuario Estadístico de la Ciudad de Buenos Aires, año 13, 1903*, 239–73. See also Caimari, *Apenas un delincuente*; and Ansolabehere and Caimari, eds., *La ley de los profanos*.

105. *Ecos del Progreso*, March 12, 1895.

Chapter 5

1. Rama, *Los gauchipolíticos rioplatenses*, 2:147–48; Sociedad Criolla Dr. Elías Regules, *Libro institucional*, 13.

2. *El Día* (Montevideo), May 26, 1894, 1, "Paseo criollo."

3. Farinetti, "Gauchos y gringos en la formación de la nación argentina," 215–20; Pisarello, "El tradicionalismo argentino en los inicios del siglo XXI," 203–13.

4. Arezo Posada, *Vigencia del tradicionalismo*, 75.

5. Vega, *Apuntes para la historia del movimiento tradicionalista argentino*, 53–54.

6. Lehmann-Nitsche, *La leyenda de Santos Vega*, 251.

7. Lehmann-Nitsche, *La leyenda de Santos Vega*, 252–54; Puccia, *Breve historia del carnaval porteño*, 75.

8. Vega, *Apuntes para la historia del movimiento tradicioanlista argentino*, 55.

9. Vega, *Apuntes para la historia del movimiento tradicionalista argentino*, 33.

10. Puccia, *Breve historia del carnaval porteño*, 75, 82; see also Collier, *The Life, Music, and Times of Carlos Gardel*, 43–44.

11. *Caras y Caretas*, March 11, 1905, 30.

12. Oliven, *Tradition Matters*, qtd. 56.

13. Oliven, *Tradition Matters*, 54–76; Arezo Posada, *Vigencia del tradicionalismo*, 46–58.

14. See, for example, *El Fogón*, February 7, 1899, 150–51.

15. *El Fogón*, May 15, 1900, 868.

16. *El Fogón*, May 15, 1900, 868.

17. *El Fogón*, June 22, 1901, 1527.

18. *El Fogón*, September 22, 1905.

19. Oliven, *Tradition Matters*, 56.

20. Vega, *Apuntes para la historia del movimiento tradicionalista argentino*, 60.

21. *El Fogón*, April 30, 1909.

22. Ratier, del Campo, Etchichury, and Iriberry, "Organizaciones rurales y cultura de las pampas."

23. Turner, *From Ritual to Theater*, 101.

24. Hammerton, *The Real Argentine*, 159–60.

25. McCleary, "Afro-Argentines, *Papás, Malevos,* and *Patotas,*" 76.

26. McCleary, "Afro-Argentines," 86, underscores this point about language.

27. *El Fogón*, May 31, 1896, 468.

28. Moore, *Cow Boys and Cattle Men*.

29. *El Fogón*, June 7, 1896, 469.

30. *El Fogón*, January 30, 1900, 720.

31. *El Fogón*, May 15, 1900, 892.

32. Hammerton, *The Real Argentine*, 168.

33. *El Fogón*, May 31, 1896, 468; *El Fogón*, April 30, 1909.

34. Rossi, *Teatro nacional rioplatense*, 84.

35. Chamosa, *The Argentine Folklore Movement*, 23.

36. Cattaruzza and Eujanian, *Políticas de la historia*, 218, 235. Also, see chapter 7 in this book for a detailed look at how this process affected Argentine historiography.

37. Regules, *Versos criollos*, 164.

38. Regules, *Versos criollos*, 164–65.

39. On the evolving legacy of Artigas, see Demasi, "La construcción de un 'héroe máximo,'" 1029–45; and Acree, *Everyday Reading*, 123–32, 143–44.

40. *El Fogón*, February 7, 1899, 151.

41. Rama, *Los gauchipolíticos rioplatenses*, 2:148–49.

42. Regules, *Versos criollos*, 172–73.

43. *El Fogón*, April 30, 1909.

44. Silva et al., "Estadísticas sobre la inmigración a la Argentina," 22; Arteaga et al., "Inmigración y estadística en el Uruguay, 1830–1940," 287.

45. Ayestarán, "Prologue," xxx.

46. Rama, *Los gauchipolíticos rioplatenses*, 2:151–53.

47. Qtd. in Arezo Posada, *Vigencia del tradicionalismo*, 29.

48. Regules, *Versos criollos*, 167–68.

49. *El Fogón*, June 7, 1896, 471.

50. Vega, *Apuntes para la historia*, 61–63; Lehmann-Nitsche, *La leyenda de Santos Vega*, 253–57.

51. Rizzo Botana, "Elías Regules en *El Fogón*," n.p.; Ayestarán, "Prologue," vii–xxxvi.

52. Vega writes of a process of "tradicionalización": see *Apuntes para la historia*, 51.

53. See Alberto and Elena, eds., *Rethinking Race in Modern Argentina*, for excellent approaches to the complexities of race in Argentina.

54. Sociedad Criolla, 13.

55. Quesada, "El 'criollismo,'" 151–53; *Caras y Caretas*, no. 281, February 20, 1904.

56. *El Fogón*, March 7, 1900, 784.

57. *El Fogón*, November 7, 1901, 4.

58. Halperín Donghi, "¿Para qué la inmigración?," 211.

59. Romero, "Los sectores populares en las ciudades latinoamericanas del siglo XIX," 215–16.

60. Prieto, *El discurso criollista en la formación de la Argentina modern*, centers on these three functions.

61. Adamovsky, "La cuarta función del criollismo y las luchas por la definición del origen y el color del *ethnos* argentino (desde las primeras novelas gauchescas hasta c. 1940)," 51–52.

62. Cattaruzza and Eujanian, *Políticas de la historia*, 218, 261–62.

63. Adamovsky, "La cuarta función del criollismo," 84–85.

64. Adamovsky, "El criollismo en las luchas por la definición del origen y el color del *ethnos* argentino, 1945–1955," 34, 43. *El Fogón*, "La cabeza de Moreira," August 22, 1901, 1627–28.

65. Oliven, *Tradition Matters*, xvi, 10.

66. Hammerton, *The Real Argentine*, 168.

67. República Argentina, *Tercer censo nacional*, 10:85.

68. Roosevelt was duly impressed by the visit. See the article he composed for *The Outlook* in 1914: "Buenos Aires: A Fine Modern Capital," March 28, 1914. Sagamore Hill National Historic Site, Theodore Roosevelt Digital Library. Dickinson State University.

69. Baily, "Las sociedades de ayuda mutua y el desarrollo de una comunidad italiana en Buenos Aires, 1858–1918," 486.

70. Gutiérrez and Romero, eds., *Sectores populares, cultura y política*, 12, note the growing political bent of club boards and how these associations connected members to civil society; see also Zubillaga, *Cultura popular en el Uruguay de entresiglos (1870–1910)*, 207–14.

71. República Argentina, *Tercer censo*, 10:94–95, 308; Devoto and Fernández, "Mutualismo étnico, liderazgo y participación política," 129–52.

72. Sábato, "On Political Citizenship in Nineteenth-Century Latin America," 1306, writes that many of these societies were "considered ideal sites for the breeding of new citizens."

73. Sábato, "On Political Citizenship in Nineteenth-Century Latin America," 1308, 1313.

74. Hobsbawm, "Mass-Producing Traditions: Europe, 1870–1914," 263–307, analyzes such involvement in Europe during a period of enthusiastic official tradition making.

75. Vega, *Apuntes para la historia*, 46.

76. Oliven, *Tradition Matters*, 60. Cattaruzza and Eujanian, "Héroes patricios y gauchos rebeldes," emphasize how Creole centers provided access to "bienes culturales" (243).

77. Hobsbawm, "Introduction: Inventing Traditions," 1–2.

78. A similar, though not parallel, instance of the transformative power of costume and play was observed by Philip Deloria in *Playing Indian*, 6–7. He wrote about how taking on traits or qualities different from one's own, specifically in the context of "playing Indian" in the United States, led to awareness and reflection about the person out of costume, or away from the club.

Chapter 6

1. Quesada, "El 'criollismo' en la literatura argentina," 152–53.

2. Veniard, *Arturo Berutti, un argentino en el mundo de la ópera*, 196–98.

3. Qtd. in Veniard, *Arturo Berutti*, 200.

4. Veniard, *Arturo Berutti*, 211–12; Seibel, *Historia del teatro argentino*, 305–6.

5. Qtd. in Veniard, *Arturo Berutti*, 229.

6. Quesada, "El 'criollismo' en la literatura argentina," 151.

7. Veniard, *Arturo Berutti*, 208–10.

8. Qtd. in Veniard, *Arturo Berutti*, 210.

9. Qtd. in Veniard, *Arturo Berutti*, 227.

10. Qtd. in Veniard, *Arturo Berutti*, 226.

11. Benzecry, *The Opera Fanatic*, 25–31; see also Rosselli, "The Opera Business and the Italian Immigrant Community in Latin America 1820–1930," 155–82.

12. Veniard, *Arturo Berutti*, 205.

13. Though beyond the scope of this chapter, impresarios like César Ciacchi, who brought a range of groups to venues throughout the region, played an important role in facilitating popular-elite exchanges.

14. *El Siglo* (Montevideo), September 1, 1897, 1.

15. *El Siglo*, September 2, 1897, 1.

16. Prieto, *El discurso criollista en la formación de la Argentina moderna*, 159–62.

17. Podestá, *Medio siglo de farándula*, 100–3.

18. *La Dinastía* (Barcelona), July 7, 1900, 3.

19. *La Dinastía*, July 10, 1900, 3; July 17, 1900, 3.

20. *Iris* (Barcelona), July 21, 1900, 18.

21. *El Día* (Madrid), July 19, 1900, 3.

22. *Heraldo de Madrid* (Madrid), July 28, 1900, 3.

23. Seibel, *El cantar del payador*, 20.

24. *La Epoca* (Madrid), July 24, 1900, 3.

25. *La Epoca*, August 2, 1900, 3; Pérez de Guzmán, "El teatro hispanoamericano," 132.

26. *La Ilustración Artística* (Barcelona), April 30, 1900. The Podestás were still identified here as the company that would be arriving in Spain.

27. *La Dinastía*, July 12, 1900; *Heraldo de Madrid*, July 28, 1900; *El Día*, July 28, 1900.

28. Fey, "Peddling the Pampas," 61–85; Uslenghi, *Latin America at Fin-de-Siècle Universal Exhibitions*.

29. Ugarte, *Crónicas del bulevar*, 253–59.

30. Ugarte, *Crónicas del bulevar*, 256.

31. *Le Matin* (Paris), September 19, 1900, 4. In addition, there was an International Congress on Theater Arts that took place as part of the Exposition, July 27–31, and theater was part of the conference.

32. See *Harper's Guide to Paris and the Exposition of 1900*, 68–85; *Guide Bleu du Figaro à L'exposition de 1900*, 113.

33. The spread of mutual aid societies and other civil associations also injected new terms and nicknames relating to solidarity, modes of dress, and political affiliation into everyday language. See Zubillaga, *Cultura popular en el Uruguay de entresiglos*, 245–73.

34. Quesada, "El 'criollismo' en la literatura argentina," 153–55; Rossi, *Teatro nacional rioplatense*, 48.

35. Robert Lehmann-Nitsche's Biblioteca Criolla is one of the richest collections of these publications. See Prieto, *El discurso criollista*, 197–241.

36. Prieto, *El discurso criollista*, 66.

37. Prieto, *El discurso criollista*, 71–72.

38. Quesada, "El 'criollismo' en la literature argentina," 158, 228–30.

39. *Caras y Caretas* (Buenos Aires), January 20, 1900, 24; March 9, 1901, 33; March 2, 1901, 38; April 19, 1905, 34; December 19, 1903; July 23, 1910, 62.

40. Podestá, *Medio siglo de farándula*, 79; Plesch, "The Guitar in Nineteenth-Century Buenos Aires."

41. *El Deber Cívico* (Melo), April 27, 1900.

42. *Tucumán Literario*, May 21, 1893 (qtd. in López, "Recepción," 136); *El Mercurio* (La Plata), July 21, 1894 (qtd. in Colombo, "Los primeros años del Juan Moreira en La Plata (1886–1894)," 37).

43. Obligado, *Prosas*, 41–43.

44. Schiaffino, *La pintura y la escultura en Argentina (1783–1894)*, 356–57.

45. Viana, "Dramas criollos: el gaucho real y el gaucho inventado," 614–19; Arózteguy, "Sobre dramas criollos," 620–21; Viana, "Sobre dramas criollos," 621–23.

46. Arózteguy, "Dramas criollos: lo bueno y lo malo," 352–61.

47. *La Tribuna*, May 23, 1896; *La Nación*, May 24, June 1, 1896; *El Tiempo*, May 28, June 6, 1896.

48. Quesada, "El 'criollismo' en la literatura argentina," 208.

49. Sánchez, "Cartas de un flojo"; "El caudillaje criminal en Sud América"; "El teatro nacional," 42–47.

50. Qtd. in Rossi, *Teatro nacional rioplatense*, 57–58, n2.

51. Rivarola, "El teatro nacional," 341–75.

52. Qtd. in Rossi, *Teatro nacional rioplatense*, 142, n2.

53. Rossi, *Teatro nacional rioplatense*, 142–43.

54. Pérez Petit, "Defensa del drama criollo," 251, 254–55; see also *El Fogón*, January 15, 1899; August 15, 1909; February 15, 1913; February 22, 1913; September 20, 1913, for continued conversation about Creole dramas and national theater.

55. Lawrence Levine, in *Highbrow/Lowbrow: The Emergence of Cultural Hierarchy in America*, 85–168, describes a process of sacralization of culture in the late nineteenth-century United States. This process did not play out in the Río de la Plata in the same way, though there was clearly was an ordering of culture, with new parameters that aimed to establish a new cultural hierarchy.

Chapter 7

1. Olivera, *En la brecha: 1880–1886*, 319.

2. García Velloso, *Memorias de un hombre de teatro*, 159.

3. Adamovsky, "El criollismo como canal de visiones críticas sobre la historia argentina," 25–50.

4. Llanes, *Teatros de Buenos Aires*, 18–20; Mazziotti, "Bambalinas," 74.

5. Mazziotti, "El auge de las revistas," 76; Silva et al., "Estadísticas sobre la inmigración a la Argentina"; González Velasco, *Gente de teatro*, 24.

6. Dirección General de Estadísticia Municipal, *Anuario Estadístico de la Ciudad de Buenos Aires, año 10, 1900*, 283–86; Dirección General de Estadísticia Municipal, *Anuario Estadístico . . . , año 13, 1903*, 287–90; Dirección General de Estadísticia Municipal, *Anuario Estadístico . . . año 17, 1907*, 339–40.

7. Dirección General de Estadísticia Municipal, *Anuaire Statistique de la Ville de Buénos-Ayres, VIme année—1896*, 543–58; Klein, "El público del *Moreira* en Buenos Aires," 39–42.

8. Klein, "El público del *Moreira*."

9. Podestá, *Medio siglo de farándula*, 98–99.

10. Podestá, *Medio siglo de farándula*, 104–5; Dubatti, "Los Podestá," 113–17.

11. Podestá, *Medio siglo de farándula*, 107, 10.

12. Podestá, *Medio siglo de farándula*, 113–25.

13. Rossi, *Teatro nacional rioplatense*, 66–67.

14. Sánchez, "Cartas de un flojo"; "El caudillaje criminal en Sud América"; "El teatro nacional," 46–47.

15. *Ecos del Progreso* (Salto), December 1900–January 1901. Throughout the region there were also adaptions of Creole dramas, like the sainete version of *Juan Cuello* (*Ecos del Progreso*, January 8, 1910), and activities that conjured the Creole spirit, such as horse-taming shows (January 6, 1910).

16. Qtd. in Rossi, *Teatro nacional rioplatense*, 165.

17. *Libro de El Siglo, 1863–1913*, 222–23.

18. Seibel, *El teatro "bárbaro" del interior*, 25–26.

19. Pellarolo, *Sainete criollo*, 62–63; Pacheco, *Los disfrazados y otros sainetes*, 5.

20. Evans, "Setting the Stage for Struggle," 52.

21. Golluscio de Montoya, "Elementos para una 'teoría' teatral libertaria (Argentina 1900)," 85–93.

22. Nouwen, *Oy, My Buenos Aires*, especially chapters 3 and 4; Garrett, Performing Everyday Life.

23. Evans, "Setting the Stage," 49–50.

24. Pellarolo, *Sainete criollo*, 59.

25. Golluscio de Montoya, "Del circo colonial a los teatros ciudadanos," 141–49.

26. Quesada, *Reseñas y críticas*, 291, 356.

27. Bianchi, *Teatro nacional*, 107, 157–61.

28. Pellarolo, *Sainete criollo*, 63.

29. See, for example, Soria, *Digesto municipal de la Ciudad de Buenos Aires*; and McCleary, "Inflaming the Fears of Theatergoers," 254–72.

30. Mazziotti, "El auge de las revistas."

31. Mazziotti, "*Bambalinas*." The Spanish titles of these were *Biblioteca "Teatro Uruguayo," Biblioteca "Teatro Argentino,"* and the *Nuevo archivo teatral de cultura popular*.

32. García, *Sobre el teatro nacional y otros artículos y fragmentos*, 15.

33. Rossi, *Teatro nacional rioplatense*, 66–67.

34. Pellarolo, *Sainete criollo*, 107; Prieto, *El discurso criollista*, 153–57.

35. *El Siglo* (Montevideo), January 6, 1910, 5; see also January and February for commentaries on these spectacles.

36. Mogliani, "El costumbrismo en el teatro argentino."

37. Mogliani, "El costumbrismo"; Seibel, *Historia del teatro argentino*, 767–75.

38. Hutcheon, with O'Flynn, *A Theory of Adaptation*.

39. Mogliani, "El costumbrismo," 206; Seibel, *Historia del circo*.

40. Podestá, *Medio siglo de farándula*, 178–80.

41. Podestá, *Medio siglo de farándula*, 184.

42. Museo de Arte Popular José Hernández, Fondo Documental Carlos G. Daws, Album 4, 185–87.

43. See *El Siglo* and *El Día*, August–September 1925.

44. Qtd. in Podestá, *Medio siglo de farándula*, 204.

45. *El Día*, September 14, 1925.

46. García Velloso, *Memorias de un hombre*, 162.

47. Blanca Podestá, *Algunos recuerdos de mi vida artística*, 19.

48. Acree, *Everyday Reading*, epilogue; Borucki, "La Republicana (1850–1950)."

49. Fondo Documental Carlos G. Daws, Album 20, 104–5.

50. Adamovsky, "El criollismo como canal de visiones críticas sobre la historia argentina," 31.

51. San Martín, *Cine mudo argentino*, 73.

52. Finkielman, *The Film Industry in Argentina*, 1–10; Richter, "Uruguayan Cinema in the 20th Century," 2.

53. Cuarterolo, "Los antecedentes del cine político y social en la Argentina (1896–1933)," 145–72; San Martín, *Cine mudo argentino*, 101–3.

54. Finkielman, *The Film Industry*, 16.

55. Tranchini, "El cine argentino y la construcción de un imaginario criollista," 101–73.

56. Fondo Documental Carlos G. Daws, Album 4, 251.

57. San Martín, *Cine mudo argentino*, 77.

58. Finkielman, *The Film Industry*, 19–21.

59. San Martín, *Cine mudo argentino*, 101–2.

60. González Velasco, *Gente de teatro*, 21–22; Legido, *El teatro uruguayo*, 29.

61. Karush, *Culture of Class*, 72–73.

62. This specific wording comes from *Caras y Caretas*, January 21, 1899, no. 16, though similar ads were published continuously throughout these years.

63. Richter, "Uruguayan Cinema," 3.

64. *Caras y Caretas*, August 23, 1902, no. 203.

65. See especially Karush, *Culture of Class*, chapters 1 and 2; and, for 1940s and 1950s Argentina, Milanesio, *Workers Go Shopping*.

66. Karush, *Culture of Class*, 53.

67. Maccarini, *Teatro de identidad popular*, 67–71.

68. Matallana, "*Locos por la radio*," 36–38, 197–207; González Velasco, *Gente de teatro*, 51.

69. Ehrick, *Radio and the Gendered Soundscape*, chapter 2.

70. Karush, *Culture of Class*, 66–67; Matallana, "*Locos por la radio*," 103–5.

71. Matallana, "*Locos por la radio*," 109, writes that radio theater shows "acted as the continuation of gauchesque narratives in a new mode of communication."

72. Seibel, *El teatro "bárbaro*," 61–62, 105–26.

73. Navarrete, "Mendoza (1892–1939)," 1:286–87.

74. Chamosa, *The Argentine Folklore Movement*, 9, 15–16, 22–26.

Curtain

1. Steiner, "From Frontier to Region," 479–501.

2. Kasson, *Buffalo Bill's Wild West*, 120.

3. Sagala, *Buffalo Bill on Stage*, 7; Kasson, *Buffalo Bill's Wild West*, 98–99.

4. *Buffalo Bill's Wild West and Congress of the Rough Riders of the World*, 2.

5. Examples include the surge of folklore movements and their study across Europe and the Americas in the nineteenth and early twentieth centuries, and invented traditions such as the Scottish kilt or the ceremony commonly associated with the British monarchy. Consider the late-twentieth-century revitalization of the centuries-old Palio di Siena horse racing competition that takes place in Italy each summer, where neighborhood pride combines with iconography celebrating tradition and a sense of regional identity. In Latin America, acts of nationalism are performed annually. Each September, Mexico's president, by ringing the same church bell used in 1810, reenacts the ritual cry, or call to arms, that transfixed the town of Dolores, marking the beginning of the fight for Mexican independence. Across the United States, war reenactments abound, especially related to the Civil War, replete with their political associations and tendency toward myth. Other forms of invention appear less politically charged, such as *sertanejo* music in Brazil that has catapulted regional notions of the countryside to the forefront of conversations on national culture and identity. Burke, *Popular Culture in Early Modern Europe*; Chamosa, *The Argentine Folklore Movement*; Hobsbawm and Ranger, eds., *The Invention of Tradition*; Dent, *River of Tears*; Reily, "*Música sertaneja* and Migrant Identity."

6. Kasson, *Buffalo Bill's Wild West*, 15.

7. Kasson, *Buffalo Bill's Wild West*, 24; Sagala, *Buffalo Bill on Stage*, 51–52.

8. Kasson, *Buffalo Bill's Wild West*, 54–55.

9. Sagala, *Buffalo Bill on Stage*, 2.

10. Kasson, *Buffalo Bill's Wild West*, 62.

11. Kasson, *Buffalo Bill's Wild West*, speaks of a "national desire" that the shows tapped into (17–18).

12. Podestá, *Medio siglo de farándula*, 102.

13. Seibel, *Historia del circo*, 55.

14. Kasson, *Buffalo Bill's Wild West*, 114–17. One of the most famous examples is that of Theodore Roosevelt, who sought refuge in the Dakota Badlands after his wife and mother died, and who wrote a four-volume history of Westward expansion laced with nostalgia, tellingly titled *The Winning of the West*.

15. Deloria, *Playing Indian*.

16. Personal correspondence with Slatta, September 9, 2016. Slatta does point to a sort of "cowboy renaissance" on display in rodeos and attempts to preserve ideas of the Old West in the late twentieth century: see "Making and Unmaking Myths of the American frontier." Yet these efforts are highly professionalized and often revolve around competition rather than serving as leisure and social spaces—the pillar of Creole societies.

17. Conway, "Charros: A Critical Introduction," 66–83; Slatta, *Comparing Cowboys and Frontiers*, 77–82.

18. Conway, "Charros," 68.

19. See also Conway, *Heroes of the Borderlands*.

20. Charros were (and still are) popular figures at rodeos and pageantlike events full of theatricality throughout Mexico and the Southwest United States.

21. Sainetes by Alberto Vacarezza, Nemesio Trejo, or Florencio Sánchez are most often the ones that have been remade over the decades.

22. Hora, *Historia del turf argentino*.

23. Alfaro, *Carnaval: una historia social de Montevideo desde la perspectiva de la fiesta*, 2:118; Remedi, *Carnival Theater*.

24. Sarlo, *El imprerio de los sentimientos*; Sarlo, *Una modernidad periférica*; Acree, *Everyday Reading*.

25. Bockelman, "Between the Gaucho and the Tango," 577–601.

26. Oliven, *Tradition Matters*, xv, 71–73, 76; Arezo Posada, *Vigencia del tradicionalismo*, 58–62.

27. At the outset of the twenty-first century there were more than 1,200 Creole clubs in the province of Buenos Aires alone. Pisarello, "El tradicionalismo argentino en los inicios del siglo XXI," 204; see also the database in Pisarello, *Presente de gauchos en la Provincia de Buenos Aires*.

28. Bassa, "Patrimonio, identidad y tradición: el caso de las asociaciones tradicionalistas."

29. From its inception the week included bronco bucking and other competitions on horseback, rural games, displays of different cattle breeds, and payadores. Though the Semana Criolla originated in the capital, smaller cities started hosting their local variant in subsequent years.

30. "Buscan reconocimiento internacional al 'gaucho,'" *El País* (Montevideo), July 18, 2015.

31. De Giorgi, *El magma interior*; Samuelle, "La fiesta más criolla en el pago más grande"; Melgar, "Miles en fiesta de la tradición," *El País*, March 6, 2016.

32. Arezo Posada, *Vigencia del tradicionalismo*, 79–80; Sociedad Criolla Dr. Elías Regules, *Libro institucional*.

33. In addition to the existence of these clubs, national holidays such as the Día de la Tradición in Uruguay, initiated in 1946 in honor of Elías Regules's birthday, and Argentina's Día Nacional del Gaucho, declared in December 1994 in recognition of the date Hernández's *El Gaucho Martín Fierro* appeared, continue to showcase the presence of Creole heritage. Arezo Posada, *Vigencia del tradicionalismo*, 48–80.

34. Some of these festivals have deep roots while others are more recent creations. In the 1960s, for instance, two of these became annual affairs in Argentina: the Festival Nacional de Doma y Folklore and the Festival Nacional de Folklore de Cosquín, both in the province of Córdoba. Both have grown to last longer than a week and offer extensive musical lineups and competitions of rural pastimes, including bronco busting. A final similar example known as the Música de la

Tierra festival in Montevideo originated in 2014. It aims to "celebrate the value of our countryside, its landscapes and sounds, as well as the musical heritage shared by Uruguayans, Brazilians, and Argentines," primarily for younger generations. http://www.musicadelatierra.org/uy/festival.

35. Centro de Documentación de Danza, Teatro y Música, carpeta Juan Moreira, Imp. Int. 615, Teatro de la Libertad.

36. Companies have resurrected adaptations or scenes from *Juan Moreira*, for example, at the elegant Cervantes National Theater in Buenos Aires, the Fiesta de la Patria Gaucha, and the Cosquín Festival. In Buenos Aires, Ariel Bufano, the director and cofounder of the San Martín Puppet Theater Group, led the production of *El Gran Circo Criollo* that presented elements of the serious and the silly that we have seen throughout this book, as well as a final Creole drama number called "The Glory of Santos Morales." Centro de Documentación de Danza, Teatro y Música, El Gran Circo Criollo, Grupo de Titiriteros, under the direction of Ariel Bufano, video from 1983. Another group from Argentina, La Musaranga, which creates automatons and puppets from found or recyclable objects, has also done a version of *Moreira* for children as part of the act they call the "Circo Neo-Criollo." In Uruguay both the Ovidio Titers Band and the Coriolis Company, for their part, have included in their repertoire an entire puppet theater rendition of *Juan Moreira*.

37. Seibel, *Historia del circo*, 235–38; Seibel, "Códigos de teatro popular en el Juan Moreira," 54–59; Seibel, *Historia del teatro argentino*, 767–75.

38. http://www.lanacion.com.ar/2027966-marcelo-tinelli-la-vida-secreta-del-gran-prestidigitador.

39. Qtd. in Rossi, *Teatro nacional rioplatense*, 165.

40. Carlos Olivera, *En la brecha: 1880–1886*, 319.

Bibliography

Archives

AGN, Ar (Archivo General de la Nación, Argentina)

BN Ar (Biblioteca Nacional Mariano Moreno, Argentina)

BN Ur (Biblioteca Nacional, Uruguay)

Centro de Documentación de Danza, Teatro y Música, Teatro San Martín, Argentina

Centro Gallego, Uruguay

CIDDAE (Centro de Investigación, Documentación y Difusión de las Artes Escénicas), Uruguay

INAPL (Instituto Nacional de Antropología y Pensamiento Latinoamericano), Argentina

INET (Instituto Nacional de Estudios de Teatro, Argentina)

Fondo Documental Carlos G. Daws, Museo de Arte Popular José Hernández, Argentina

MHN (Museo Histórico Nacional, Uruguay; collections at the Casa Giró; Casa Lavalleja; Museo Romántico; and Casa Rivera)

Sociedad Criolla Elías Regules, Uruguay

Newspapers and Magazines

El Argentino (Paraná, Argentina)

Caras y Caretas (Buenos Aires, Argentina)

El Comercio (Lima, Perú)

Daily Alta California (San Francisco, CA, USA)

El Deber Cívico (Melo, Uruguay)

El Departamento: periódico de la tarde, noticioso y comercial (Mercedes, Uruguay)

Diario Oficial de Avisos de Madrid (Madrid, Spain)

El Día (Madrid, Spain)

El Día (Montevideo, Uruguay)
El Diario (Buenos Aires, Argentina)
La Dinastía (Barcelona, Spain)
Ecos del Progreso (Salto, Uruguay)
La Epoca (Madrid, Spain)
El Fígaro (Buenos Aires, Argentina)
El Fogón (Montevideo, Uruguay)
Heraldo de Madrid (Madrid, Spain)
Iris (Barcelona, Spain)
La Ilustración Artística (Barcelona, Spain)
Le Matin (Paris, France)
El Mercurio (La Plata, Argentina)
El Mosquito (Buenos Aires, Argentina)
El Nacional (Buenos Aires, Argentina)
La Nación Argentina (Buenos Aires, Argentina)
El Negro Timoteo (Montevideo, Uruguay)
El Observador (Montevideo, Uruguay)
La Opinión Pública (Montevideo, Uruguay)
El Orden (Buenos Aires, Argentina)
El País (Montevideo, Uruguay)
La Patria Argentina (Buenos Aires, Argentina)
El Paysandú (Paysandú, Uruguay)
El Porvenir (Monte Caseros, Argentina)
La Prensa (Buenos Aires, Argentina)
La Prensa (Diario de la Tarde) (Salto, Uruguay)
El Progresista: Publicación Independiente y Liberal (Carmelo, Uruguay)
La República (Montevideo, Uruguay)
El Siglo (Montevideo, Uruguay)
The Standard (Buenos Aires, Argentina)
Sud América (Buenos Aires, Argentina)
El Tiempo (Buenos Aires, Argentina)
El Tribuno (La Plata, Argentina)
La Tribuna (Buenos Aires, Argentina)

Published Primary and Secondary Sources

Abella, Walter Serrano, and Javier Vaz. *Martín Aquino: el matrero*. Montevideo: Fin de Siglo, 2009.

Acree, William G. *Everyday Reading: Print Culture and Collective Identity in the Río de la Plata, 1780–1910*. Nashville, TN: Vanderbilt University Press, 2011.

———. "The Creole Circus and Popular Entertainment in 19th-Century Argentina and Uruguay." *Oxford Research Encyclopedia of Latin American History*, 2016.

————. "Hemispheric Travelers on the Rioplatense Stage." *Latin American Theatre Review* 47, no. 2 (2014): 5–24.

Adamovsky, Ezequiel. "El criollismo como canal de visiones críticas sobre la historia argentina (desde el *Martín Fierro* hasta c. 1945)." *Anuario IEHS* 32, no. 1 (2017): 25–50.

————. "El criollismo en las luchas por la definición del origen y el color del *ethnos* argentino, 1945–1955." *Estudios Interdisciplinarios de América Latina y el Caribe* 26, no. 1 (2015): 31–63.

————. "La cuarta función del criollismo y las luchas por la definición del origen y el color del *ethnos* argentino (desde las primeras novelas gauchescas hasta c. 1940)." *Boletín del Instituto de Historia Argentina y Americana "Dr. Emilio Ravignani,"* 3ra serie 41 (2014): 50–92.

Aisemberg, Alicia. "Compañías." In *Historia del teatro argentino en Buenos Aires.* Vol. 1, *Período de la constitución del teatro argentino (1700–1884),* edited by Osvaldo Pellettieri, 506–16. Buenos Aires: Galerna, 2005.

————. "Espectáculos y público." In *Historia del teatro argentino en Buenos Aires.* Vol. 1, *Período de la constitución del teatro argentino (1700–1884),* edited by Osvaldo Pellettieri, 528–40. Buenos Aires: Galerna, 2005.

Alberto, Paulina L., and Eduardo Elena, eds. *Rethinking Race in Modern Argentina.* New York: Cambridge University Press, 2016.

Alfaro, Milita. *Carnaval: una historia social de Montevideo desde la perspectiva de la fiesta.* Vol. 2, *Carnaval y modernización: impulso y freno del disciplinamiento (1873–1904).* Montevideo: Trilce, 1998.

Andrews, George Reid. *The Afro-Argentines of Buenos Aires, 1800–1900.* Madison: University of Wisconsin Press, 1980.

————. *Blackness in the White Nation: A History of Afro-Uruguay.* Chapel Hill: University of North Carolina Press, 2010.

Anonymous. *A Five Years' Residence in Buenos Ayres, During the Years 1820 to 1825.* London: G. Herbert, 1825.

Anonymous. *Descripción de las fiestas cívicas celebradas en Montevideo, Mayo de 1816, and Oración inaugural pronunciada por Larrañaga en la apertura de la Biblioteca Pública de Montevideo, 1816.* Facsimile ed. With an introduction by Edmundo M. Narancio. Montevideo: Facultad de Humanidades y Ciencias, Instituto de Investigaciones Históricas, Universidad de la República (Uruguay), 1951.

Anonymous. *Fiestas mayas celebradas por el ejército republicano en el Cerro Largo.* Imprenta del Ejército, 1828.

Anonymous. "El valiente fanfarrón y criollo socarrón o El gaucho." In *Antología de obras de teatro argentino: desde sus orígenes a la actualidad,* edited and with a prologue by Beatriz Seibel, 201–62. Buenos Aires: Instituto Nacional del Teatro, 2006.

Anonymous. *Relación de las fiestas mayas de Buenos Aires en el presente año de 1813.* Buenos Aires: Imprenta de Niños Expósitos, 1813.

Ansolabehere, Pablo, and Lila Caimari, eds. *La ley de los profanos: delito, justicia y cultura en Buenos Aires (1870–1940)*. Buenos Aires: Fondo de Cultura Económica, 2007.

Arezo Posada, Carlos. *Vigencia del tradicionalismo: la patria gaucha*. Montevideo: Ediciones de la Plaza, 2011.

Arózteguy, Abdón. *Ensayos dramáticos*. Buenos Aires: Librairie Nouvelle "La Anticuaria," 1896.

———. *Julián Giménez*, in *Ensayos dramáticos* (Buenos Aires: Librairie Nouvelle "La Anticuaria," 1896), 1–94.

———. "Sobre dramas criollos." *Revista Histórica* 32, nos. 94–96 (1962): 620–21.

Arteaga, Juan José, et al. "Inmigración y estadística en el Uruguay, 1830–1940." In *Inmigración y estadísticas en el cono sur de América*, edited by Hernán Asdrúbal Silva, 261–372. México, D.F.: Instituto Panamericano de Geografía e Historia; Washington, DC: Organización de los Estados Americanos, 1990.

Ayestarán, Lauro. *La música en el Uruguay*. Vol. 1. With a prologue by Juan E. Pivel Devoto. Montevideo: SODRE, 1953.

———. "Prologue" to Regules, *Versos criollos*, xxx. Clásicos Uruguayos, vol. 57. Montevideo: Ministerio de Instrucción Pública y Previsión Social, 1965.

Baily, Samuel L. "Las sociedades de ayuda mutua y el desarrollo de una comunidad italiana en Buenos Aires, 1858–1918." *Desarrollo Económico* 21, no. 84 (1982): 485–514.

Barrán, José Pedro. *Historia de la sensibilidad en el Uruguay*. Vol. 1, *La cultura "bárbara" (1800–1860)*. Montevideo: Ediciones de la Banda Oriental; Facultad de Humanidades y Ciencias, 1990.

Barrán, José Pedro, Gerardo Caetano, and Teresa Porzecanski, eds. *Historia de la vida privada en el Uruguay*. Vol. 1, *Entre la honra y el desorden, 1780–1870*. Montevideo: Ediciones Santillana, 1996.

Bassa, Daniela Noemí. "Patrimonio, identidad y tradición: el caso de las asociaciones tradicionalistas." Conference presentation, VII Jornadas Santiago Wallace de Investigación en Antropología Social, Instituto de Ciencias Antropológicas, Facultad de Filosofía y Letras, UBA, 2013.

Beezley, William H. "Introduction." Special Issue: Mexican Puppets as Popular and Pedagogical Diversions. *The Americas* 67, no. 3 (2011): 307–14.

Benítez, Rubén. *Una histórica función de circo*. Buenos Aires: Universidad de Buenos Aires, Departamento Editorial, 1956.

Benzecry, Claudio. *The Opera Fanatic: Ethnography of an Obsession*. Chicago: University of Chicago Press, 2011.

Beruti, Juan Manuel. *Memorias curiosas*. Buenos Aires: Emecé Editores, 2001.

Bianchi, Alfredo A. *Teatro nacional*. Buenos Aires: Imprenta Cuneo, 1920.

Bilbao, Manuel. *Buenos Aires desde su fundación hasta nuestros días*. Buenos Aires: Imprenta de Juan A. Alsina, 1902.

Blanco Amores, Ángela. "Pablo Podestá. El niño acróbata y el circo nómade. El comediante criollo y el teatro gauchesco." *Boletín de Estudios de Teatro 7*, nos. 24–25 (1949): 3–14.

Bockelman, Brian. "Between the Gaucho and the Tango: Popular Songs and the Shifting Landscape of Modern Argentine Identity, 1895–1915." *American Historical Review* 116, no. 3 (2011): 577–601.

Bonatti, María. "Juan Moreira en un contexto modernista." *Revista Iberoamericana* 44, no. 104–5 (1978): 557–67.

Borges, Jorge Luis. "Prólogo" In *El gaucho*, by José Luis Lanuza, 9–11. Buenos Aires: Muchnik Editores, 1968.

Borucki, Alex. *From Shipmates to Soldiers: Emerging Black Identities in the Río de la Plata*. Albuquerque: University of New Mexico Press, 2015.

———. "La Republicana (1850–1950)." Unpublished essay.

———. "Tensiones raciales en el juego de la representación: Actores afro en Montevideo tras la fundación republicana (1830–1840)." *Gestos* 42 (2006): 33–56.

Bosch, Mariano G. "Viejos circos porteños." *Boletín de Estudios de Teatro* 6 (1944): 157–61.

Bourdieu, Pierre. *Distinction: A Social Critique of the Judgement of Taste*. Cambridge, MA: Harvard University Press, 2010.

Brackenridge, H. M. *Voyage to Buenos Ayres Performed in the Years 1817 and 1818*. London: Sir Richard Phillips and Co., 1820.

Buffalo Bill's Wild West and Congress of the Rough Riders of the World. Chicago, 1893.

Burke, Peter. *Popular Culture in Early Modern Europe*, 3rd ed. Farnham, England; Burlington, VT: Ashgate, 2009.

Burucúa, José Emilio, and Fabián Alejandro Campagne. "Mitos y simbologías nacionales en los países del cono sur." In *Inventando la nación: Iberoamérica siglo XIX*, edited by Antonio Annino and François-Xavier Guerra, 433–74. México, DF: Fondo de Cultura Económica, 2003.

Caimari, Lila. *Apenas un delincuente: crimen, castigo y cultura en la Argentina, 1880–1955*. Buenos Aires: Siglo Veintiuno Editores, 2004.

Caldcleugh, Alexander. *Travels in South America during the Years 1819–20–21*. Vol. 1. London: John Murray, 1825.

Carmeli, Yoram S. "Text, Traces, and the Reification of Totality: The Case of Popular Circus Literature." *New Literary History* 25, no. 1 (1994): 175–205.

Carril, Bonifacio del. *Monumenta iconográphica: paisajes, ciudades, tipos, usos y costumbres de la Argentina, 1556–1860*. Buenos Aires: Emecé Editores, 1964.

Castagnino, Raúl H. *El circo criollo: datos y documentos para su historia, 1757–1924*. Buenos Aires: Lajouane, 1953.

———. *Esquema de la literatura dramática argentina (1717–1949)*. Buenos Aires: Instituto de Historia del Teatro Americano, 1950.

———. "Juan Moreira: Entre Paradigmas Gauchescos." *Revista del Instituto Nacional de Estudios de Teatro* 5, no. 13 (1986): 23–29.

————. *Literatura dramática argentina, 1717–1967.* Buenos Aires: Editorial Pleamar, 1968.

————. *El teatro en Buenos Aires durante la época de Rosas.* 2 vols. Buenos Aires: Academia Argentina de Letras, 1989.

Castilho, Celso Thomas. "Recrear *La cabaña de Tom* en la Ciudad de México y América Latina. Intercambio anti-esclavista e intelectual en el mundo Atlántico del siglo XIX." *Historia Mexicana,* forthcoming.

Cattaruzza, Alejandro, and Alejandro Eujanian. *Políticas de la historia: Argentina 1860–1960.* Buenos Aires: Alianza Editorial, 2003.

Chamosa, Oscar. "Lúbolos, Tenorios y Moreiras: reforma liberal y cultura popular en el carnaval de Buenos Aires de la segunda mitad del siglo XIX." In *La vida política en la Argentina del siglo XIX: armas, votos y voces,* edited by Hilda Sábato and Alberto Lettieri, 115–35. Buenos Aires: Fondo de Cultura Económica, 2003.

————. *The Argentine Folklore Movement: Sugar Elites, Criollo Workers, and the Politics of Cultural Nationalism, 1900–1955.* Tucson: University of Arizona Press, 2010.

————. "'To Honor the Ashes of Their Forebears': The Rise and Crisis of African Nations in the Post-Independence State of Buenos Aires, 1820–1860." *The Americas* 59, no. 3 (2003): 347–78.

Chasteen, John Charles. "Anything Goes: Carnivalesque Transgressions in Nineteenth-Century Latin America." In *Building Nineteenth-Century Latin America: Re-rooted Cultures, Identities, and Nations,* edited by William G. Acree Jr. and Juan Carlos González Espitia, 133–49. Nashville, TN: Vanderbilt University Press, 2009.

————. "Black Kings, Blackface Carnival, and Nineteenth-Century Origins of the Tango." In *Latin American Popular Culture: An Introduction,* edited by William H. Beezley and Linda A. Curcio-Nagy, 43–59. Wilmington, DE: SR Books, 2000.

————. *Heroes on Horseback: A Life and Times of the Last Gaucho Caudillos.* Albuquerque: University of New Mexico Press, 1994.

————. *National Rhythms, African Roots: The Deep History of Latin American Popular Dance.* Albuquerque: University of New Mexico Press, 2004.

————. "Violence for Show: Knife Dueling on a Nineteenth-Century Cattle Frontier." In *The Problem of Order in Changing Societies: Essays on Crime and Policing in Argentina and Uruguay,* edited by Lyman L. Johnson, 47–64. Albuquerque: University of New Mexico Press, 1990.

Cientofante, Manuel M. *Amores de Cocoliche.* Buenos Aires: Casa Editora de Salvador Matera, 1909.

————. *Napolitano Cocoliche.* Buenos Aires: Casa Editora de Salvador Matera, 1909.

Collier, Simon. *The Life, Music, and Times of Carlos Gardel.* Pittsburgh: University of Pittsburgh Press, 1986.

Colombo, María Susana. "Los primeros años del Juan Moreira en La Plata (1886–1894)." *Revista del Instituto Nacional de Estudios de Teatro* 5, no. 13 (1986): 30–38.

Conway, Christopher B. "Charros: A Critical Introduction." In *Modern Mexican Culture: Critical Foundations*, edited by Stuart A. Day, 66–83. Tucson: University of Arizona Press, 2017.

———. *Heroes of the Borderlands: The Western in Mexican Film, Comics, and Music.* Albuquerque: University of New Mexico Press, 2019.

———. *Nineteenth-Century Spanish America: A Cultural History.* Nashville, TN: Vanderbilt University Press, 2015.

Cuarterolo, Andrea. "Los antecedentes del cine político y social en la Argentina (1896–1933)." In *Una historia del cine político y social en Argentina (1896–1969)*, edited by Ana Laura Lusnich and Pablo Piedras, with a prologue by Fernando Birri, 145–72. Buenos Aires: Nueva Librería, 2009.

Cúneo, Dardo. *Frank Brown.* Buenos Aires: Editorial Nova, 1944.

Darío, Rubén. "Psicologías carnavelescas." In *Páginas olvidadas*, 77–82. Buenos Aires: Ediciones selectas América, 1921.

Davie, John Constance. *Letters from Paraguay: Describing the Settlements of Montevideo and Buenos Ayres. . . .* London: G. Robinson, 1805.

de Giorgi, Alvaro. *El magma interior: política, cultura y territorio en la Fiesta de la Patria Gaucha.* Montevideo: Trilce, 2002.

Deloria, Philip. *Playing Indian.* New Haven, CT: Yale University Press, 1998.

de María, Isidoro. *Montevideo Antiguo.* 2 vols. With a prologue by Juan E. Pivel Devoto. Montevideo: Ministerio de Instrucción Pública y Previsión Social, n.d.

———. *El Teatro Solís: reseña histórica en el vigésimo noveno aniversario de su inauguración.* Montevideo: Tipografía José Pedro Varela, 1885.

Demasi, Carlos. "La construcción de un 'héroe máximo': José Artigas en las conmemoraciones uruguayas de 1911." *Revista Iberoamericana* 71, no. 213 (2005): 1029–45.

Dent, Alexander Sebastian. *River of Tears: Country Music, Memory, and Modernity in Brazil.* Durham, NC: Duke University Press, 2009.

Devoto, Fernando, and Alejandro Fernández. "Mutualismo étnico, liderazgo y participación política. Algunas hipótesis de trabajo." In *Mundo urbano y cultura popular: estudios de historia social argentina*, edited by Diego Armus, 129–52. Buenos Aires: Sudamericana, 1990.

Dillon, Elizabeth Maddock. *New World Drama: The Performative Commons in the Atlantic World, 1649–1849.* Durham, NC: Duke University Press, 2014.

Dirección General de Estadística Municipal. *Anuario Estadístico de la Ciudad de Buenos Aires, año 3, 1893.* Buenos Aires: Compañía Sud-Americana de Billetes de Banco, 1894.

———. *Anuario Estadístico de la Ciudad de Buenos Aires, año 4, 1894.* Buenos Aires: Compañía Sud-Americana de Billetes de Banco, 1895.

——. *Anuario Estadístico de la Ciudad de Buenos Aires, año 6, 1896.* Buenos Aires: Imprenta, Litografía y encuadernación de G. Craft, 1897.

——. *Anuario Estadístico de la Ciudad de Buenos Aires, año 10, 1900.* Buenos Aires: Compañía Sud-Americana de Billetes de Banco, 1901.

——. *Anuario Estadístico de la Ciudad de Buenos Aires, año 13, 1903.* Buenos Aires: Compañía Sud-Americana de Billetes de Banco, 1904.

——. *Anuario Estadístico de la Ciudad de Buenos Aires, año 17, 1907.* Buenos Aires: Imprenta "La Bonaerense" de Gerónimo Pesce, 1908.

——. *Anuaire Statistique de la Ville de Buénos-Ayres, VIme année—1896.* Buenos Aires: G. Kraft, 1897.

——. *Year-Book of the City of Buenos Aires, Years 20 and 21, 1910 and 1911.* Buenos Aires: "El Centenario" Alegre & Quincoces, 1913.

Dubatti, Jorge. "Los Podestá." In *Historia del teatro argentino en Buenos Aires*, vol. 2, edited by Osvaldo Pellettieri, 113–17. Buenos Aires: Galerna, 2002.

——. "'Martín Fierro' de Elías Regules: una parábola nativista." In *Martin Fierro* and *El Entenao*, by Elías Regules. With notes by Teodoro Klein, Beatriz Seibel, Eneida Sansone de Martínez, and Jorge Dubatti, 31–34. Buenos Aires: Ediciones del Jilguero, 1996.

Duffau, Nicolás. *Armar al bandido: prensa, folletines y delincuentes en el Uruguay de la modernización: el caso de El Clinudo (1882–1886).* Montevideo: CSIC; Universidad de la República, 2014.

Ehrick, Christine. *Radio and the Gendered Soundscape: Women and Broadcasting in Argentina and Uruguay, 1930–1950.* New York: Cambridge University Press, 2015.

Estrada, Santiago. *Teatro: colección de artículos.* With a critical and biographical study by Antonio Peña y Goñi. Barcelona: Imprenta Henrich y Cía. 1889.

Evans, Judith. "Setting the Stage for Struggle: Popular Theater in Buenos Aires, 1890–1914." *Radical History Review* 21 (1979): 49–61.

Falkner, Thomas. *Description of Patagonia, and the Adjoining Parts of South America.* London: C. Pugh, 1774.

Farinetti, María. "Gauchos y gringos en la formación de la nación argentina." *Apuntes de Investigación del CECYP*, no. 13 (2008): 215–20.

Fernández, Mauro A. ("Fénix"). *Historia de la magia y el ilusionismo en la Argentina: desde sus orígenes hasta el siglo XIX inclusive.* With a prologue by Teodoro Klein and a "prólogo mágico" by Ricardo "Fantasio" Roucau. Buenos Aires: 1996.

Fey, Ingrid E. "Peddling the Pampas: Argentina at the Paris Universal Exposition of 1889." In *Latin American Popular Culture: An Introduction*, edited by William H. Beezley and Linda A. Curcio-Nagy, 61–85. Wilmington, DE: Scholarly Resources, 2000.

Fiestas mayas celebradas por el ejército republicano en el Cerro Largo. Imprenta del Ejército, 1828.

Finch, Laura I. "All about 'Rama.'" *The Annals of Psychical Science* 6 (1907): 426–34.

Finkielman, Jorge. *The Film Industry in Argentina: An Illustrated Cultural History.* Jefferson, NC: McFarland & Co., 2004.

Garavaglia, Juan Carlos. *Construir el estado e inventar la nación: el Río de la Plata, siglos XVIII–XIX.* Buenos Aires: Prometeo Libros, 2007.

———. "El *teatro del poder*: ceremonias, tensiones y conflictos en el estado colonial." *Boletín del Instituto de Historia Argentina y Americana 'Dr. Emilio Ravignani' tercera serie,* no. 14 (1996): 7–30.

García, Juan Agustín. *Sobre el teatro nacional y otros artículos y fragmentos.* Buenos Aires: Agencia General de Librería, 1921.

García Velloso, Enrique. *Memorias de un hombre de teatro.* With a prologue by Ricardo Halac. Buenos Aires: Fondo Nacional de las Artes, 1999.

Garrett, Victoria Lynn. *Performing Everyday Life in Argentine Popular Theater, 1890–1934.* Cham, Switzerland: Palgrave Macmillan, 2018.

Ghiano, Juan Carlos. *Teatro gauchesco primitivo.* Buenos Aires: Ediciones Losange, 1957.

Golluscio de Montoya, Eva. "Del circo colonial a los teatros ciudadanos: proceso de urbanización de la actividad dramática rioplatense." *Cahiers du monde hispanique et luso-brésilien* 42 (1984): 141–49.

———. "Elementos para una 'teoría' teatral libertaria (Argentina 1900)." *Latin American Theatre Review* 21, no. 1 (1987): 85–93.

González Urtiaga, Juan. *José J. Podestá y 'Pepino el 88.'* Montevideo: Centro de Estudios de Teatro Rioplatense, n.d.

———. *Los Podestá: el teatro rioplatense a través de "la Gran Familia."* Montevideo: Organización Nacional Pro Laboral para Lisiados ONPLI, 2001.

———. *Nuevas canciones inéditas del Gran Pepino José J. Podestá.* Montevideo: Centro de Estudios de Teatro Rioplatense, 1997.

González Velasco, Carolina. *Gente de teatro: ocio y espectáculos en la Buenos Aires de los años veinte.* Buenos Aires: Siglo XXI Editores, 2012.

Gottlieb, Robert. *Sarah: The Life of Sarah Bernhardt.* New Haven, CT: Yale University Press, 2010.

Gottschalk, Louis Moreau. *Notes of a Pianist, During his Professional Tours in the United States, Canada, the Antilles, and South America.* Edited by Clara Gottschalk. Translated by Robert E. Peterson. Philadelphia: J. B. Lippincott & Co., 1881.

Graziano, Frank. *Cultures of Devotion: Folk Saints of Spanish America.* New York: Oxford University Press, 2007.

Groussac, Paul. "La temporada teatral: Fedora Bernhardt." *Boletin de Estudios de Teatro* año 2, no. 4 (1944): 37–43.

Guide Bleu du Figaro à L'exposition de 1900. Paris: Le Figaro; Taride, 1900.

Gutierrez, Eduardo. *Juan Moreira.* With a prologue by Josefina Ludmer. Buenos Aires: Perfil Libros, 1999.

Gutiérrez, Eduardo, and José J. Podestá. *Juan Moreira.* Edited with a prologue and notes by Angel Mazzei. Buenos Aires: Ministerio de Cultura y Educación, 1970.

Gutiérrez, Leandro H., and Luis Alberto Romero, eds. *Sectores populares, cultura y política: Buenos Aires en la entreguerra*. Buenos Aires: Editorial Sudamericana, 1995.

Haigh, Samuel. *Sketches of Buenos Ayres and Chile*. London: James Carpenter, 1829.

Halperín Donghi, Tulio. "¿Para qué la inmigración? Ideología y política inmigratoria en la Argentina, 1810–1914." In Halperín Donghi, *El espejo de la historia: problemas argentinos y perspectivas latinoamericanas*, 189–238. Buenos Aires: Editorial Sudamericana, 1987.

Hammerton, John Alexander. *The Real Argentine: Notes and Impressions on a Year in the Argentine and Uruguay*. New York: Dodd, Mead, & Co., 1915.

Harper's Guide to Paris and the Exposition of 1900. London & New York: Harper & Brothers, 1900.

Hernández Desplats, Marcos. *Martín Aquino: Batllismo y barbarie. La verdadera historia del último matrero oriental*. Montevideo: Ediciones de la Plaza, 2017.

Hidalgo, Bartolomé. *Obra Completa*. With a prologue by Antonio Praderio. Montevideo: Ministerio de Educación y Cultura, 1986.

Hinchliff, Thomas Woodbine. *South American Sketches, or A Visit to Rio Janeiro, The Organ Mountains, La Plata, and the Paraná*. London: Longman, Green, Longman, Roberts, & Green, 1863.

Hobsbawm, Eric. "Introduction: Inventing Traditions." In *The Invention of Tradition*, edited by Eric Hobsbawm and Terence Ranger, 1–14. Cambridge: Cambridge University Press, 1992.

———. "Mass-Producing Traditions: Europe, 1870–1914." In *The Invention of Tradition*, edited by Eric Hobsbawm and Terence Ranger, 263–308. Cambridge: Cambridge University Press, 1992.

Hobsbawm, Eric, and Terence Ranger, eds. *The Invention of Tradition*. Cambridge: Cambridge University Press, 1992.

Hora, Roy. *Historia del turf argentino*. Buenos Aires: Siglo Veintiuno Editores, 2014.

———. *Los terratenientes de la pampa argentina: una historia social y política, 1860–1945*. Buenos Aires: Siglo Veintiuno Editores, 2002.

Huizinga, Johan. *Homo Ludens: A Study of the Play-Element in Culture*. Boston: Beacon, 1955.

Hutcheon, Linda, with Siobhan O'Flynn. *A Theory of Adaptation*, 2nd ed. London: Routledge, 2013.

Irigoyen, Emilio. "La ciudad como escenario: poder y representación hasta 1830." In *Uruguay: imaginarios culturales. Desde las huellas indígenas a la modernidad*, edited by Hugo Achugar and Mabel Moraña, 95–124. Montevideo: Ediciones Trilce; Pittsburgh: Instituto Internacional de Literatura Iberoamericana, 2000.

Johnson, Lyman L. "Why Dead Bodies Talk: An Introduction." In *Death, Dismemberment, and Memory: Body Politics in Latin America*, edited by Lyman L. Johnson, 1–26. Albuquerque: University of New Mexico Press, 2004.

————. *Workshop of Revolution: Plebian Buenos Aires and the Atlantic World, 1776–1810.* Durham, NC: Duke University Press, 2011.

Karush, Matthew B. *Culture of Class: Radio and Cinema in the Making of a Divided Argentina, 1920–1946.* Durham, NC: Duke University Press, 2012.

Kasson, Joy S. *Buffalo Bill's Wild West: Celebrity, Memory, and Popular History.* New York: Hill & Wang, 2000.

Klein, Teodoro. *El actor en el Río de la Plata.* Vol. 1, *De la colonia a la independencia nacional.* Buenos Aires: Ediciones Asociación Argentina de Actores, 1984.

————. *El actor en el Río de la Plata.* Vol. 2, *De Casacuberta a los Podestá.* Buenos Aires: Ediciones Asociación Argentina de Actores, 1994.

————. "El manuscrito de Martín Fierro." In *Martín Fierro: 1890; El entenao: 1892: obras inéditas de Elías Regules.* With notes by Teodoro Klein, Beatriz Seibel, Eneida Sansone de Martínez, and Jorge Dubatti, 35–37. Buenos Aires: Ediciones del Jilguero, 1996.

————. "El público del *Moreira* en Buenos Aires." *Revista del Instituto Nacional de Estudios de Teatro* 5, no. 13 (1986): 39–42.

————. "Los Podestá-Scotti y el género criollo." In *Martin Fierro* and *El Entenao*, by Elías Regules. With notes by Teodoro Klein, Beatriz Seibel, Eneida Sansone de Martínez, and Jorge Dubatti, 5–18. Buenos Aires: Ediciones del Jilguero, 1996.

Lanuza, José Luis, and René Burri. *El gaucho.* With a preface by Jorge Luis Borges. Buenos Aires: Muchnik Editores, 1968.

Legido, Juan Carlos. *El teatro uruguayo: de Juan Moreira a los independientes, 1886–1967.* Montevideo: Ediciones Tauro, 1968.

Leguizamón, Martiniano. "*Calandria: costumbres campestres en diez escenas.*" In *Dramaturgos post-románticos*, edited and with a prologue and notes by Angel Mazzei. Buenos Aires: Ministerio de Cultura y Educación, 1970.

Lehmann-Nitsche, Robert. *La leyenda de Santos Vega: documentos para la sociología argentina.* In *Anales de la Facultad de Derecho y Ciencias Sociales*, vol. 2. Buenos Aires, 1916.

Lenchantín, José Antonio. *Moreira en ópera: juguete lírico en un acto y dos cuadros en prosa y verso.* Buenos Aires: Imprenta, Litografía, Encuadernación de Guillermo Kraft, 1897.

Levine, Lawrence W. *Highbrow/Lowbrow: The Emergence of Cultural Hierarchy in America.* Cambridge, MA: Harvard University Press, 1988.

————. "The Folklore of Industrial Society: Popular Culture and Its Audiences." *American Historical Review* 97, no. 5 (1992): 1369–99.

Levy, Aiala. "Sarah Bernhardt en São Paulo: una musa para la 'capital artística.'" Translated by Sara Hidalgo. *ISTOR* 14, no. 53 (2013): 11–22.

Llanes, Ricardo M. *Teatros de Buenos Aires: referencias históricas.* Buenos Aires: Secretaria de Cultura y Acción Social, 1968.

López Cantos, Ángel. *Juegos, fiestas y diversiones en la América española.* Madrid: Editorial MAPFRE, 1992.

López, Liliana B. "Recepción." In *Historia del teatro argentino en Buenos Aires*. Vol. 2, *La emancipación cultural (1884–1930)*, 131–43. Edited by Osvaldo Pellettieri. Buenos Aires: Galerna, 2002.

Lusnich, Ana Laura, and Susana Llahí. "El circo: compañías." In *Historia del teatro argentino en Buenos Aires*. Vol. 1, *Período de la constitución del teatro argentino (1700–1884)*, edited by Osvaldo Pellettieri, 358–64. Buenos Aires: Galerna, 2005.

Maccarini, Manuel. *Teatro de identidad popular: en los géneros sainete rural, circo criollo y radioteatro argentino*. Buenos Aires: INET, 2006.

Marial, José. "Los enemigos de Juan Moreira." *Revista del Instituto Nacional de Estudios de Teatro* 5, no. 13 (1986): 60–65.

Marks, Patricia. *Sarah Bernhardt's First American Theatrical Tour, 1880–1881*. Jefferson, NC: McFarland & Co., 2003.

Matallana, Andrea. *"Locos por la radio": una historia social de la radiofonía en la Argentina, 1923–1947*. Buenos Aires: Prometeo Libros, 2006.

Mazziotti, Nora. "El auge de las revistas teatrales en 1910–1934." *Cuadernos Hispanoamericanos* no. 425 (1985): 73–88.

———. *"Bambalinas*: el auge de una modalidad teatral-periodística." In *Mundo urbano y cultural popular: estudios de historia social argentina*, edited by Diego Armus, 69–89. Buenos Aires: Sudamericana, 1990.

McCleary, Kristen. "Afro-Argentines, *Papás, Malevos,* and *Patotas*: Characterizing Masculinity on the Stages and in the Audiences of Buenos Aires, 1880–1920." In *Modern Argentine Masculinities*, edited by Carolina Rocha, 73–88. Bristol: Intellect, 2013.

———. "Inflaming the Fears of Theatergoers: How Fires Shaped the Public Sphere in Buenos Aires, Argentina, 1880–1910." In *Flammable Cities: Urban Conflagration and the Making of the Modern World*, edited by Jordan Sand, Uwe Lubken, and Greg Bankoff, 254–72. Madison: University of Wisconsin Press, 2012.

———. "Popular, Elite, *and* Mass Culture? The Spanish Zarzuela in Buenos Aires, 1890–1900." *Studies in Latin American Popular Culture* 21 (2002): 1–27.

Melgar, Pablo. "Miles en fiesta de la tradición." *El País*, March 6, 2016.

Milanesio, Natalia. *Workers Go Shopping: The Rise of Popular Consumer Culture*. Albuquerque: University of New Mexico Press, 2013.

Miranda Silva, Francisca, and William H. Beezley. "The Rosete Aranda Puppets: A Century and a Half of an Entertainment Enterprise." *The Americas* 67, no. 3 (2011): 331–54.

Mirza, Roger. "Los orígenes coloniales de la escena oriental." In *Sociedad y cultura en el Montevideo colonial*, compiled by Luis Ernesto Behares and Oribe Cures, 307–18. Montevideo: Facultad de Humanidades y Ciencias de la Educación, 1997.

———. "Para una revisión de la historia del teatro uruguayo: desde los orígenes hasta

1900." In *Uruguay: imaginarios culturales. Desde las huellas indígenas a la modernidad*, edited by Hugo Achugar and Mabel Moraña, 179–202. Montevideo: Ediciones Trilce; Pittsburgh: Instituto Internacional de Literatura Iberoamericana, 2000.

Mogliani, Laura. *El costumbrismo en el teatro argentino*, PhD diss. Buenos Aires: UBA, 2006.

———. "*Julián Giménez* de Abdón Arózteguy." In *Teatro, memoria, identidad*, edited by Roger Mirza, 195–207. Montevideo: Facultad de Humanidades y Ciencias de la Educación, UDELAR, 2009.

Montaldo, Graciela R. *Museo del consumo: archivos de la cultura de masas en Argentina*. Buenos Aires: Fondo de Cultura Económica, 2016.

Monzón, Antonio. "El teatro porteño en el histórico año de la Revolución de Mayo." *Boletín de Estudios de Teatro* 28 (1950): 3–12.

Moore, Jacqueline M. *Cow Boys and Cattle Men: Class and Masculinities on the Texas Frontier, 1865–1900*. New York: New York University Press, 2010.

Moratorio, Orosmán. *Juan Soldao, drama criollo, satírico-político*. Montevideo: José Escribanis, 1894.

Moya, Ismael. "El circo y el payador." *Revista del Instituto Nacional de Estudios de Teatro* 1, no. 1 (1959): 19–28.

Myers, Jorge. "Una revolución en las costumbres: las nuevas formas de sociabilidad de la elite porteña, 1800–1860." In *Historia de la vida privada en la Argentina*, vol. 1, edited by Fernando Devoto and Marta Madero, 111–45. Buenos Aires: Taurus, 1999.

Nasaw, David. *Going Out: The Rise and Fall of Public Amusements*. Cambridge, MA: Harvard University Press, 1999.

Navarrete, José Francisco. "Mendoza (1892–1939)." In *Historia del teatro argentino en las provincias*, vol. 1, edited by Osvaldo Pellettieri, Laura Mogliani, Patricia Fischer, and Martín Rodríguez, 257–90. Buenos Aires: Galerna, 2005.

Negus, Keith. "The Work of Cultural Intermediaries and the Enduring Distance Between Production and Consumption." *Cultural Studies* 16, no. 4 (2002): 501–15.

Nixon, Sean, and Paul Du Gay. "Who Needs Cultural Intermediaries?" *Cultural Studies* 16, no. 4 (2002): 495–500.

Nouwen, Mollie Lewis. *Oy, My Buenos Aires: Jewish Immigrants and the Creation of Argentine National Identity*. Albuquerque: University of New Mexico Press, 2013.

Obligado, Rafael. *Prosas*, edited and with a prologue by Pedor Luís Barcía. Buenos Aires: Academia Argentina de Letras, 1976.

Oliven, Ruben. *Tradition Matters: Modern Gaúcho Identity in Brazil*. Translated by Carmen Chaves Tesser. New York: Columbia University Press, 1996.

Olivera, Carlos. *En la brecha: 1880–1886*. Buenos Aires: F. Lajouane; París: Ch. Bouret, 1887.

Pacheco, Carlos M. *Los disfrazados y otros sainetes*. With an introduction by Marta Lena Paz. Buenos Aires: EUDEBA, 1964.

El País. "Buscan reconocimiento internacional al 'gaucho.'" July 18, 2015.

Parish Robertson, John, and William Parish Robertson. *Letters on South America: Comprising Travels on the Banks of the Paraná and the Río de la Plata*, vol. 3. London: John Murray, 1843.

Pellarolo, Silvia. *Sainete criollo: democracia/representación. El caso de Nemesio Trejo*. Buenos Aires: Corregidor, 1997.

Pellettieri, Osvaldo. "Cambios en el sistema teatral de la gauchesca rioplatense." *Gestos* 2, no. 4 (1987): 115–24.

——. *Cien años de teatro argentino (1886–1990): del Moreira a Teatro Abierto*. Buenos Aires: Galerna, 1990.

——. "'Juan Cuello,' Novela y obra teatral de la gauchesca al nativismo." Paper presented at the Segundas Jornadas de Investigación, UBA, 1987. http://www.teatrodelpueblo.org.ar/dramaturgia/pellettieri004.htm

Pellettieri, Osvaldo, ed. *Historia del teatro argentino en Buenos Aires*. Vol. 1, *Período de la constitución del teatro argentino (1700–1884)*. Buenos Aires: Galerna, 2005.

——. *Historia del teatro argentino en Buenos Aires*. Vol. 2, *La emancipación cultural (1884–1930)*. Buenos Aires: Galerna, 2002.

——. *Inmigración italiana y teatro argentino*. Buenos Aires: Galerna/Instituto Italiano de Cultura de Buenos Aires, 1999.

Pellettieri, Osvaldo, Laura Mogliani, Patricia Fischer, and Martín Rodríguez, eds. *Historia del teatro argentino en las provincias*, vol. 1. Buenos Aires: Galerna/INET, 2005.

Pereira, Antonio N. *Recuerdos de mi tiempo*. Montevideo: Imprenta "El Siglo Ilustrado," 1891.

Pérez de Guzmán, Juan. "El teatro hispanoamericano." *La España moderna* año 12, 141 (1900): 114–34.

Pérez Petit, Víctor. "Defensa del drama criollo." *Nosotros* 2, no. 16 (1937): 239–55.

——. *Teatro*. Vol. 1, *Cobarde, Claro de luna, Yorick*. Montevideo: Barreiro y Ramos, 1912.

Pisarello, María Cecilia. "El tradicionalismo argentino en los inicios del siglo XXI." *Cuadernos del Instituto Nacional de Antropología y Pensamiento Latinoamericano* 21 (2006–2007): 203–13.

——. *Presente de gauchos en la Provincia de Buenos Aires*. Buenos Aires: Unión del Personal Civil de la Nación, 2004.

Plesch, Melanie. "The Guitar in Nineteenth-Century Buenos Aires: Towards a Cultural History of an Argentine Musical Emblem." PhD diss., University of Melbourne, 1998.

Podestá, Blanca. *Algunos recuerdos de mi vida artística*. Buenos Aires: Artes Gráficas Bartolomé U. Chiesino, 1951.

Podestá, José J. *Medio siglo de farándula: memorias de José J. Podestá*. Edited and with a preliminary study by Osvaldo Pellettieri. Buenos Aires: Galerna; Instituto Nacional de Teatro, 2003.

Pollero, Raquel. "Historia demográfica de Montevideo y su campaña (1757–1860)." PhD diss., Universidad de la República, Montevideo, 2013.

Prieto, Adolfo. *El discurso criollista en la formación de la Argentina moderna.* Buenos Aires: Siglo XXI Editores, 2006.

Puccia, Enrique. *Breve historia del carnaval porteño.* Buenos Aires: Municipalidad de la Ciudad de Buenos Aires, 1974.

Quesada, Ernesto. "El 'criollismo' en la literatura argentina." In *En torno al criollismo: textos y polémicas,* edited and with a critical study by Alfredo V. E. Rubione, 103–230. Buenos Aires: Centro Editor de América Latina, 1983.

———. *La propiedad intelectual en el derecho argentino.* Buenos Aires: Librería de J. Menéndez, 1904.

———. *Reseñas y críticas.* Buenos Aires: Félix Lajouane, 1893.

Rama, Ángel. *Los gauchipolíticos rioplatenses,* vol. 2. Buenos Aires: Centro Editor de América Latina, 1994.

Ratier, Hugo E., Eugenia del Campo, Leandro Etchichury, and Magdalena Iriberry. "Organizaciones rurales y cultura de las pampas: la construcción social de lo gauchesco y sus implicaciones." Conference presentation at the IV Reunión de Antropología del Mercosur. November 2001, Curitiba, Brazil.

Regules, Elías. *Martín Fierro: 1890; El Entenao: 1892: obras inéditas de Elías Regules.* With notes by Teodoro Klein, Beatriz Seibel, Eneida Sansone de Martínez, and Jorge Dubatti. Buenos Aires: Ediciones del Jilguero, 1996.

———. *Los guachitos: comedia criolla.* Montevideo: Peña Hnos., 1927.

———. *Versos criollos.* Clásicos Uruguayos, vol. 57. With a prologue by Lauro Ayestarán. Montevideo: Ministerio de Instrucción Pública y Previsión Social, 1965.

Reily, Suzel Ana. "*Música sertaneja* and Migrant Identity: The Stylistic Development of a Brazilian Genre." *Popular Music* 11, no. 3 (1992): 337–58.

Relación de las fiestas mayas de Buenos Aires en el presente año de 1813. Buenos Aires: Imprenta de Niños Expósitos, 1813.

Remedi, Gustavo. *Carnival Theater: Uruguay's Popular Performers and National Culture.* Minneapolis: University of Minnesota Press, 2004.

República Argentina. *Tercer censo nacional,* vol. 10. Buenos Aires: Talleres Gráficos de L. J. Rosso y Cía, 1917.

Richter, Daniel Alex. "Uruguayan Cinema in the 20th Century." *Oxford Research Encyclopedia of Latin American History,* December 2016. doi: 10.1093/acrefore/9780199366439.013.341

Ristori, Adelaide. *Studies and Memoirs: An Autobiography.* Boston: Roberts Brothers, 1888.

Rivarola, Enrique E. "El teatro nacional: su carácter y sus obras." *Revista de la Universidad de Buenos Aires* 3, no. 14 (1905): 341–75.

Rizzo Botana, Ángela Raquel. "Elías Regules en *El Fogón.*" Unpublished essay.

Roach, Joseph. *Cities of the Dead: Circum-Atlantic Performance.* New York: Columbia University Press, 1996.

Rojas, María A. "El público asistente a los circos, hasta la aparición de 'Juan Moreira.'" *Revista de Estudios de Teatro* 3 (1960): 50–58.

Rolleri, Santiago (L. Irrelor). *Cocoliche en carnaval*. Buenos Aires; Montevideo: Santiago Rolleri, 1902.

———. *Nuevas canciones de Cocoliche*. Buenos Aires; Montevideo: S. Rolleri, n.d.

Romero, Luis Alberto. "Los sectores populares en las ciudades latinoamericanas del siglo XIX: la cuestión de la identidad." *Desarrollo Económico* 27, no. 106 (1987): 201–22.

Rosselli, John. "The Opera Business and the Italian Immigrant Community in Latin America 1820–1930: The Example of Buenos Aires." *Past & Present* 127 (1990): 155–82.

Rossi, Vicente. *Cosas de negros*. Buenos Aires: Taurus, 2001.

———. *Teatro nacional rioplatense: contribución a su análisis y a su historia*. Buenos Aires: Solar, 1969.

Rubione, Alfredo V. E., ed. *En torno al criollismo: textos y polémicas*, with a critical study by Rubione. Buenos Aires: Centro Editor de América Latina, 1983.

Sábato, Hilda. "On Political Citizenship in Nineteenth-Century Latin America." *American Historical Review* 106, no. 4 (2001): 1290–1315.

Sagala, Sandra K. *Buffalo Bill on Stage*. Albuquerque: University of New Mexico Press, 2008.

Salgado, Susana. *The Teatro Solís: 150 Years of Opera, Concert, and Ballet in Montevideo*. Middletown, CT: Wesleyan University Press, 2003.

Samuelle, Juan. "La fiesta más criolla en el pago más grande." *El Observador*. Montevideo, March 3, 2015.

Sánchez, Florencio. "Cartas de un flojo." Montevideo, 1962.

———. "El caudillaje criminal en Sud América." Montevideo, 1962.

———. "El teatro nacional." Montevideo, 1962.

Sánchez de Thompson, Mariquita. *Intimidad y política: diario, cartas y recuerdos*. Edited with a preliminary study by María Gabriela Mizraje. Buenos Aires: Adriana Hidalgo Editora, 2003.

———. "Madame Mendeville Recalls Viceregal Buenos Aires." In *Latin American Independence: An Anthology of Sources*. Edited and translated by Sarah C. Chambers and John Charles Chasteen, 15–26. Indianapolis & Cambridge: Hackett, 2010.

San Martín, Fernando. *Cine mudo argentino: 1896/1932*. Buenos Aires: Gráfica Laiglon, 2016.

Sansone de Martínez, Eneida. "A manera de prólogo." In *Martin Fierro* and *El Entenao*, by Elías Regules. With notes by Teodoro Klein, Beatriz Seibel, Eneida Sansone de Martínez, and Jorge Dubatti, 27–30. Buenos Aires: Ediciones del Jilguero, 1996.

———. *El teatro en el Uruguay en el siglo XIX: desde los orígenes a la independencia*. Montevideo: Surcos, 1995.

Santillán, Juan José. "Juan Moreira: historia del gaucho traicionado." *Clarín*, November 6, 2015.

Sarlo, Beatriz. *El imprerio de los sentimientos: narraciones de circulación periódica en la Argentina, 1917–27*. Buenos Aires: Grupo Editorial Norma, 2000.

———. *Una modernidad periférica: Buenos Aires 1920 y 1930*. Buenos Aires: Ediciones Nueva Visión, 1988.

Sarmiento, Domingo Faustino. "El teatro como elemento de cultura." *Boletín de Estudios de Teatro* 1, no. 1 (1943): 3–5.

Schiaffino, Eduardo. *La pintura y la escultura en Argentina (1783–1894)*. Buenos Aires: Edición del Autor, 1933.

Seibel, Beatriz. *Los artistas trashumantes*. Buenos Aires: Ediciones de la Pluma, 1985.

———. "Buenos Aires 1890: Los espectáculos." In *Martin Fierro* and *El Entenao*, by Elías Regules. With notes by Teodoro Klein, Beatriz Seibel, Eneida Sansone de Martínez, and Jorge Dubatti, 19–23. Buenos Aires: Ediciones del Jilguero, 1996.

———. *El cantar del payador*. Buenos Aires: Ediciones del Sol, 1988.

———. "Códigos de teatro popular en el Juan Moreira: fiesta y creación dramática." *Revista del Instituto Nacional de Estudios de Teatro* 5, no. 13 (1986): 54–59.

———. *Historia del circo*. Buenos Aires: Ediciones del Sol, 2005.

———. *Historia del teatro argentino: desde los rituales hasta 1930*. Buenos Aires: Corregidor, 2002.

———. *El teatro "bárbaro" del interior*. Buenos Aires: Ediciones de la Pluma, 1985.

Seibel, Beatriz, ed. *Antología de obras de teatro argentino: desde sus orígenes a la actualidad*. With a prologue by Seibel. Buenos Aires: Instituto Nacional del Teatro, 2006.

Seigel, Micol. "Cocoliche's Romp: Fun with Nationalism at Argentina's Carnival." *TDR* 44, no. 2 (2000): 56–83.

Selgas, José. *Hojas sueltas y más hojas sueltas*. Madrid: Imprenta de A. Pérez Dubrull, 1883.

Silva Francisca Miranda, and William H. Beezley, "The Rosete Aranda Puppets: A Century and a Half of an Entertainment Enterprise." *The Americas* 67, no. 3 (2011): 331–54.

Silva, Hernán Asdrúbal et al. "Estadísticas sobre la inmigración a la Argentina." In *Inmigración y estadísticas en el cono sur de América*, edited by Hernán Asdrúbal Silva, 13–68. México, DF: Instituto Panamericano de Geografía e Historia; Washington, DC: Organización de los Estados Americanos, 1990.

Slatta, Richard W. *Comparing Cowboys and Frontiers*. Norman: University of Oklahoma Press, 1997.

———. "Making and Unmaking Myths of the American Frontier." *European Journal of American Culture* 29, no. 2 (2010): 81–92.

Sociedad Criolla Dr. Elías Regules. *Libro institucional*. Montevideo, 1991.

Soria, Eugenio F. *Digesto municipal de la Ciudad de Buenos Aires: leyes, ordenanzas, acuerdos y decretos vigentes*, 4th ed. Buenos Aires: Imprenta de M. Biedma e Hijo, 1907.

Steiner, Michael. "From Frontier to Region: Frederick Jackson Turner and the New Western History." *Pacific Historical Review* 64, no. 4 (1995): 479–501.

Taullard, Alfredo. *Historia de nuestros viejos teatros*. Buenos Aires: Imprenta López, 1932.

Torre Revello, José. *Del Montevideo del siglo XVIII: fiestas y costumbres*. Montevideo: Imprenta El Siglo Ilustrado, 1929.

Tranchini, Elina Mercedes. "El cine argentino y la construcción de un imaginario criollista." In *El Premio FAIGA*, 101–73. Buenos Aires: Editorial Federación Argentina de la Industria Gráfica y Afines, 1999.

Trigo, Abril. "Ideología y política en el teatro gauchesco (primitivo)." *Prisma/Cabral: Revista de Literatura Hispánica/Caderno Afro-Brasileiro Asiático Lusitano* 11 (1983): 45–56.

Turner, Victor. *Dramas, Fields, and Metaphors: Symbolic Action in Human Society*. Ithaca: Cornell University Press, 1975.

———. *From Ritual to Theater: The Human Seriousness of Play*. New York: PAJ, 1982.

———. *The Antoropology of Performance*. With a preface by Richard Schechner. New York: PAJ, 1988.

Ugarte, Manuel. *Crónicas del bulevar*. With a prologue by Rubén Darío. Paris: Garnier Hermanos, 1903.

Uslenghi, Alejandra. *Latin America at Fin-de-Siècle Universal Exhibitions: Modern Cultures of Visuality*. New York: Palgrave Macmillan, 2016.

Vega, Carlos. *Apuntes para la historia del movimiento tradicionalista argentino*. Buenos Aires: Secretaria de Cultura de la Presidencia de la Nación; Instituto Nacional de Musicología "Carlos Vega," 1981.

Veniard, Juan María. *Arturo Berutti, un argentino en el mundo de la ópera*. Buenos Aires: Instituto Nacional de Musicología "Carlos Vega," 1988.

Viana, Javier de. "Dramas criollos: el gaucho real y el gaucho inventado." *Revista Histórica* 32, nos. 94–96 (1962): 614–19.

———. "Sobre dramas criollos." *Revista Histórica* 32, nos. 94–96 (1962): 621–23.

Vicuña Mackenna, Benjamín. *La Argentina en el año 1855*. With a prologue by V. Lillo Catalán. Buenos Aires: La Revista Americana de Buenos Aires, 1936.

Vidal, Daniel. *Florencio Sánchez y el anarquismo*. Montevideo: Banda Oriental/ Biblioteca Nacional, 2009.

Viqueira Albán, Juan Pedro. *Propriety and Permissiveness in Bourbon Mexico*. Translated by Sonya Lipsett-Rivera and Sergio Rivera Ayala. Wilmington, DE: SR Books, 1999.

Wilde, José Antonio. *Buenos Aires desde setenta años atrás (1810–1880)*. Buenos Aires: EUDEBA, 1960.

Yunque, Alvaro. "Estudio preliminar" to *Croquis y siluetas militares: escenas contemporáneas de nuestros campamentos*, by Eduardo Gutiérrez, 7–40. Buenos Aires: Librería Hachette, 1956.

Zubillaga, Carlos. *Cultura popular en el Uruguay de entresiglos (1870–1910)*. Montevideo: Linardi y Risso, 2011.

Index

Page numbers in italic text indicate illustrations.